CONCEPTS OF MISSION

CONCEPTS OF MISSION

The Evolution of
Contemporary Missiology

FRANCIS ANEKWE OBORJI

ORBIS BOOKS

Maryknoll, New York 10545

Founded in 1970, Orbis Books endeavors to publish works that enlighten the mind, nourish the spirit, and challenge the conscience. The publishing arm of the Maryknoll Fathers and Brothers, Orbis seeks to explore the global dimensions of the Christian faith and mission, to invite dialogue with diverse cultures and religious traditions, and to serve the cause of reconciliation and peace. The books published reflect the opinions of their authors and are not meant to represent the official position of the Maryknoll Society. To obtain more information about Maryknoll and Orbis Books, please visit our website at www.maryknoll.org.

An earlier version of this book was published in 2005 in Rome and Lagos by Ceedee Publications.

Cover: Saint Paul the Apostle from a marble in the crypt of the Maryknoll chapel, Maryknoll, New York.

Library of Congress Cataloging-in-Publication Data

Oborji, Francis Anekwe.
    Concepts of mission : the evolution of contemporary missiology /
Francis Anekwe Oborji.
        p. cm.
    Includes bibliographical references and index.
    ISBN-13: 978-1-57075-663-4 (pbk.)
    ISBN-10: 1-57075-663-5
    1. Missions—Theory. I. Title.
BV2063.O26 2006
266'.201—dc22
                                    2006017580

In Loving Memory
of
My Parents

CONTENTS

Part Three
NEW PERSPECTIVES

ABBREVIATIONS

References to the entries listed below will use the following abbreviations. In the case of Vatican II conciliar decrees and papal encyclicals, the abbreviation will be followed by article numbers that refer to the numbering system used in the official texts.

AA   *Apostolicam Actuositatem*, Vatican II decree on apostolate of lay people
AAS   *Acta Apostolicae Sedis*
AFER   *African Ecclesial Review*
AG   *Ad Gentes*, Vatican II decree on the missionary activity of the church
ATR   African Traditional Religion
CCC   *Catechism of the Catholic Church*
CD   *Christus Dominus*, Vatican II decree on the pastoral office of bishops
CDF   Congregation for the Doctrine of the Faith
CHL   *Christifidelés Laici*, apostolic exhortation of Pope John Paul II on the vocation and mission of the laity in the church
CT   *Catechesi Tradendae*, apostolic exhortation of Pope John Paul II on catechesis
DeV   *Dominum et Vivificantem*, encyclical letter of Pope John Paul II on the Holy Spirit
DH   *Dignitatis Humanae*, Vatican II declaration on religious liberty
DI   *Dominus Iesus*, declaration *Dominus Iesus* from Congregation for Doctrine of the Faith
DV   *Dei Verbum*, Vatican II dogmatic constitution on divine revelation
EATWOT   Ecumenical Association of Third World Theologians
EN   *Evangelii Nuntiandi*, apostolic exhortation of Pope Paul VI on evangelization
ES   *Ecclesiam Suam*, encyclical letter of Pope Paul VI on dialogue
GS   *Gaudium et Spes*, Vatican II pastoral constitution on the church in the modern world
IMC   International Missionary Council
LCWE   Lausanne Committee for World Evangelization

LG	*Lumen Gentium*, Vatican II dogmatic constitution on the church
NA	*Nostra Aetate*, Vatican II declaration on the relations of the church to non-Christian religions
NCE	*The New Catholic Encyclopedia*
NT	New Testament
OT	Old Testament
PO	*Presbyterorum Ordinis*, Vatican II decree on the ministry and life of priests
PP	*Populorum Progressio*, encyclical letter of Pope Paul VI on human progress
PUG	Pontifical Gregorian University
PUU	Pontifical Urban University
RH	*Redemptor Hominis*, encyclical letter of Pope John Paul II on Christ as universal redeemer
RM	*Redemptoris Missio*, encyclical letter of Pope John Paul II on the missionary mandate
SA	*Slavorum Apostoli*, encyclical letter of Pope John Paul II on Saints Cyril and Methodius
SC	*Sacrosanctum Concilium*, Vatican II constitution on sacred liturgy
UR	*Unitatis Redintegratio*, Vatican II decree on ecumenism
UUS	*Ut Unum Sint*, encyclical letter of Pope John Paul II on ecumenism
WCC	World Council of Churches

FOREWORD

As Christianity enters the twenty-first century, the church and its mission studies stand at a critical juncture. Francis Anekwe Oborji's *Concepts of Mission: The Evolution of Contemporary Missiology* is an important guide to what is at stake. Written by a Nigerian, this book is the first attempt by an African Catholic missiologist to take account of the full range of theologies and theories of mission that ground the modern missionary movement. It is an important book, first, as a synthesis of missiology that carefully attends to the Catholic Church's teaching and to theologians' progressive understanding of concepts of mission; and second, as a reading of the issues that confront the world Christian movement.

My initiation into understanding Christianity as a world religion and as something larger than what was then called the "Church Universal" began in 1958, when I started training for life as a Divine Word Missionary. Born in small-town Iowa in the heartland of the United States, I had a totally Catholic, mono-religious view of the universe. Studies at the Gregorian University, five wonderful years in Papua New Guinea, life in an African American parish as I pursued doctoral studies at the University of Chicago, marriage, and seventeen years at Orbis have broadened that outlook. They have not, however, made me doubt the value and integrity of what I began with. My current understanding of how what was healthiest in my rural Iowa Catholic roots is profoundly connected with what is emerging globally today began dawning in a new manner while I worked with Lamin Sanneh and Andrew Walls on several of their books that Orbis had the privilege of publishing, and while I was a participant in a series of annual consultations at Yale and Edinburgh Universities organized by Sanneh and Walls. In Francis Anekwe Oborji I sense a similar voyage, perhaps even what David Tracy once wisely called "disenchantment with disenchantment" (Tracy 1975, 10-12).

My understanding began to coalesce in 1996, when I started working with Dale Irvin on his *Christian Histories, Christian Traditioning: Rendering Accounts*. The botanical image that Dale uses there describing world Christianity and the Christian tradition as having a "rhizomatic" structure was extremely helpful. He refers to a family of plants called "rhizomes," that have "subterranean, horizontal root systems, growing below and above ground at once" (Irvin 1998, 47). As I joined Dale, Scott Sunquist, a host of valued advisors working on a new history that would do justice to Christianity as a world religion, I began thinking of what unites Christians globally as analogous to the rhizomatic root system of princess pines common in northern Wisconsin. Their root system can stretch over great distances. To the untutored eye all that is visible are single small trees, yet all share the same root system.

In Dale Irvin's *Traditioning* book, he uses the analogy of a subterranean rhizomatic root system to suggest that something more organic than their conjunctions in regional, national, and international bodies links the world's Christian traditions, despite their visible differences. Some think of world Christianity as post-denominational today. I am less sure of that than I am that more than doctrines, Scriptures, traditions, bureaucracy, codes of canon law, or organizational associations unites the thousands and thousands of local churches around the world into what we began calling the "world Christian movement." The two-volume book on which Scott and Dale have been working since 1998—*The History of the World Christian Movement*—took its title from that insight. Volume 1 (Irvin and Sunquist 2001) has now been published, and volume 2 is in preparation. We might have called it *The History of the World Christian Rhizome.*

What does this have to do with the study of mission? Just this. If missiology is the discipline that attempts to understand what Christ calls his disciples to do, we need to understand the role of the church in mission in relation to the peoples of other faiths and cultures. Tomes, of course, have been written on that topic. I simplify—but not by much—when I say that many become incoherent when they try to describe the relationship between the "local" and the "universal" church. Which is real? The local community? The church universal? And if they are both real, how are they real and how does one explain their relationship? At another level, history is studded with stories of conflicts and rivalries that followed the separation among the churches. In a bid to address these divisions, some authors, like David Bosch in his *Transforming Mission*, have proposed common witness in mission as a new missionary paradigm. Coming from an African background, however, and without downplaying the urgency of ecumenical dialogue in promoting the Christian mission, Oborji brings into relief the question of intercultural dialogue in mission. He does not enter into the polemics in ecclesiology or leadership struggles that are still major themes in ecumenical discussions and modern theology. These themes, important as they are, are marginal for an African Christian whose ancestors never took part in those issues that caused division in Christendom. What is of paramount importance to him as an African is to strive to link the worldview of his ancestors and people with the self-revelation of God in Christ; to explore the universal dimensions of such ancestral heritage, their origins in the One Supreme God; and to show how all these have their foundation in the kingdom of God inaugurated in Jesus Christ.

One major point that Oborji illustrates very well in the book is something I have noted in international Catholic and ecumenical discussions. It's something congenial to me, as well, since it dovetails with my own experience in Papua New Guinea. I am talking of the way Oborji as an African missiologist stresses inculturation, intercultural dialogue, and the search for elements that bring the church-family together. Under that rubric he sees action for human promotion and liberation, I will say, but his theology brings to the fore the fact that the ties we share in baptism and our common origin in the one God ought to be the basis of unity in human and church community, and within that search there should be a shared effort to end neo-capitalist and neo-colonialist hegemony. The tone of this book, I will add, is one that seeks justice but does so without stridency and in the voice of someone who is talking to brothers and sisters, not adversaries.

While Oborji does not pose the question in this way, the challenge of his book, it seems to me, lies in seeing that the key issue is something like the following. Since the Christian landscape has changed rapidly in recent times from the Northern Hemisphere to the South, can the churches become the kind of communion that will accommodate the voices and sensibilities of these new Christians from the global South . . . for the sake of carrying on the mission of Christ? I am not suggesting here that I know what shape that communion would take. That is clearly a matter for dialogue. But I do want to suggest that Father Oborji presents here a perspective on the church's concept of mission and theologians' contributions to the debate that is faithful to the church's magisterium and to Scripture. I think those principles deserve serious attention.

Francis Anekwe Oborji offers his reader insight into the mind of an African missiologist coming to grips with the missiological tradition. He articulates those principles of universal ecclesial communion that mission must exemplify if world Christianity is to live up to the teaching of Vatican II that "the Church on earth is by its very nature missionary" (*AG* 2). Oborji's *Concepts of Mission* is the best book I know for gaining a synthetic view of contemporary thought from Vatican II and the papal magisterium on mission. It is irenic throughout, but the discerning eye will see that what is at stake is whether the church's understanding and practice of mission are to be rooted in full Trinitarian theology or reduced now to this and now to that contemporary vogue. In his brief treatment of the main trends of thought on the nature of the church's mission in the writings of contextual theologians in Latin America, Asia, and Africa, what comes into relief is the need for a church that practices communion in seeking to carry out that mission in a spirit of dialogue. The way that Father Oborji articulates the African image of the *church-family* as God's way of uniting all humanity is worth taking note of. If the world Christian movement becomes that kind of family, it will be well on the way to manifesting God's way of rooting the followers of

Jesus in the mystery by which, in God's Spirit (Eph 3:16), the world is being saved:

> With all wisdom and insight he has made known to us the mystery of his will, according to his good pleasure that he set forth in Christ, as a plan for the fullness of time, to gather up all things in him, things in heaven and things on earth. (Eph 1:8-10; see also 3:5-13)

William R. Burrows

ACKNOWLEDGMENTS

One of the most decisive moments of my life occurred when I had the priv-ilege of studying missiology at the Pontifical Urbaniana University in Rome after some years of pastoral work and teaching in my home diocese of Onitsha, Nigeria. I express my indebtedness to the late Archbishop Stephen Ezeanya of Onitsha, who recommended that I specialize in missiology, and to the academic council of the faculty of missiology of the Urbaniana Uni-versity, which assigned me this project in 1998 as a research program for the teaching of mission theology. This book is the fruit of that research program. I am grateful to the past and present deans of the faculty, the Most Reverend Giuseppe Cavallotto (the former rector magnificus of the university), Profes-sor Alberto Trevisiol, IMC, and the late Professor Paolo Giglioni, as well as to Professor Joseph Dinh Duc Dao for serving as *tutores* for the project and for their support and encouragement. I learned much from the reactions of colleagues at the early stage of my presence there and especially when this project began. Such experience changed the way I see things and made me resolve to go ahead with the project. I am particularly grateful to my students in Rome, whose interests in my courses and methodology of teaching are a constant source of strength and encouragement. They will find the results of many discussions with them inside and outside the classroom in this book. Many thanks to the staff of the library of the Urbaniana University for their efficient services.

I cannot forget the research program with which I began this project at the Philosophische-Theologische Hochschule of the Society of the Divine Word at Sankt Augustin (near Bonn), Germany. The assistance given me by Eugen Nunnenmacher, SVD, and the late Karl Müller, SVD, is greatly appreciated. I remember with gratitude the inestimable library assistance given to me by Angelika Striegel and Martina Ludwig. I thank Father Manfred Müller, SVD, my former rector at St. Peter's Pontifical College in Rome, through whose good offices I was offered accommodation at Sankt Augustin as I carried on my research. I thank also Father Josef Rieger, SVD, then the rector of Sankt Augustin, for his concern for my well-being displayed throughout my stay with him and his confreres.

I also appreciate the evaluation of the original manuscript of the book by Professor Jesús López-Gay, SJ, of the Pontifical Gregorian University in Rome, and his review of my other book, *Teologia della Missione: Storia e*

Nuove Sfide. Dr. Ortrud Stegmaier, SSpS, gave me special encouragement by her appreciative note after going through the initial draft of the work. If Sister Stegmaier's note gave the work the needed assurance from an experienced woman missiologist, the critical observations made by Professor Jan A. B. Jongeneel of the University of Utrecht, the Netherlands, have helped to increase and update the ecumenical dimensions of this book. From the beginning of the work, it has always been my desire to give it a full ecumenical posture. Professor Jongeneel's observations have helped me to keep this focus in relief. In addition, I benefited greatly from my many contacts while I served as the executive secretary of the International Association of Catholic Missiologists (IACM).

The Congregation for the Evangelization of Peoples was of great help financially at the early stages of my stay in Rome. I thank, in particular, the administration of the Pontifical Mission Works of St. Peter Apostle for their help and understanding. I am grateful also to the administration of the John XXIII Foundation as well as to the Sisters of the Oblates of Saint Benedict of Joseph Labre, who look after the house of the foundation where I live in Rome. I remain grateful to the bishops of my home diocese in Nigeria: Valerian M. Okeke (the present archbishop of Onitsha) and Albert K. Obiefuna (archbishop emeritus of Onitsha). Nor can I forget everything I owe to Francis Cardinal Arinze (the former archbishop of Onitsha, now the prefect of the Congregation for the Divine Worship and Sacramental Discipline).

I appreciate the love and support that I have continued to enjoy from the members of my family, from the parish community of my hometown, Aguleri, and from the presbyterium of Onitsha archdiocese, especially during my summer vacations at home. I remain grateful to all of them for their company and warmth, which do not allow me to give way to despair and discouragement.

It is very satisfying to have this book published by Orbis Books. I thank my good friend Bill Burrows, the managing editor of Orbis Books, for making this possible and for all his encouragement. Publication by Orbis will bring this little book to a wider network of readers than I dreamed of when I was writing in my small room in Rome.

I thank all my friends and acquaintances for their closeness and prayers, which, I believe, have helped to sustain me all this while. May the one who has called us to participate in his mission continue to sustain and enlighten us in his way.

Part One

BASIC ISSUES

1

MISSION IN CONTEMPORARY MISSIOLOGY

Vatican II opened new roads to missiological reflection, especially on the concepts of mission (*AG* chaps. 1-2), the values and functions of local churches (*AG* chap. 3), the meaning of cultures (*GS* 53-63), the fundamentals of interreligious dialogue (*NA* 2), promotion of liturgical adaptation and inculturation (*SC* 37-40), and human promotion (*GS* 64-82). Theological reflection on some of these themes has continued to enrich the traditional concept of mission. Although there have been some ideological tendencies in the mission theology of some authors, the teaching of Vatican II still provides the needed insight on the meaning and concept of mission. It is in the light of this that we wish to examine in this opening chapter the concept of mission from the perspective of conciliar and postconciliar mission theology and in relation to the historical facts and currents of thought that are found in contemporary missiology. This approach will not only serve as a good introduction to the whole study but will also help one appreciate the relevance of missiology as a science of its own in theological education. It will also furnish us with the historical context in which the concerns of mission theology today are discussed.

Let us begin with the basic question: What are the sources that inform the writings of missiologists today? We can only mention the principal ones: Scripture as the fundamental text; Christian tradition; history of mission and theology, which helps to guide against undesirable ways of thinking; the magisterium, which ensures fidelity to the common faith in Christ and the pursuit of the Christian mission; ecumenical discussion; and enhanced discussion of inculturation, interreligious dialogue, human promotion, the role of women, modern means of mass communication, the North-South economic divide, and globalization, which receive special attention in the works of Third World theologians. In addition, missiologists are concerned with how to respond to the process of secularization among Christians of the North Atlantic and also of the global South (culture of modernity); challenges coming from the greater awareness of other religions, cultures, and their political influence; and the problem created by the emergent new religious movements (see Sundermeier 1997, 437ff.). Again, among these concerns, missiologists are faced with certain challenges: exegetical insights on the question of salvation and other religions (see *LG* 16; *NA* 2; Brennan 1990, 50ff.). In other words, contemporary missiology is faced with the serious problem posed by radical relativism in the theology of religions and the concerns of Asian theologians in that regard. At the same time, however, mission theology continues to appreciate the way in which the theologians (in particular, African authors) emphasize culture and its role in evangelization (theology of inculturation). Mission theology in the postconciliar era battles also with the influences from the so-called theology of liberation and the effort to define human promotion (development) in relation to the proclamation of the gospel, a matter which Latin American theologians emphasized more than others when that theology flourished in the 1960s and 1970s, and even into the 1980s.

Mission studies are also influenced by the problem of the discrepancy between the message that the church proclaims and the lifestyle of its members. Some authors have noted that the un-Christian nature of the life of many Christians exists on all the continents. And recently, missiologists have started to explore new ways of relating between the churches of the North Atlantic nations and those of the Third World. This may imply that a new missionary ecclesiology is under way.

Mission theology is always confronted with the particular and specific goal of the Christian mission. The most onerous task has been to emphasize the urgency and importance of the Christian mission, in particular the mission *ad gentes* and the role of the church in that regard, even as we grapple with the influence of secularization in the countries with ancient Christian roots. Again, be it theology of religion or the discussion on cultures (inculturation), mission theology emphasizes the need for compatibility with the gospel and communion with the universal church (see *RM* 52, 54; *Ecclesia in Africa* 59-62). The same principle guides research in the areas of human promotion. Mission is to be pursued in the context of proclamation of the gospel through which the church offers a force of liberation that leads to conversion of heart and ways of thinking that promote human dignity, development, and healthy solidarity among people (*RM* 59).

Mission in the Theology of Vatican II

The debate in mission theology since Vatican II consists essentially of the meaning and purpose of Christian mission. The Vatican II missionary decree *Ad Gentes* has already clarified this in its teaching: "'Missions' is the term usually given to those undertakings by which the heralds of the Gospel are sent by the church and go forth into the whole world to carry out the task of preaching and planting the church among peoples or groups who do not yet believe in Christ. . . . The special purpose of this missionary activity is evangelization and the planting of the church among those peoples and groups where she has not yet taken root" (*AG* 6). The conciliar decree adds that "all over the world indigenous particular churches ought to grow from seed of the word of God, churches which would be adequately organized and would possess their own proper strength and maturity. With their own hierarchy and faithful, and sufficiently endowed with means adapted to the full Christian life, they should contribute to the good of the whole church" (*AG* 6). It is within this definition and purpose of mission that the council presents a broader meaning of the term "evangelization": "Evangelization is that activity through which, in obedience to Christ's command and moved by the grace and love of the Holy Spirit, the church makes itself fully present to all persons and peoples in order to lead them to the faith, freedom and peace of Christ by example of its life and teaching, and also by the sacraments and other means of grace" (*AG* 5).

Though the council defines mission in simple terms of evangelization and church implantation, it is all embracing. Theologically, its foundation is divine. The emphasis is always on the mandate from Christ. Pastorally, it includes all the paths of mission itself and evangelization (in the strict sense of the word, that is, the kerygma or rather the initial proclamation to non-Christians or neophytes), and the implanting of the church as a sign of its visible presence among any people and place. Furthermore, it embraces the issue of integral development of humanity as it relates to the church's evangelizing mission. Through her life and teaching the church brings the freedom and peace of Christ to people. Again, by means of the sacraments and other means of grace, the church makes available to people those means established by Christ for the sanctification and the eschatological salvation of humanity (see Oborji 1998, 58).

In this theology of mission, the council also speaks of the nature and foundation of the church in relation to missionary activity: "The Church is missionary by nature" (*AG* 2). The basis of the church's missionary nature is the divine mandate that it has been "sent to the nations to be the *universal sacrament of salvation*" (*AG* 1). The two distinctive characteristics of the church's mission are preserved here. First, both the church and its mission are defined in distinctive instrumental terms, "in the service of and in the function of the divine intervention in favor of all humanity of all times and of the whole world." Second, the mission of the church is given its ultimate theological foundation, "the Trinitarian mystery itself, thus coming as a historical extension, from God's eternal saving plan which was expressed in sending the Word made flesh in Jesus Christ and in sending the Holy Spirit, with the Father as the original supreme source" (Nunnenmacher 1993, 118).

But the most vital aspect, in this context, is that which speaks of being "fully present to all persons and peoples," and one could add, to all cultures. Vatican II is fully oriented to this fact. The church in her missionary activity is the visible sign of Christ's presence to all peoples and nations (see *LG* 1). This is the summary of the council's orientation to the theology of mission (see *GS* 53-62). However, the various dimensions of mission and ecclesial activities that go with the former are given broader meaning in postconciliar documents, in particular, in *Evangelii Nuntiandi* and *Redemptoris Missio* (see Oborji 1998, 58-59).

Furthermore, one of the hallmarks of Vatican II is its rediscovery of the theology of reciprocity (*LG* 13; *AG* 22). This theology is based on the gospel image of the sowing of the good news and on the council's theology of local churches, which are established in every place. This theology informed the council's missionary juridical system of *mandatum*, which replaces the *ius commissionis*. The conciliar system of *mandatum* empowers the local bishops as fully responsible for evangelization in their dioceses. The missionaries are to enter into contract with the bishops in whose dioceses they wish to serve. Again, this new awareness is centered on the council's theology of mission as reciprocal activity between sister churches. This new theology of mission applies universally to all the churches, even while not denying their differences (see *AG* 6). Thus, the council's mission theology should not be confused with the prevailing missiology of the old (see Dupuis 1994, 276). The bottom line in the conciliar mission theology is the emphasis on cultural diversity in the church and the role of local churches (in communion with the universal church-family) in the work of evangelization and implanting of the church in their various cultural contexts. This is reciprocity. In addition to assuming all that the church has acquired in its earthly pilgrimage, each local church is challenged to contribute something from its cultural setting to enrich the patrimony of the universal church-family. In other words, the council developed a theology of coresponsibility in evangelization and of trust in the local churches.

The foregoing discussion underscores the importance of the Vatican II theology of mission, particularly the rediscovery of the local churches as the primary agent of mission. This awareness has led to a fundamentally new interpretation of the purpose of mission and the role of missionaries and mission agencies. The council still affirms, however, and rightly so, that in the midst of these new circumstances and relationships there is still need for formation of experts or, rather, trained missionaries. But the missionaries are to recognize that their task pertains to the whole church, and they are to appreciate that they are sent as ambassadors of one local church to another local church (where such a local church already exists), as witnesses of solidarity and partnership, and as expressions of mutual encounter, exchange, and enrichment (see *AG* 26).

Mission in Postconciliar Thought

The postconciliar mission theology initiated a new debate on the concept of mission; this led to the so-called crisis of postconciliar missiology.

Mission as Evangelization

The debate here is on the relationship between the terms "mission" and "evangelization." Some missiologists began to question the use of the term "mission," and in its place preferred the use of the word "evangelization." But what are the reasons for the attack against the "mission"? Why are some authors reluctant to hear about it any longer, and even less so "missions" in the plural, in the sense of geographical territories dependent on a Roman dicastery?

In the first place, some authors misinterpreted Paul VI's apostolic exhortation *Evangelii Nuntiandi* to have suggested the use of "evangelization" over and above "mission." Evangelization (*missio ad gentes* or "first proclamation"), according to these authors, exists everywhere, because in every church there are people to be evangelized. Thus, the *missio ad extra* may mean that one has to go outside one's own frontiers to go to other churches with the spirit of dialogue and inculturation. But one must avoid speaking of the *missio ad gentes*. Again, it is within this camp that we find those authors who do not like to use any longer the terms "mission" and "missiology," but rather would speak mainly of "six continents," world Christianity, and Crosscultural Communication. "Mission in six continents" was the response of the World Missionary Conference in Mexico City in 1963. The conference somehow altered the traditional concept of mission and declared: where the church is, it is missionary in its being and in its proclamation. "Everywhere the church is to be concerned with overcoming disbelief and awakening faith, with overcoming enmity with love, with transforming social despair with hope. Everywhere *the whole Church* is responsible for bringing *the whole message to the whole world*. This was the message of the Mexico City Conference" (Sundermeier 1997, 437-38; see Scherer 1985, 454).

This ecumenical assembly on Word and Evangelism held in Mexico City in 1963 claims that today the seed of the gospel has been sown in nearly the whole world and churches have been established and are developing everywhere. In some parts they appear to be still in a stage of growth; in others in a stage of maturity, and in still others they are in a state of recession. Particular churches already have their own pastors and their own institutes for theological formation with their own reviews as a means of expression. This school of thought believes also that in the churches of the North Atlantic there is a noticeable lack of vitality: they need or they will need missionaries sent by young churches from the Third World. Mission is present everywhere, and all countries are in a state of mission. Authors of this school speak of "reverse mission," "mission as a two-way street," and so forth. They also raise some spontaneous questions: why should one leave and set out for a distant mission *ad gentes* when in one's own territory, though it was Christian, there is so much need and so many real mission lands (see López-Gay 1993, 15-16)? This school of thought has continued to influence the understanding of mission in the works of some authors.

In addition, the twentieth century witnessed a school of thought that believes that the "missions" belong to the past. It connotes an activity from outside, from an alien place into someone's else's territory. With the advent of the *local church*, no one should come in from outside and do what the local church is expected to do or remove the missionary initiative from it. "Mission" in the singular or, even better, "evangelization" might be more acceptable than "missions" (see Bellagamba 1993, 41). Here, also, we have some authors who particularly attack the term *gentes*. The usual and most widely accepted meaning of this term is "nations," "pagans," "non-Christians." The authors believe that, quite often especially for those outside the church, the term sounds offensive and unacceptable. Again, since the church professes the universality of salvation, of the Spirit, to speak of pagans, of nonbelievers, does not make sense. This term is offensive to the followers of other religions, who feel equated with the nonbelievers and resent being called non-Christians.

These attacks brought very devastating confusion on the traditional meaning of "mission" in general and on the expression *missio ad gentes* in particular. Precisely for this reason, John Paul II, in the encyclical *Redemptoris Missio,* devoted many of its chapters to safeguarding the term from negative interpretations. In the first three chapters, for instance, *Redemptoris Missio* highlights the theological basis for mission in modern times. Mission is essentially the self-communication and the self-giving of God to humans. In communicating and giving his very being to humans, God has willed to use the Word, who became Christ, as the only mediator and savior. He uses the power of the Spirit to apply it to ever-changing historical situations. For John Paul II, humanity under the impetus of Christ proceeds on its journey in an ascensional movement toward greater depth of participation in and wider response to the offer of God. Thus the kingdom of God on earth is established. The church is the first and most blessed beneficiary of God's self-revelation and self-giving. It believes and professes the centrality of Christ in the plan of God. The church is assisted in a unique way by the Holy Spirit; it has to be a sign and sacrament of all that God has done to people and has to involve itself in historical situations to promote what it believes and what it stands for. Hence, her mission on earth (see Bellagamba 1993, 40).

Mission ad Gentes

The development in mission theology after Vatican II has brought to the fore the importance of safeguarding the validity of mission *ad gentes*. The mission of the church is one; it is the same as Christ's and the Spirit's. Yet, it has its own specific activities to make it distinctive and particular. One of these specific activities is *missio ad gentes*. This aspect of the church's mission is special and specific. Therefore, *missio ad gentes* must be safeguarded. It cannot be compromised. John Paul II does not accept that "evangelization" should replace "mission" (*RM* 34). In fact, "mission" must be kept. It has biblical and theological foundations and its own richness too.

Moreover, in Vatican II mission theology, the term "mission" regained all its depth. When considered in the light of the Trinitarian mystery, the church's mission finds its origin in the love of the Father and is the continuation of the mission of the Son and of the Holy Spirit (*AG* 2-5). Mission is not something abstract, but it is part of human history with its problems and values (*AG* 9, 11). The conciliar missionary decree *Ad Gentes* presents the evangelizing initiatives in territories dependent on the Roman dicastery and speaks of them as either places where Christ has not yet been announced or where the church is not sufficiently established. The decree adds: these "are generally called 'missions'" (*AG* 6). Thus, the geographical term "missions" is not presented as something absolute. Again, what is referred to as "missionary activity" is a different activity from pastoral or ecumenical activity only for external reasons, that is, because of the means it uses and the goal it seeks. But all these activities "flow immediately from the very nature of the church." A real specificity of the mission *ad gentes* is found in the response to a special call from the Spirit, who demands that they "go forth (*exeunt*) in faith and obedience to those who are far from Christ as ministers of the Gospel so that the offering up of the Gentiles may be sanctified by the Holy Spirit" (*AG* 23).

In fact, Paul VI, in the exhortation *Evangelii Nuntiandi*, speaks of the "universal mission" with a geographical connotation (*EN* 50) and of the "missionary endeavor" as an activity different from the "new evangelization," because it consists of a "first proclamation of Jesus Christ" addressed to those who have never heard the Good News (*EN* 51, 52). The exhortation, in particular, presents the "missionary action" of the church (*EN* 76). The church "born of such a mission [Christ's mission] is sent" and called to "prolong and continue the saving mission of Christ himself in the power of the Holy Spirit." Thus, the whole church has received the "mission to evangelize" (*EN* 15, 51). For this reason, the church has the obligation to keep alive its missionary spirit, and even more to intensify it in the historical moment in which we live. This is a responsibility which the church has for all of humanity (*EN* 53). In other words, the term "missions" as used here by Paul VI refers to the geographical sense of the word, as in the conciliar decree (*AG* 6). In this regard, Paul VI recalls the declaration of the synod fathers: "We wish to confirm once more that the task of evangelizing all people constitutes the essential mission of the Church," and he adds, "it is a task and mission which the vast and profound changes of present-day society make all the more urgent" (*EN* 14).

Therefore, Paul VI, in *Evangelii Nuntiandi,* preserves the traditional meaning of the terms "mission," "missions," and "missionary." These words still have their universal dimension and maintain their relevance. However, the novelty of the apostolic exhortation consists in the fact that it emphasizes that the fulfillment of this mission becomes "evangelization," which is not limited to the first proclamation or to a second evangelization, but it embraces many other elements, such as the sacraments, means of Christian initiation, work for true human promotion and liberation, and so forth (*EN* 17, 24).

In the same context, John Paul II, in *Redemptoris Missio,* defines mission within the three concrete situations in which the church's evangelizing activities are carried out in the modern world. Today, the mission of the church is pursued in a complex and changing reality. Faced with this picture, the church directs its various activities toward three concrete situations: mission *ad gentes,* pastoral activity, and reevangelization or new evangelization.

- *Mission* ad gentes: This expression, when properly used, describes the mission of the church directed to "peoples, groups, and socio-cultural contexts in which Christ and his Gospel are not known, or which lack Christian communities sufficiently mature" (*RM* 34). Mission *ad gentes* is the effort of evangelization directed to peoples or groups who do not yet believe in Christ, who are far from Christ, in whom the church has not yet taken root, and whose culture has not yet been influenced by the gospel.

- *Pastoral activity:* This is the evangelization effort of the church in those areas or Christian communities where adequate and solid structures exist. It is the giving of pastoral attention to the cultures and the practicing Christians who live in areas that have already been evangelized or are still in the process of deepening the faith just received (*RM* 33).

- *Reevangelization or new evangelization:* This new terminology was introduced and popularized by John Paul II himself. It is a new direction in the church's evangelizing efforts aimed at addressing the emerging situations in the field of evangelization, directed to those "groups of the baptized who have lost a living sense of the faith . . . and live a life far removed from Christ and his Gospel. The situation that calls for a new evangelization is particularly found in countries with ancient Christian roots, and occasionally in the younger churches as well" (*RM* 33).

The encyclical cites examples of where the new evangelization is most needed: in today's world, which is characterized by rapid and profound transformation; in urban areas where massive growth creates great demographic pressure, where human problems are often aggravated by feelings of anonymity; where there are immigrants from various religious backgrounds and among refugees; and also in situations of poverty, which is today of an intolerable scale (*RM* 37).

Another situation that calls for this new effort of evangelization is what the pope describes as *cultural sectors*, the modern equivalent of the Areopagus. This includes the "world of communications, . . . commitment to peace, the development and liberation of peoples, the rights of minorities, the advancement of women and children and safeguarding the created world . . . the immense *Areopagus* of culture, scientific research and international relations, with all the vast opportunities as well as challenges they offer to mission" (*RM* 37-38).

Therefore, *Redemptoris Missio* insists that the old categories related to *missio ad gentes* are still useful and should be retained: "Care must be taken to avoid the risk of putting very different situations on the same level and of reducing, or eliminating, the church's mission and missionaries *ad gentes* (*RM* 32). Mission *ad gentes* is not a threat to religious freedom, "which remains the premise and guarantee of all freedom . . . because the church proposes; she imposes nothing" (*RM* 39). The encyclical accepts that there is only one mission: "This mission is one and undivided, having one origin and one final purpose . . . the church's one mission" (*RM* 31, 33). However, within the one mission of the church, there are different tasks and kinds of activity (*RM* 31). The reason for that diversity is not intrinsic to mission, but it depends on the circumstances within which the same mission is exercised (*RM* 33). Thus, at present, there are three major situations that require a different approach to mission.

Among the three situations, the first and most important is *missio ad gentes*. Its importance and its priority are derived from its object: non-Christians. These are people in the world who are most in need of the mission of the church in order to be enlightened in a credible and intelligible manner as to God's plan, and the way that plan has been carried out in Christ, and to be offered the chance to hear it and embrace it. These people "have the right to hear" this good news (*RM* 44). In fact, the church cannot withdraw from her permanent mission of bringing the gospel to the multitudes—the millions of men and women who as yet do not know Christ, the redeemer of humanity (*RM* 44). It is therefore necessary to ensure that this specifically missionary work that Jesus entrusted and still entrusts each day to the church does not become an indistinguishable part of the overall mission of the whole people of God and as a result become neglected and forgotten (*RM* 34).

The New Evangelization

With the introduction of "new evangelization" or "reevangelization" in the documents of the church in recent times have come some negative interpretations. "New evangelization" was used by John Paul II for the first time in his pontificate in 1983 in Haiti at the meeting with the Latin American Conference of Bishops (CELAM: *Consejo Episcopal Latinoamericano*). But it is in *Redemptoris Missio* that the pope developed the theology and the real practical meaning of the term. However, what the Haiti meeting did was to make "new evangelization" the central theme within the issues to be discussed in the later conference at Santo Domingo in October 1992 by the Latin American bishops.

Some authors have interpreted the expression "new evangelization" to mean that the same missionary situation can be found everywhere. Given that a new evangelization is needed everywhere, this cannot be taken as exclusive. The reevangelization of the Christian communities of the North Atlantic can be pursued without harming the force of the mission *ad gentes*. When Vatican Council II speaks of the "grace of renewal" of our churches and communities, it also emphasizes that this will grow and bear much fruit when "each of them expands the range of its charity to the ends of the earth, and has the same concern for those who are far away as it has for its own members" (*AG* 37). The great missionaries, beginning with St. Paul, did not wait until all the problems of the churches founded by them were solved in order to "set out and go forth" to preach the gospel elsewhere. Their characteristic was "anxiety for *all* the churches" (2 Cor 11:28; *PO* 10). The emphasis is on the phrase "all the churches," not only their own (see López-Gay 1993, 15).

Latin American bishops at the Santo Domingo Conference (1992) employed the principle of deduction in defining the new evangelization. For the bishops, the starting point for the new evangelization is the assurance that Christ holds "unfathomable riches" (Eph 3:8) that no age or culture exhausts and to which we human beings can ever turn to be enriched. To speak of a new evangelization is to acknowledge that an old one or first one has already taken place. It would be incorrect to speak of a new evangelization of tribes or peoples who never received the gospel. In Latin America, we can speak in this fashion because a first evangelization took place here five hundred years ago. Thus, the bishops continued:

> To speak of a new evangelization does not mean that the previous one was invalid, sterile, or short-lived. Rather, it means that today Christians face new challenges and new questions that urgently require a response. To speak of a new evangelization . . . does not mean proposing a new gospel different from the first. There is only one Gospel, but it can shed new light on those new problems. The expression "new

evangelization" does not mean re-evangelizing. In Latin America, the point is not to act as though there were no first evangelization but, rather, to start from many rich values it has left in place and proceed to complement them by correcting previous shortcomings. The new evangelization has emerged in Latin America as a response to the problems plaguing a continent where a divorce between faith and life leads to situations of injustice, social inequality, and violence that cry out. It means taking up the magnificent endeavor of energizing Latin American Christianity. (Hennelly 1993, 81-82)

The Latin American bishops define the new evangelization also as a new realm of vitality, a new Pentecost in which the acceptance of the Holy Spirit will give rise to a renewed people made up of free human beings conscious of their dignity and able to forge a truly human history. It is the combination of means, activities, and attitudes that can put the gospel into active dialogue with modernity and with the postmodern, in order to challenge them and to be challenged by them. It is likewise the effort to inculturate the gospel into the emerging cultures of our present world.

It is in the light of the above points that John Paul II mentions three dynamisms that should accompany the missionary activity of the new evangelization. The new evangelization must be *new in zeal* (fervor or ardor), *new in methods,* and *new in expression.* For John Paul II, evangelization is new in its zeal only if in the measure in which it is carried out it renews and brings us always closer and in fellowship with Christ, the first evangelizer. The new evangelization begins with conversion of the heart. It invites believers to rediscover once more that the Christian vocation is the call to holiness of life. It is sin that draws back the ardor of evangelization (*RM* 23; Giglioni 1996, 170-73).

In addition, the new evangelization should also be new in its methods. *New in method* is an invitation to every member of the church to become a protagonist of the diffusion of the message of Christ. Evangelization is the duty of all members of the church. Also, evangelization should be today new in its methods for the simple reason that it ought to meet the challenges of the new realities in which the gospel proclamation is addressed (*AA* 11; *RM* 2, 37).

Finally, for John Paul II, evangelization should be new in its expression. Evangelization that is *new in its expression* is that which strengthens the fiber of the ecclesial community. In other words, evangelization is new in expression when it strengthens and accompanies the growth and maturity of the faithful in their consciousness of the truth and treasure that they have in Christ. This includes, also, the Christians' awareness of being bearers of the truth that saves, and which, from the beginning of the church, has been decisive in stimulating missionary commitment. Thus, the primary condition of evangelization is the promotion of that which strengthens the missionary

commitment of the ecclesial community. New in its expression means form-
ing mature Christian communities from which the faith emits and realizes all
its original meaning and adhesion to Christ and his gospel (*CHL* 34; Giglioni
1996, 176-78).

The foregoing discussion, when evaluated from the perspective of the aim
of the present study, shows that the whole debate, be it about the term "mission" or the "new evangelization," has achieved one simple fact. It has made
visible the new phase in the church's missionary and pastoral commitments
in the contemporary world. Again, missionary activity in its relation to the
new evangelization refers to the call for the renewal of the evangelizing activity of the church in our modern world. It is an awareness of the missionary
commitment that awaits the church in diverse cultural contexts and in every
territory of the globe. The dynamism for the realization of this commitment
has been expressed in the three terms of an evangelization that is new in zeal,
new in method, and new in expression.

Emergent Dimensions of Mission Thought

In addition to the debate on the concept of mission, postconciliar mission
theology witnessed an enhanced understanding of new dimensions of mission. Of particular importance here are the discussion on what some have
described as new forms of mission: (1) ecumenical dialogue, (2) inculturation, (3) dialogue with the religions, and (4) human promotion or liberation.
To these, we may add the emerging trend (which is implicit in all of the
above), namely, mission as dialogue with the local contexts.

Mission as Ecumenical Dialogue

In recent works of missiologists, ecumenical dialogue has been identified as
one of the emergent dimensions of mission (Bosch 1991, 457). It is a new perspective in mission studies with its problems and challenges. This awakening
has a direct link with mission. In Protestantism, for example, the ecumenical
idea was a direct result of the problem of rivalry experienced by various
denominations and mission agencies from the West operating in various parts
of what is known today as the global South (Rosenkranz 1977, 198). It is
dreadful to think that a continent such as Africa and some parts of Asia are
condemned by history to know only a divided Christianity. Most people of
the global South have in fact embraced the form of Christianity proposed to
them without an exact knowledge of the origins of schism and Protestantism
in the church. The emerging form of ecumenism, therefore, should be one
that will reject useless sterile controversies in favor of the serene and humble
meaning of Christ's message to the people (Rom 6:16-22). The concern is

for a fervent cooperation in mission among the various confessions. Catholics, Orthodox, and Protestants are invited to question themselves and to share what they have understood and discovered in Christ according to their respective confessions. They must work together to proclaim Jesus Christ effectively in the world today and tomorrow. Collaboration already exists in several areas: social progress, religious education, theological research, etc. (Oborji 2002b, 27-30). Any reflection on mission trends today must include this renewed invitation to an ecumenical dialogue.

In taking this direction, Vatican II intimately links the call to Christian unity to the church's mission (*AG* 6). All baptized people are called upon to come together in one flock that they might bear unanimous witness to Christ their Lord before the nations. The Vatican II missionary decree goes on to say, "And if they cannot yet fully bear witness to one faith, they should at least be imbued with mutual respect and love" (*AG* 3, 19-23). And the council's dogmatic constitution on the church states categorically that those "who are sealed by baptism which unites them to Christ . . . are indeed in some real way joined to us in the Holy Spirit" (*LG* 15). The Vatican II decree on ecumenism (*Unitatis Redintegratio*) also speaks in favor of improved relations and mutual acceptance. In general, Vatican II considers ecumenism as one of its principal concerns and states that division among Christians contradicts the will of Christ, scandalizes the world, and damages that most holy cause, the preaching of the gospel to every creature.

This new development is also experienced in the Protestant churches. The formation of the World Council of Churches (WCC) in 1948 has been described as a great new fact leading toward Christian unity. Churches became aware that, today, it is impossible to say "church" without at the same time saying "mission"; by the same token it has become impossible to say "church" or "mission" without at the same time talking about the *one* mission of the *one* church. This is the new trend in mission (Bosch 1991, 464).

There is a growing awareness of the relationship of the question of Christian unity and the unity of the human family. In fact, some have asked whether the unity of the human family is not somehow linked to visible unity among Christians joined in a single faith. There is also a strong view that stresses that the coming of the kingdom of God and the second coming of Christ must not be separated from this invitation for the unity of the human family. Mission aims toward the unification of all in Christ. For this to come about, missionary activities must also be directed toward building bridges across those things that divide diverse peoples: religious beliefs, ethnicity, race, ideologies, etc. As recent events and conflicts in the world are showing, the reign of God also means tolerance, reconciliation, peace, and justice. All this means that humanity is in dire need of ethnic and racial redemption (Mushete 1991, 152).

Christian mission is rooted in the common faith that all Christians profess in Jesus Christ. The proclamation of this faith calls for communion if not unity among all the churches founded in the name of Christ. This also shows that ecumenical dialogue is linked to other new forms of mission, such as inculturation and interreligious dialogue. Among the principal motives behind these new ways of understanding mission practice are the need for a dynamic approach to mission and the concern to cultivate the good will that will enable the structures of communion among the churches to function properly. One thinks particularly of how the historical experiences that led to the schism of the eleventh century and the Protestantism that originated in the fifteenth century could become sources of unity and better understanding among the churches. Moreover, what experience will the young churches of the global South bring to the call for unity and communion among the churches? The nature of the Christian unity that is envisioned by these young churches surpasses the traditional vision of a church that breathes with only two lungs, East and West, as is often said (*UUS* 54).

The shift of Christianity to the global South means that the churches of Africa, Asia, and Latin America will also have to make their contributions to the development of the common Christian patrimony. And so unity among Christians is constructed around the common faith in Jesus Christ, his gospel message, and in communion with all the local churches or ecclesial communities of the universal church-family, with the chair of St. Peter as the center of communion, for the building up of the kingdom of God on earth. The renewed emphasis on inculturation and dialogue with the religions may mean that the dream of the local churches of the global South is that in the near future, with the churches of the North Atlantic, they will all assemble around the chair of St. Peter as the center of communion, each with its own traditions and disciplines, liturgy and theology, arising from various historical experiences and cultural contexts and rooted in the common faith in Jesus Christ and his gospel. In this way, all the Christians of the six continents, in a rich symphony of languages and songs, of colors and liturgical vestments, and of bodily gestures, will render honor and praise to God the Father through Christ and in the Holy Spirit. This is a necessary step toward achieving the desired unity of the human family. The churches need to unite first to become the catalyst of human unity.

Therefore, ecumenical dialogue in the light of the emergent churches of the global South will assume a new role and perspective. It will become, then, one of the principal ways for the churches to enter into a relationship of enriching communion, of giving and receiving, within the universal church-family that has the chair of St. Peter as the center of communion. This effort must be carried out with the understanding that everyone is working for the good of humanity, for the church of Christ, and for the authentic expression, witnessing, and living of the Christian faith. It must be pursued, above all, with the understanding that the Holy Spirit is actively present in all and is leading all gradually to greater knowledge of the mystery of God revealed in Jesus Christ (Oborji 1998, 200).

The conclusion that could be drawn from the above points is that the renewed way of reflecting on the intimate link between mission and Christian unity is nonnegotiable. It is not simply derived from the Third World experience of mission or from changed realities, but from God's gift of unity in the one body of Christ and the mission of the same Christ for the unification of all things in him. God's people is one; Christ's body is one. In the same way, the relation between mission and Christian unity does not presume uniformity and reductionism or denying the differences. The differences may be genuine and therefore may have to be treated as such. What is required here is repentance. Mission in unity and unity in mission are impossible without a self-critical attitude, particularly where Christians meet with others, fellow-believers or nonbelievers, who, by human standards, should be their enemies. Ecumenism is possible where people accept one another despite their differences. So, the new challenge is how Christians and, indeed, the whole human family are to live their unity in diversity and diversity in unity. The center of the diversity and the unity is always Jesus Christ. He is the foundation and point of orientation. The Bible, which is the common sacred book for all Christians, is also a source for Christian unity and common witness in mission (Bosch 1991, 464-67).

Mission as Inculturation

For some time now, the term "inculturation" has assumed a central place in mission studies. Mission theology studies inculturation as a means of evangelization. However, the reality that inculturation expresses is as old as Christianity itself, since the church has always sought ways of expressing its message in a local culture. Moreover, the church since its inception has always seen the scope of its mission as universal and all embracing. It entails crossing all human boundaries and meeting peoples of all cultures and religious traditions. Hence, no culture or people could monopolize it. Though this fact looks very clear today, it took the apostolic church some time to appreciate the universal dimension of their mission. The question of the admission of Gentiles into the church without imposing Jewish law on them initiated a general council that sought the answer (Acts 15). That was the first major inculturation in the early church: a transition from a Judaeo-Christianity to a Christianity of the Gentiles (Rahner 1981, 83). When this initial problem was resolved, Christianity spread gradually beyond its original Jewish surroundings into the Gentile world. In the process, the church came to appropriate new structures, categories, and symbols in an effort to make Christianity relevant to the people of the new sociocultural milieu. Philosophical categories and some cultural elements of the people of the Mediterranean region (especially Greeks and later Romans) were adopted to formulate central theological categories (e.g., Christology) and forms of liturgical celebrations. Once that was done, the category or symbol so adopted acquired a new meaning that transcended its original meaning because of the novelty of the Christian faith (Oborji 1998, 70). As David Bosch argues, the early Christians did not simply express in Greek thought what they already knew; rather they discovered through Greek religious and philosophical insights what had been revealed to them (Bosch 1991, 190). In the same way, Christian liturgy would not have emerged if it had not developed with structures adopted from elements of Roman culture (Newman 1989, 373).

Therefore, the exigency of inculturation is not new in the life and history of the church. What appears new, in any case, is the term "inculturation" itself and the shift of emphasis that came with it. In the previous studies of missiologists and in many magisterial documents until recently, the term used was "missionary adaptation." Adaptation, as noted earlier, refers to a more creative method of missionary activity, by which the missionary tries to adapt the Christian message and liturgy to the customs of those he works among (Schineller 1990, 16-17). But for many contemporary theologians of the Third World, adaptation is a process that seeks to adapt the practices of the church of the missionary's homeland as much as possible to the sociocultural life of the people being evangelized. A good number of authors have tried to articulate the defects of the theology of adaptation. Naturally, their approach has been very critical, but has, nonetheless, helped to clarify the meaning and newness of inculturation as a missionary theory.

Three main theories are easily associated with the adaptation model of the past: (1) the missionary theory of salvation of souls; (2) the missionary theory of the implanting of church (as it has materialized in the homeland of the missionary—also referred to as the theology of *tabula rasa*); and (3) the theory of the search for stepping stones. In whatever case, one major shortcoming of the theology of adaptation, according to some authors, is *concordism*, which consists in the attempts and tendency to equate the Christian revelation with the systems of thought in which it has found its historical expression. The result of such endeavor has been minimal. Again, some argue that the theology of adaptation implies that the young churches of the global South should not assume the cultural coloring and customs of their local culture, but rather, they remain, forever, "paralyzed Christian communities—copies ground out on a foreign model, deprived of initiative, creativity, and originality, praying with borrowed words and thinking by proxy" (Mushete 1994, 14-15).

In spite of this criticism, it has to be acknowledged that the present buoyant churches in many parts of the global South were born out of the missionary effort of the adaptation theory. Again, it would be easy for us today to judge past missionary theory negatively, but the situation would be understood differently if one considers the historical circumstances under which those missionary efforts were formulated and executed. For instance, at the time Christianity was spreading to most parts of the global South, beginning with the fifteenth-century missionary expansion, the Protestant Reformation had just begun. As a result of the latter, the Council of Trent (1545-1563) was convoked. This council, intending to safeguard the unity of the church in the face of the Protestant Reformation, initiated a Counter-Reformation. It called for the uniformity of the entire church, including the young churches. Therefore, missionaries had no choice but to join in the effort toward the unity of the church and of the Christian faith (Oborji 1998, 72).

Again, in the nineteenth century, in the midst of a divided church in the West, there arose the modernist movement. The unity of the Christian faith was once more threatened. And in an effort to safeguard the unity of the faith, Vatican Council I (1870) presented a theology of revelation that left little room for recognition of elements of revelation outside the Catholic Church (Dulles 1983, 51-52). In all this, one needs to compare the mentality or attitude of the church with that of the rest of the world at the time. Other world cultures or religions were as well not engaged in dialogue. Furthermore, the underdeveloped state of social sciences, especially cultural anthropology at the time, did not help the matter either. Cultural anthropology at the time judged most peoples outside the North Atlantic world as peoples without culture and civilization. Africans, more than any other race of the human family, seemed to have suffered most from this kind of stereotype.

Invariably, this underdeveloped nature of cultural anthropology influenced missionary theories and practice during that time. To be noted as well is the fact that up to the beginning of twentieth century, there was no well-developed theology of mission in both Catholic and Protestant circles. And when it came to be developed, it started when the theology of adaptation was in vogue: the salvation of souls and the implanting of the church throughout the world as the universal means of salvation intended by God for humankind. The two perspectives, salvation of souls and implanting of the church, are two aspects of the church's missionary endeavor. The latter persisted until Vatican Council II. The former has been broadened by the term evangelization, especially with the modern emphasis on integral evangelization. Furthermore, several documents of Vatican II speak positively of the necessity of adaptation in describing the same reality that the word "inculturation" today addresses (SC 37-40).

The theological foundation of inculturation is the incarnation. The basic argument is that just as Jesus Christ, the Word of God, became incarnate in a human culture, in the Jewish milieu, the gospel of Jesus Christ should be allowed to be inculturated (or incarnated) in the local culture and context (Matt 5:17; Acts 10:34). In this case, incarnation as the theological model of inculturation could be explained in two senses. In the first sense, it means the process of mutual penetration of the gospel and culture so that Jesus Christ may be present "today" in every culture. In this particular sense, the event of the incarnation continues in time; it happens each time the gospel is made to penetrate a cultural milieu so that the people can welcome Christ in their midst as their savior.

The second sense refers to the unique event of Bethlehem, when "the Word became flesh and dwelt among us" (John 1:14). It is the primordial inculturation of the Word of God in human flesh and history, and therefore the foundation and model for all subsequent inculturation. It is the redemption of humanity in Christ. This is the basis of the universal claim of the Christ-event. It is humanity that Christ redeemed. Whoever shares in humanity and in creation by God has been redeemed in Christ. This is why the Christian mission is universal and why any people (of any race, nationality, or color) can claim Christ as their savior and redeemer. This is why, for example, an African Christian can call Christ an African *ancestor*. And why Christ can also be called an Asian by the Asians, and so forth. In fact, it is in Christology that inculturation assumes its most important significance.

Put together, in its broad sense and general, universal aspect, incarnation means God became man; he belongs to a particular people and shares all their peculiarities; he became this man in this people. The general sense of incarnation insists on "man like all men," while the inculturation side points to the differences and peculiarity: a man unlike all men because he belonged to a particular people and culture. Like the incarnation, inculturation does not take place in the abstract; it happens in a concrete cultural space (Charles 1996, 74). But it is in analogous terms that one can say that the gospel should be inculturated or incarnated in a culture just as Jesus Christ, the Word of God, took flesh and lived among us (John 1:14), became incarnate in a human culture. Analogy does not mean total identity between the realities so compared. The incarnation of Jesus Christ is a mystery. It is a divine act, a unique and entirely singular event. The mystery of the incarnation points to other realities beyond the issues of inculturation. Therefore, its usage by theologians should be understood in terms of analogy. In fact, it is for this reason that the International Theological Commission spoke of eight theological principles as the doctrinal foundations of inculturation, while giving primary place to the mystery of incarnation (Giglioni 1996, 132).

Some definitions of inculturation have been offered by theologians. According to Pedro Arrupe, inculturation is the "incarnation" of the Christian life and of the Christian message in a particular cultural context, in such a way that this experience not only finds expression through elements proper to the culture in question but becomes a principle that animates, directs, and unifies the culture, transforming and remaking it so as to bring about a new creation (Arrupe 1978, 97ff.). In the words of Justin Ukpong, inculturation involves immersing Christianity in the local cultures of the people so that just as Jesus became man, so must Christianity become the cultural religion of the people (1984, 27).

All this shows that inculturation is an indispensable means of evangelization. It involves vigorous research and patience, but it is something that must be encouraged if Christianity is to make sense to the people being evangelized.

Mission as Dialogue with the Religions

Dialogue with the religions has been recognized as an emergent dimension of mission. In this context, it has often been said that one of the most serious problems the church will face in the twenty-first century will be that of explaining the Christian meaning of soteriology in a plurireligious world, where religions have acquired such an important role. Mission theology has already made great progress in its study of the relationship between Christianity and other world religions. Today, Christians have come to admit not only that the great religions are *praeparatio evangelica* ("preparation for the gospel"), but also that each of them has its own proper life center, from the midst of which they have found fulfillment in Christianity.

Though this teaching is clear and sound, the subject has given rise to some radical positions in the writings of theologians, particularly authors of the radical theology of religions. We are faced with an ambiguous concept: on the one hand, the church, which has always accepted the "possibility of the salvation of people who have not heard the Gospel"; on the other, "the soteriological significance of the same church." With regard to the first point, Vatican II affirms the possibility of salvation in non-Christian religions (*NA* 2). This fact has already been explained by Catholic missiologists associated with fulfillment theory. Today, however, some radical authors, such as Knitter, Hick, and others, speak of soteriology (soteriocentrism) in a context outside real theocentricism and even in opposition to Christocentrism (see Bellagamba 1993, 18ff.).

But the teaching of the church continues the biblical tradition, recognizing the irreplaceable, unique role of the mediation of Christ, the savior; and one reaches salvation through faith in Christ himself and membership in his church on earth. However, because of the same Christ-event, since he is the only way to salvation, those who have not heard the gospel can attain salvation through ways only God knows, for we are dealing with a mystery: "Everyone, therefore, ought to be converted to Christ, who is known through the preaching. . . . So, although in ways known to himself God can lead those who, through no fault of their own, are ignorant of the Gospel to that faith . . ." (*AG* 7). Yet, this possibility of salvation outside the Christian religion does not lesson the missionary urgency (*RM* 4-9).

Mission as Human Promotion

The theological discussion on human promotion (known also in some quarters as liberation theology), in its various expressions, arises out of the concern of theologians to address the people's experience of exploitation, oppression, and injustice. The theology seeks to address the causes of poverty, especially in the countries of the global South, which for a long time have suffered from domination by various forms of imperialism. In the words of Barnabas Okolo, the theology emerged as a response to experiences of negation, grinding poverty caused by greed, exploitation, and oppression. It is a critical reflection on these experiences in the light of the gospel, with the aim of inspiring in the impoverished people a sincere commitment to build a more just and humane society (1994, 102-3).

Generally speaking, the theologians of human promotion take as their point of departure the local situation, especially the sociopolitical and economic reality of the people. Human promotion also studies issues of justice, peace, and solidarity. It is now argued that failure to act in support of these issues will cause evangelization to lose its credibility. And this is not all. Action for justice and participation in the transformation of the world are integral parts of evangelization. They are a meeting ground for Christians and non-Christians, a place reserved for dialogue and solidarity, a sign of authentic love for humanity, which is at the center of the gospel message (Mushete 1991, 150). The point being emphasized in all this is that in the presence of God, people matter, people count. And so does their welfare.

Special attention is always given to poverty and economic crisis. Some theologians base their reflections on internal factors: sociocultural crisis engendered by the clash between modernity and traditional cultural values and meaning; the political instability caused by bad governments and dictatorial rule, poor economic planning, corruption, and natural disasters, such as epidemics, frequent droughts, and the desertification of the countries in the global South. However, most of the theologians base their reflections on the external factors, such as unfair trade terms of the world economic order, the manipulation of Third World countries by the industrialized nations and financial institutions, the heavy burden of external debts incurred and money squandered by corrupt regimes, and the harsh conditions of the "Structural Adjustment Programs" imposed by the International Monetary Fund and the World Bank on these poor countries to make the latter loan-worthy for development projects that make them more dependent on the industrialized nations. All this involves issues of justice, peace, and development. What is the role of Christian mission in all these?

The real inspiration of theologians in discussing human promotion in the contemporary reality comes from their Christian conviction. It is on the basis of their Christian faith that theologians offer their reflections and address the poor conditions of Third World countries. Indeed to neglect this duty is for the theologians to feel a sense of indifference to the situation of the Two-Thirds World. In other words, the theologians want to be part of the church's efforts in the area of human promotion. This means that the social teachings of the church are at the base of the sources of the theologians' reflection on human promotion. Thus, in their writing, most theologians emphasize the two basic dimensions of human promotion. On the one hand, human promotion requires the liberation of human beings from all that holds them in subhuman or oppressive conditions, so that they may enjoy their full dignity as children of God. On the other hand, it involves an integral development of the people and the values they possess, so that they may assume full responsibility for their own destiny. The former brings out the theological basis for human promotion: the immense dignity that the human person enjoys before God. The latter shows that the integral salvation of the whole human person, and not merely the extrication of the soul from the body, is the goal of evangelization (*RH* 13-14).

All this shows that there is a link between evangelization and human promotion. The theological foundation of human promotion is the incarnation. Through the redemptive incarnation of Christ, God himself enters, in a very radical way, into a new solidarity with humanity in history, liberates men and women from sin, and reestablishes them as sons and daughters. Both in his teaching and in his actions Jesus witnessed to this radically new and liberative solidarity of God with humanity (Luke 4:16-22; see Isa 61:1-2; Mark 1:15; Rev 21:1-4).

Seen in this wider context, it becomes clear that human promotion, if well understood, is an aspect of the church's evangelizing mission (see Congregation for the Doctrine of the Faith 1984, 867-77). This is why Vatican II discusses human promotion and its equivalents in the context of the church's evangelizing mission in the modern world (*GS* 42-84). The same orientation is found in postconciliar documents. For example, in the encyclical letter *Populorum Progressio* (1967), Paul VI spoke of an integral development that goes beyond mere economic growth to include the promotion of each person, the whole person, and indeed all of humanity (Paul VI 1967, 14). In the apostolic exhortation *Evangelii Nuntiandi* (1975), he said that evangelization is incomplete without human promotion, because the two are intimately connected in the anthropological, theological, and evangelical order (*EN* 29-31). Some years earlier, in 1971, the synod of bishops on "Justice in the World" had said that "action on behalf of justice and participation in the transformation of the world is a constitutive dimension (*ratio constitutiva*) of the church's evangelizing mission for the redemption of the human race and its liberation from every situation of oppression." The same orientation is given by John Paul II in the encyclical letter *Redemptoris Missio* (*RM* 58-59), by the Latin American bishops (CELAM 1979, 37-60), and by the African bishops (SECAM 1984, 143).

All this confirms the teaching that socioeconomic and political concerns have vital links with evangelization. Therefore, the church in the contemporary world, as she reflects on and pursues her mission of salvation, cannot neglect becoming actively involved in the efforts for human promotion, justice, and peace. Through evangelization the church aims at internally transforming human beings so that they can live in renewed relationship with God and with their brothers and sisters. The link between human promotion and evangelization is a necessary one. It consists of the fact that the mission to preach the gospel and the promotion of the human person concern the salvation of the total person, soul and body. Through the proclamation of the gospel and the works of justice and mercy, the human person is built up. To separate the works of development from the love that prompts them and that is preached in the gospel is to deny the profound unity of Christian involvement. This link above all brings out the communitarian nature of the human vocation and hence of the necessity of a more than individual ethic and of the importance of social responsibility and participation (*GS* 23-32). In fact, human promotion in the modern era should be made to develop in the perspective of this deeper awareness of the close link it has with evangelization.

The foregoing point, however, does not mean that one has to reduce the mission of the church to only social services or human promotion. The mission of the church is specifically a "religious" one and, therefore, is eschatological. This religious foundation of the church's mission is the source of its commitment, direction, and vigor to establish and consolidate the human community according to the law of God. In fact, "the church is able, indeed it is obliged, if times and circumstances require it, to initiate action for the benefit of all humankind, especially of those in need, like the works of mercy and similar undertakings" (*GS* 42b).

Moreover, if we are to give a theological reason for the eschatological dimension of mission, it is that the *eschaton* does not pertain only to the future; eschatology affects the present world and is already being realized in history through mission. Thus the notion of Christian time: history has a progressive character, and time is the condition for the realization of the last day, the fulfillment of salvation. The time has already arrived (*kairos*), the opportunity of carrying out the mission and of actualizing salvation. This is because the salvation that is already realized in Christ is not yet being brought to all men and women. We are at the last days, in the fullness of times, in which salvation already realized objectively has to be applied to all non-Christians (Rom 5:6; 13:11; 2 Cor 6:2; etc.). And salvation is not only for men and women, but it also includes that of human and religious cultural values. Christ through the mission of the church has come to save all (*AG* 9, 11). The church's time is the time of mission. In this last day of eschatology, the kerygma, or rather the gospel, has to be proclaimed to all; only then will the end arrive (Matt 24:14). The last element of this teaching on eschatology is the reign of Christ—Christ the Lord of all and in all (Col 1:15-19; Eph 1:10). Mission transforms the world in a Christian manner, purifies all its values, takes all that is good in the religions and cultures and restores them to Christ. This dynamism of creation through Christ passes through mission (Rom 8:19; Heb 2:5-6; 1 Cor 15:24ff.).

Thus, Vatican II confirms that the event of Christ is the event that gives meaning and fulfillment to this world and to history. This meaning continues to receive its progressive and successive fulfillment through the mission of the church. Sacred and profane history are touched; cosmic time and sacred are implied in turn. The risen Christ, an example of the power of God which transforms nature, becomes the sacrament of this transformation. Another example of the divine transforming power is the Eucharist, where the created things, cultivated by human hands, are transformed (*GS* 38; Forte 1975). Indeed, eschatology is explained best in terms of recapitulation of all in Christ (CCC 831-32).

Mission and Dialogue with Contextual Theologies

One of the emergent realities in mission studies is the increasing interest in the theologies of the Third World. It may not be wrong to say that the new ways of mission came about, largely, as a result of the realities of the Third World and the emergent theological reflections there. Thus, in this twenty-first century, contextual theologies may assume a new dimension in mission studies. One of the critical issues facing Christian mission has always been to respect and preserve the cultural identity of the people being evangelized and to help them find and recover all their cultural and religious heritage in Christ. Christian mission is about the encounter of the gospel message of Jesus Christ with different peoples and their ever-newer religious-cultural and sociopolitical contexts. It is about the impregnation of these contexts by the gospel, the assimilation of people's cultures by the gospel and that of the gospel by cultures, and the history of the consequent changes in the process of evangelization and of people's cultures.

Again, if mission theology until now has been dominated by the works of theologians from the North Atlantic, recent studies are showing that the future of mission and indeed of Christian theology will be determined by emerging contributions from Third World theologians. Theology, as is often said, is born of mission and of the concrete situation in which the evangelizing church finds itself. Even North Atlantic theology has started to become conscious of its contextualized nature despite its traditional claim to universalism. And Third World theologians are also becoming increasingly aware that the sociocultural, religious, economic, and political realities that make up the respective contexts of their theologies are inseparably linked with this claim of North Atlantic theology to universalism. Thus, as is already evident, North Atlantic and Third World theologians are now engaged in a fruitful and mutually critical dialogue. This dialogue, or rather the renewed interest for a new vision of relationship between the churches of the North Atlantic and those of the global South, is inspired by the same reality (Jenkins 2002). Rather than talk of "displacement" of the North by the South, it is better to view the shift in terms of emergence of "new centers of Christianity's universality." Whenever the faith is preached, assimilated, and incarnated in the cultural context of people, there emerges a new center of "Christianity's universality" (Bediako 1995, 163). In Catholic parlance, there emerges a local church in which one lives the fullness of the universal church. This points to the importance of dialogue with emergent contextual theologies and of a new vision of missionary ecclesiology of communion and autonomy in the universal church-family. Therefore, it is not so much a question of putting in danger the significance of the human agencies of mission or of the Christians from the South displacing their counterparts from the North. Rather, what is required is a new language that will take into consideration these emerging realities. This will help to guard against prejudiced attitudes of one zone against the other and the frequent tendency to discredit some concrete and genuine developments in the churches of the global South. All churches would like to be regarded and accepted as subjects in God's saving plan and as full participants in the work of Christian mission.

All this shows that the emergence of theological reflection in the young churches of Third World countries should not create tensions. In this age of globalization and interculturality, it is necessary to encourage an exchange of opinions and information between local churches on theological and pastoral levels. Thus, dialogue with contexts is an emerging trend in mission studies.

Tendencies and Factors Influencing Mission Thinking

What are the factors and currents of thought responsible for the emergence of the new understanding of mission? Since the last century, mission studies have been influenced by certain social and cultural factors occasioned by reality in the mission field and by some theological currents. Among the sociocultural factors, we have the shift in Christianity from the North to the global South, the decline in missionary vocations in the churches of the North Atlantic, the enhanced appreciation of modern studies on cultural anthropology, indigenization, etc. The theological currents concern the notion of mission as service to the kingdom, the theories of *missio Dei*, Christology, the role of the Holy Spirit, and the church in mission. There were also influential currents of thought on proclamation and conversion. A brief overview of some of these factors and tendencies may deepen our insight further on the concept of mission and will help us to appreciate the relevance of missiology in theological education.

Sociological Factors

It is no longer a secret to admit that Christianity in the global South presents a very bright future for Christendom when compared with the present situation in the North, where Christianity is struggling anew to recapture its pristine glory and to make itself understandable to a new generation. This reality has recently assumed new attention in the writings of some missiologists. Thus, as already indicated, the challenge rests on reading this new development from the positive viewpoint of Christian expansion and not as a displacement of one zone by the other. In addition to this, there is a noticeable decrease in the number of missionaries from the North Atlantic churches and a lack of truly missionary spirit. There is also a concern about the continuing decline in vocations in these zones that were noted for their missionary enterprise in the Third World countries in the last centuries (see Motte and Lang 1982, 274). This factor has caused some authors to play down the missionary urgency and to see the formation of new groups of lay persons as mission volunteers *ad tempus,* just as in the social field, as a "sign of the times." But the question is: Should the consecrated missionary who before worked all his life in missions leave the coast clear for the lay person who commits himself for some years to a rather human task (see López-Gay 1993, 11).

Behind this reality, however, the good news is that the churches in the global South are today witnessing a great increase in vocations and in the number of new mission societies. Though apostolic workers in the young churches are still a minority in proportion to the churches of the North Atlantic, their increasing numbers are a reality of vitality and of clear growth. Indeed, the vitality of the young churches is not only a question of numbers (of workers), but above all of missionary spirit. The missionary spirit remains active, especially when it is expressed in "missionary departures," in missionaries "sent out" to the nations. Also in this field, the young churches seem to be particularly active (see Dinh Duc Dao 1993, 37-38). The continents of Africa, Asia, and Latin America, which were often regarded as objects of mission enterprise, are themselves sending out missionaries. This challenges the older sister-churches of the North Atlantic to be disposed to receive and accept missionaries from these young churches as equals and in the spirit of Pius XII's encyclical letter *Fidei Donum* (see nos. 128-139). Therefore, notwithstanding the actual numerical crisis of missionaries in many churches of the Northern Hemisphere, one can conclude that God wants and seeks missionaries. Moreover, God provides the church in every age with the needed manpower in the missions. Mission is God's work.

However, the above realities, among others, inspired the so-called theory of "moratorium" which was proposed by some theologians in the Third World toward the end of the twentieth century. The theologians called for a moratorium on foreign missionaries. This theory, which was proposed for the first time in 1972 in Kenya and is still today the object of discussion in some circles, was meant to create a kind of pause of about ten years, during which the young churches were expected to discover their own identities and develop their own specific character without the control or interference of foreign missionaries. The theory, which forgets that the particular churches had a de facto right to ask foreigners to leave anyway, saw their departure as necessary for local Christians to resolve issues like the proper use of vernacular languages, the place of indigenous cultural elements, and getting nationals into leadership positions occupied by expatriates.

Again, at the 1974 synod on evangelization, the bishops, in particular the African delegates, rejected the theory of moratorium. For the African bishops, there should not arise the question of a moratorium or of stopping material assistance to younger churches. The bishops spoke of "promoting evangelization in coresponsibility." They said that, starting with the ecclesiology of Vatican II, there should develop in the churches a new relationship based on coresponsibility in evangelization. It was at the synod also that the African bishops issued a statement concerning the old form of the so-called missionary adaptation. The bishops chose as a new strategy for evangelization the model of the incarnation (inculturation) of the gospel into cultures.

In this context, it is clear that the moratorium does not solve the real problem of the particularity of the young churches either theologically or practically. For instance, theologically, starting with the conciliar theology of the "communion of churches," *all* the particular churches, including the young ones, have something to offer and to receive. None of them is self-sufficient. They will always need one another and *new forces* (see AG 20, RM 85). It needs to be emphasized, however, that among other things, the theme of moratorium also implies that the missionary must try to change some of his previous attitudes toward the people of the mission lands. He must avoid a paternalistic attitude and the temptation to impose his own culture. New missionaries must have an attitude of service, of openness and respect and acceptance of the local populace, their cultures and institutions. They must also cooperate with local missionaries and learn from them. Therefore, as the ecumenical commission on "Mission and Evangelization" affirms, there can never be a real moratorium on mission.

Thus, the goal of mission as evangelization and formation of particular churches, a community rooted in a concrete context with its proper cultural values, cannot be compromised in the name of a utopian or abstract theory like that of a moratorium (see AG 19a; EN 62; RM 85). In fact, the type of particularity of the church proposed in the theory of moratorium, its call to stop the sending and the presence of foreign missionaries in a bid to develop an indigenous church, is unattainable. The response of the African bishops in 1974 is still valid: we still have need of foreign missionaries, but what needs to be changed is the style of those who come; they must come with a spirit of service and not to impose their own ideas (see *International Review of Mission* [1975]: n. 254).

Another historical factor or reality that has continued to influence mission studies and which is also closely related to the previous one is the influence that developments in social anthropology and celebrated congresses on indigenization have had on the subject. These congresses, which have been so frequent since the 1970s (at Xicotepec and Iquitos in 1971), in spite of some overgeneralizations, have helped mission studies appreciate the value of local cultures in evangelization. This effort gained momentum immediately after the attainment of political independence of countries in the Third World. This reality was very much felt at the 1974 synod on evangelization, in which a good number of the delegates came from the young churches. At the synod, these young churches tried to identify their own identity and specificity in the context of the conciliar teaching on church communion and the role of cultures in evangelization. The real sense of authenticity in the young churches is later expressed in the postsynodal exhortation (see *EN* 62-64). The issue of indigenization receives new emphasis in the present practice of the theology of inculturation and contextual theology.

Again, one major positive aspect of this development is the interest in social and religious anthropology and the discovery of the role of the latter in missiological studies. This development has at least helped to rediscover the important place culture has in the process of evangelization. The new scholarship and its subsequent application to missionary activity opened up new prospects for evangelization. People considered uncivilized and uncultured were discovered, after careful study, to have complex cultural systems, religious beliefs, and high moral standards. It was also realized that culture had much deeper influence on the person than was previously thought. Merely converting individuals and isolating them from their cultural milieu so as to protect their faith was a useless endeavor. Rather, what is required is authentic conversion through a real penetration of the cultural milieu itself with gospel values (see Oborji 1998, 73-74). This aspect of the new development in social anthropology needs to be maintained.

Theological Tendencies

For some time now, contemporary missiology has been dominated by a certain type of debate concerning research about mission and theocentrism as well as by the theme of ecumenism. But underneath this is the discussion of the term *missio Dei* ("mission of God") (see Rosin 1972). As we shall see, the debate on *missio Dei* began with Protestants at the Wellingen Congress of 1952 and was inspired by the thesis of Karl Barth on the term *actio Dei*. This was taken up by Vicedom in his book: *From Christ-centrism to Theology of God's Sovereignty* (1958; Eng. 1965). This tendency emphasizes the fact that God is the protagonist of mission. The real aim of the *missio Dei* is the reign of God, not the *ecclesia viatorium*. Thus, mission is defined as God's action (Ghana Congress 1958). God's presence in the world and human history are also emphasized (New Delhi Congress 1961). From these beginnings we arrive at the Uppsala Congress, where the term *missio Dei* is accepted in its historical evolution.

Mission as Missio Dei and Service to the Kingdom. The main thesis of this theory can be re-stated thus: "Mission today is action meant for the discovery of God's action in the world." God saves when and as God wants. The mission of God is not bequeathed to the church nor is it an extension of the church itself. Hence, the expression *missio Dei* brings with it a real danger. It wants to establish the divine initiative in mission (which is right), but this is explained vaguely by its understanding of the entire action through time and space as if God, in his own case, had wished to realize the renewal of the world today and humankind's redemption without Jesus Christ and the church. According to this theory, the church and the missionary are only a "sign" that God is present and actual in the world. The theological consequence of this tendency is the attempt to bring into relief the theology of the kingdom of God and to give attention to the perceived signs of the kingdom, principally, to peace initiatives, which are interpreted as secular events. It is the secularization of mission (see *RM* 22-30).

Mission and Christology. The recent crisis in Christological formulation is having a great influence on contemporary debates in missiology. There is a tendency today to try to relativize what some consider the abstract formulations of traditional Christological formulas with regard to the cardinal teaching on the final role of God's action in Jesus. This approach is especially found in the works of theologians for whom Western tendencies to "Christomonism" need correction. Another version of this tendency is found in the works of theologians of radical pluralism of religion such as John Hick and Paul Knitter. Their pluralistic theology of religions effectively downgrades Jesus Christ and what he stands for in traditional Christian theology. Some authors explain this tendency as something caused by the reality of post-Enlightenment Europe and its developments in science and technology, which have pushed religion to the sidelines as the secularization of society grows (Pannenberg 1990, 96). The Enlightenment paradigm of mission, as characterized and utilized by liberal theology, has resulted in a critical juncture with regard to mission in churches that have adopted this way of seeing things (Bosch 1991, 186).

In the first chapter of *Redemptoris Missio*, John Paul II responded to this tendency in Christology and mission. Indeed, it is possible to read the whole of this encyclical as an extended *apologia* for a return to a renewed, orthodox, Trinitarian Christology from which Christian mission can take its bearings and not be reduced to a kind of social service. *Dominus Iesus*, a document of the Congregation for the Doctrine of Faith, also addressed this problem. What, then, is the real concern in contemporary Christology from the Roman magisterium's perspective? The central issue is how to articulate adequately the way God saves people, who Jesus is, and the role of Jesus, of the church, and of other religious founders and the traditions they founded in the mystery of salvation.

There are various currents of thought related to this problem. First, there is the so-called *exclusivist theory*, which excludes any mediator of salvation other than Christ and the church he instituted. This theory excludes all other religious figures and all other peoples who are outside Christianity from achieving salvation in a regular and normal way and, in its more rigorous manifestations, teaches that outside explicit faith in Christ no one can be saved.

Second, there are inclusivist theories, which hold that Christ and the church have a unique role in salvation. They accept, however, the possibility of salvation for all, even if some do not have explicit faith in Christ, but wherever one is saved, it is the work of Christ that is ultimately the cause of that salvation. This trend has two aspects.

The first can be called an "inclusive Christocentric" strand. It puts major stress on the role of Christ, with a subordinate role for the church. For some theologians, God saves normally in and through Christ and the church. Christ and the church remain constitutive (essential) to salvation. This salvation won by Christ is available to all, even those who do not know Christ and are not members of the church, but who are truly men and women of good will. In this view of the matter, however, salvation is available publicly and visibly in and through Christ and the church, which are God's chosen ways of making divine grace manifest.

The second can be called an "inclusive theocentric" strand. It says that God saves in and through anyone or any institution God chooses. The Father of Jesus, the first person of the Trinity, may use other religious leaders and religious institutions as models of salvation, but they are not mediators of salvation in their own right. Christ and the church, though, retain a prominent role in this process. They are normative. In this perspective Christ "indicates that he is the revelation and mediation from God which corrects and fulfils all other mediations. . . . If God desires all to be saved, much of his saving activity will be accomplished in a religious milieu which is non-Christian" (Schineller 1976, 556). But if Christ is not normative in this view, much less can the church be considered normative. The church is intended to be the community in which the truest and fullest revelation of his love is manifest, the measure by which other religious communities are judged (see Schineller 1976, 559).

There are also pluralistic views—theories that assert that salvation comes to people in many ways, through many mediators, who, in principle, are equal and whose role is equivalent. Langdon Gilkey does not see this as an orthodox Christian view of the matter. He does, however, maintain that from a philosophical or history-of-religions perspective the great world religions exist in what he calls a situation of "rough parity," and that none of them can demonstrate decisive superiority over the others (Gilkey 1987). There are two theological responses to this sort of insight. The first is a *theocentric* view that claims God saves in and through the classic founders of religion, and through present-day religious leaders and institutions. They are all pictured as achieving the same basic goal and thus functionally performing the same role. The theory claims further that neither Christ nor the church has a special function in salvation history: they are one possibility among many. In this view, then, there are many mediators of salvation, and Christ is one of them. And in its ecclesiological position, there are many communities of salvation, for God has no special, favored way in which we are to achieve salvation (Hick 1973; 1980). In this theory, the maxims, "outside Christ no salvation," and, a fortiori, "outside the church no salvation," disappear altogether.

The second pluralistic orientation can be called a *soteriocentric* view. This theory claims that all followers of religions believe that there is salvation in the world. They do not agree on its origin, though the majority relate the source of salvation to God; but others do not (chiefly Buddhists). So, the advocates of this theory assert that the important thing is not to find out who grants salvation, nor how or when it is granted, but for followers of every religious way to help one another attain it, develop it, let it work in and through people. The best way to do it is through interfaith dialogue and cooperation in solving the world's concrete problems, which are viewed as impeding the fullness of salvation (see Bellagamba 1993, 23).

There is a tendency in some forms of contemporary Christology to posit an opposition between Christ-Logos and the historical Jesus. Jesus of Nazareth, it says, had a restricted role, and the Word or Logos, who illumines all and saves all, is absolute. From this viewpoint, we get the so-called Logos Christology, the Cosmic Christology, the Unknown Christ of Hinduism (Raimundo Panikkar), and the Omega Christology (Pierre Teilhard de Chardin). There is also a theory that speaks of "Christian presence in the religions." Some authors arrive at the conclusion that "Christianity without Christ" has for the world today more actuality than that which presents the revelation and communication of God in Christ. A second trend eschews Christology in any way that resembles the classic doctrine of the church and attempts to create a vision of Jesus from critical reconstructions of the biblical record. One thinks of works by the members of the so-called Jesus seminar, in particular the books of John Dominic Crossan. The Christology of Roger Haight (1999) has received attention from the Congregation for the Doctrine of Faith for developing what is sometimes called "Spirit Christology" in ways that empty Jesus of full divine personhood and that portray him not as a consubstantial member of the Trinity but merely as one in whom the Spirit of God was present ("Notification" 2004).

Moreover, such Christological tendencies do not have a point of departure in the Trinity, but from Jesus the human being, who, in the memorable phrase of Dietrich Bonhoeffer, is defined by his "being for the others." The interest is not so much in the incarnation of the preexisting Logos by the plan of God for eschatological salvation and the fulfillment of creation or in the divinity of Christ. Rather, interest falls on his "pro-existence," his "being-for-us," which amounts to his being a symbol of a God who is benevolent toward all humanity, especially the oppressed. This Christological position stands in the tradition of the great prophets of Israel in their efforts to denounce injustice and institute a truly just society. In this view Christ is distinguished by his solidarity with others in the face of worldly powers. As such, there is little to criticize and much to praise in retrieving this man-for-others and prophetic dimension. Indeed there is much to praise. But orthodoxy, tutored by the early Trinitarian councils and creeds, asks, "Is this all the Scriptures and tradition record?"

Some authors arrive at completely secular and radical conclusions: God and transcendence are eliminated in favor of a unidimensional, "horizontal" Christian *atheology*. The message of Christ in this case is to be interpreted only when we have the human being as the background. Christ was a free man, who preached liberation and who liberates humankind. Thus, the figure of Christ is reduced to a model in the struggle for liberation, for work in favor of others—and these are the new focus for mission. Other authors more theological in approach see in Christ the normative means but not the constitutive element of salvation. It seems fair to say, too, that in this understanding salvation is viewed primarily in this-worldly, historical, and sociopolitical liberationist terms, not as an eschatological event in which we participate now but anticipate the fullness thereof at the parousia.

To evaluate such trends in Christology, we need to begin by looking at the mission of Christ in the New Testament. There he is portrayed as the definitive missionary who was sent by the Father for the salvation of all and who has communicated this mission to the church. From the moment of its inception, the church kept in mind this view, as one sees in texts such as "There is no salvation in any other name" (Acts 4:12), and no other mediator "between God and humankind" (1 Tim 2:4-6). Furthermore, in very clear terms, Christ describes himself as the life, the truth, and the way (John 10:6). As we said above, John Paul II in *Redemptoris Missio* points out the inadequacies of such theories in contemporary Christology and affirms that Jesus the Christ is the foundation of the church's internal life and of all her activities, and Jesus is the reason for its most essential activity, the mission *ad gentes* (*RM* 4). Furthermore, since salvation is possible only in and through Christ in whom God revealed himself, and since he is the Word, he is also the unique, universal, and absolute savior (*RM* 5-6). Thus, Christ must be proclaimed to those who do not yet know him (*RM* 9-11). John Paul II's insistence on the uniqueness of Christ, however, as mediator does not exclude other "participated forms of mediation of different kinds and degrees"; but these "acquire meaning and value only from Christ's own mediation, and they cannot be understood as parallel or complementary to his" (*RM* 5). Christ is the only mediator between God and humanity; all the other great founders of religions can be considered mediators only in relationship with and in the power of Christ (*LG* 62; *RM* 5; *DI* 13-15).

From this perspective, the church, the first beneficiary of Christ's salvation, also becomes a sign of that sacrament to all and has the mission to offer it to all. Salvation, which is offered by God to all, must always be viewed in relationship to Christ and the church. The church derives its boldness in and its strength for its missionary proclamation as well as its centrality in the life of all humanity from Jesus' unique role. It is through the church that Christ, the only mediator between God and man, continues his mission on earth (*LG* 6-8, 14, 20, 14; *UR* 4; *RM* 9-11; *UUS* 11; *DI* 16-22). Therefore, the church is not another mediator of salvation, or a different mediator over, above, or together with Christ. The church is a sign and means of Christ's unique role of salvation. But it remains true that everybody is influenced by the redemptive act of Christ and the work of the church (see Bellagamba 1993, 23-24).

Mission and the missionary church. Related to the above tendencies is the ecclesiological crisis in contemporary missiology. Under the influence of the authors of the missionary theory of *missio Dei*, interpreted in an exclusive sense, the lordship of God or, rather, the concept of the "kingdom of God" is emphasized, while an understanding of the church as an essential element in the mediation of the mystery, of the church as a sacrament of salvation, and of its missionary mandate is forgotten or pushed aside. In fact, the problem begins when this kingdom tries to replace the mission of Jesus Christ and the present role of the church. Missionaries, in the opinion of these authors, work for the coming of the kingdom, and its prime manifestations are qualities such as liberty, peace, and justice in this world. Certainly Christ proclaimed the kingdom and was its first servant. This school of thought, however, reduces the church to and then takes into consideration only its juridical structure, forgetting that the church is portrayed as much more than this in both Scripture and doctrine. See, for example, *Lumen Gentium* chap. 1, which speaks eloquently of the church as intimately involved in the mystery of salvation and as a complex reality in which the visible and invisible elements cohere "in a powerful analogy, to the mystery of the incarnate Word" (*LG* 8). The necessity to move out into the world in mission, accordingly, is an undertaking that one carries out for love of God and of one's fellow human beings. But the question whether we can separate the structure of the church from Christ's saving presence in the church itself is answered negatively in Paul VI's *Evangelii Nuntiandi*, article 15. This statement also speaks to those who do not want to hear again of the goal of missionary activity as evangelization and *plantatio ecclesiae* ("planting the church").

The new understanding of the relationship between mission and human promotion, however, as pointed out already, has tried to correct most of the excesses in this type of interpretation of the *missio Dei* and the kingdom. The salvation brought by the church is not only eschatological, the salvation of souls, but is also on behalf of people who live in today's world and in today's history. Human promotion is an integral part of the church's mission (*EN* 33ff.; *RM* 59). Jesus inaugurated his church by preaching the good news, that is, the coming of the kingdom of God (Mark 1:15). This kingdom shone out before men in the word, in the works, and in the presence of Christ (*LG* 5). The kingdom of God is inseparable from the presence and the proclamation of Christ, because the church "receives the mission of proclaiming and establishing among all peoples the Kingdom of Christ and of God, and she is, on earth, the seed and the beginning of that Kingdom" (*LG* 5). The proclamation of the kingdom is the center of evangelization (*EN* 8), but this is inconceivable without the explicit announcement of the life and mystery of Jesus of Nazareth (*EN* 22, 27; *RM* 16). Therefore, in the midst of these tendencies in contemporary missiology, we have to come back and take our inspiration from the definitive economy of the incarnation, of the missionary mandate, and of the gospel: "proclaim the Gospel to all creation. Whoever believes will be saved" (Mark 16:15); "there is no other name by which we must be saved" (Acts 4:12-13); "the Christian economy, therefore, since it is new and definitive Covenant, will never pass away; and no new public revelation is to be expected" (*DV* 4).

Taking papal and conciliar teaching to heart, one realizes that there are both acquisitions to be considered and lost value and vigor that must be recovered (*GS* 4, 11). Contemporary missiology is influenced by the debate on the intimate and inseparable relationship between the Holy Spirit and the missionary church. In the teaching of the church, the salvific activity of God is realized through the mission of the church. This mission is a historical mediation, visible, salvific, as on that day God saved the world through the mission of his Son, whose mission the church continues today (*EN* 15). This is the "ordinary means" (*via ordinaria*) established by God. But there is an intimate and inseparable relationship between the Holy Spirit and the missionary church. According to Vatican II, the fundamental rule for the realization of salvation today is "the Lord Jesus, the ordinary way, his apostolic ministry and promise of the sending of the Holy Spirit, in a way that both always collaborate and in each case for the realization of the work of salvation" (*AG* 4; *LG* 8, 48b; *EN* 15, 80). The Holy Spirit and missionaries are "agents" of salvation, true collaborators, cooperators. The church is the "sign and instrument of the Holy Spirit" (López-Gay 1988, 3). Thus, the significance of Pentecost for the church at Jerusalem (Acts 2) and for other particular churches (Acts 13:1ff.; *RM* 24-29). Therefore we can talk of the Holy Spirit in missionaries. It is the Holy Spirit that calls the missionaries and sends them on mission. It is the same Holy Spirit that works in the hearts of non-Christians and invites them to listen and accept the offer of salvation through the gospel proclamation of the missionaries. However, in this case, it is pertinent to remark that the Holy Spirit gives to all the possibility of coming into contact with the paschal mystery in a way known only to God (*GS* 22).

Proclamation and mission. Another theological trend that has had great influence on mission studies today is the debate on the relationship between proclamation and mission. The historical origins of this can be located within the theological approach of the last century that advocated a movement from kerygma to anthropology and to politics. Kerygmatic theology was given its concretization at the Eichstätt Catechetical-Missionary Study Week. This was part of the continental Catechetical-Missionary Study Weeks organized under the auspices of the Austrian Jesuit Johannes Hofinger at the close of the 1960s. The aim was to promote catechetical renewal. The Eichstätt study week observes that for catechetical renewal, the problem is not so much methodology, but reflection on the content of the faith. The interest is not so much in how to evangelize but the content of the proclamation, the message and the person of Christ. Methodologically, the study week accepted a four-fold emphasis: biblical, liturgical, witness, and doctrinal (see Warren 1983, 30ff.).

In the similar study week in Bangkok (1962), the center of attention was no longer on the content of the message to humankind. The study week discussed the theme of preevangelization and noted the crisis of the kerygma (Warren 1983, 40ff.). Furthermore, in the study week of Katigondo, Uganda (1964), the issues of anthropology and ethnology were tabled. In order to develop in the ministers of the word a strong apostolic personality modeled on that of the Good Shepherd, the study week asked that these ministers be initiated into human, personal, and community contacts both with the faithful and with those outside the fold (see Warren 1983, 6). The key word of this anthropocentric trend is found in the Manila (Philippines) study week (1967). Here the "anthropological approach," as well as secularization and pluralism, received the attention of the participants at the congress. The initial approach to persons of other faiths (religions) and to nonbelievers was investigated, and a question was raised as to the type of culture that should be taken into consideration in the adaptation of the church to the local cultures of Asia. Through commitment to human values, especially the struggle for social reform, Christians must bear witness to their spirit of loving service. They should, through such common work, endeavor to reveal to others the deepest nature of the Christian mystery that motivates them. Christ could, where opportunity presents itself, be presented as the fulfillment of human aspirations. Again, local cultures are continually changing. Consequently, adaptation to local culture today means adaptation to the present culture of a nation that has roots in the past and is open to the assimilation of what is best in the technological and scientific culture of the West.

The Manila study week recommended that theology and catechesis be reoriented to give prominence to the universal dimension of the reality of God revealed in Jesus Christ. The deepest truths of Christianity have all of humankind as their participants and beneficiaries, whether these be aware of it or not. God is the creator and father of all; Christ is the lord of history and redeemer of humanity; and the Holy Spirit works in every human heart from the first moment of creation. These truths can make Christians aware of the spiritual riches of all humankind and at the same time make others see in Christianity the fulfillment of their own highest aspirations. These truths must be put in the forefront of our theology and our catechesis (see Warren 1983, 60ff.).

The next moment of the theology of missionary proclamation as political reading was at the Medellín conference in 1968, where the liberation of the oppressed under social and political structures was subsumed into a vision of a praxis of integral evangelization. The Medellín documents remark that Latin America is racked by acute and rapid changes in the economic, demographic, social, and cultural spheres. As a consequence, those responsible for catechesis face a series of tasks that are complicated and difficult to combine. They must

- promote the evolution of traditional forms of faith characteristic of a great part of the Christian people and bring about new forms;

- evangelize and catechize masses of simple people, frequently illiterate, and at the same time meet the needs of students and intellectuals who are the most alive and dynamic sectors of society;

- purify traditional forms of influence and at the same time discover a new way of influencing contemporary forms of expression and communication in a society that becomes increasingly secularized;

- put to use all the resources of the church in accomplishing these tasks and at the same time renounce forms of power and prestige that are not evangelical (see Warren 1983, 66ff.).

Mission and conversion. Contemporary missiology witnessed and still witnesses a heated debate on the concept of "conversion" in relation to missionary activity. Some missiologists adhered to the theory of "nonconversion," which is said to have been a maxim of Gandhi. This theory received its theological orientation in the missionary thought of authors such as Bede Griffiths, Kaj Baago, etc. (see *Missiology* 6 [1978], 149). These authors think that the word "conversion" means "breaking off" people from their culture in order for them to embrace a new religion. J. López-Gay contests this way of interpreting conversion (1988, 28). The fact is that conversion forms part of the mission of Christ and of his proclamation (Mark 4:17; Luke 5:32). It also formed part of the mission of the precursor, John the Baptist (Matt 3:6, 8ff.), and of the apostles (Acts 2:38). In the missionary mandate, we found the proclamation of conversion (Luke 24:47). In fact, the term "conversion" is joined to missionary work among the nations (Acts 11:18; 14:22; 17:30; 26:18).

Biblical vocabulary explains the profound theology of conversion in relation to themes such as the "way" and "covenant." In the Old Testament, conversion (*shub*) is an attitude of the heart (which is not purely legal) that makes the person called by God (following the vocation) to leave the wrong path and turn to God, to return to God, abandoning his sins (Amos 4:7-11; Joel 2:12ff.); and so God turns to the person and makes a new covenant with him (Zech 1:3; Lam 5:21; Jer 31:18; 32:29). God who is love takes the initiative in conversion. The human person on his part is expected to acknowledge his own sin, confess it, and be sorry as he returns to God. Thus, conversion is tied to the heart (Jer 4:1-4; 3:19-25).

The New Testament used two verbs for "conversion" (*metanoien* and *epistrephein*), and these developed the same sense of the term in the Old Testament. Conversion is explained thus in the sense of "leaving the mistaken path and returning to Christ" (as the parable of the prodigal son dramatizes). It is in this sense that some of these terms are applied to non-Christians: "For they themselves report concerning us what a welcome we had among you and how you turned to God from idols, to serve a living and true God, and to wait for his son from heaven" (1 Thess 1:9; Acts 9:35; 11:21; 15:3; 26:18f.); conversion means abandoning darkness and the power of Satan (Acts 28:18; Eph 5:8).

Thus, in missions conversion is necessary. It is not for the saints but for salvation, which comes after a second conversion. The first conversion is necessary, because he who believes will be saved (Acts 13:38ff.). It brings with itself the forgiveness of sins (Acts 11:18; Rom 8:6; 7:6). Interior conversion is manifested in sacramental signs and by entry into the ecclesial community (*EN* 28, 47, 23; *RM* 46-48). In other words, there are theological elements which show that, in conversion, every step is a process. In the first place, God is the principal protagonist in conversion. Conversion is the work of God. He calls (conversion and vocation, Mark 10:25ff.), and he gives grace (John 6:44). God changes the heart and life of man and converts him to his Son; and so, in the Son, the Father reconciles us (2 Cor 5:18f.; Rom 5:11). Second, the grace of conversion is attributed to the Holy Spirit (1 Corinthians), who works in the depth of the heart. A conversion to the church is also treated as a conversion to Christ, who is present today in the church; "be converted to the church" is an expression of St. Irenaeus, and it is applied to Gnostics who have abandoned the church (*Adv. Haer.* I, III, 24, 1; 1, 6, 3; 13, 5).

The second point touches the question of man and his part in this process of conversion. As López-Gay puts it, it is a free adhesion (of the heart) with the following elements:

- intellectual element: acceptance of the gospel, kerygma, objectively accepting new values in Christ as the only savior (Mark 1:15b; Acts 20:21b). The word transmits this element (Jer 2:4, 31; 17:15-16).

- a moral factor: to leave the path of sin (Luke 13:2-3; Acts 3:19; 26:20; Matt 5:20; Rom 6:2ff.; Eph 4:22). It is an exodus or passage from darkness to light, from death to life.

- a personal experience with the person of Christ: the meeting with the person (Jer 3:19, 21, 23ff.) and, in our context, with Christ. In every conversion, there is the joy of meeting (Luke 15:24; Mark 2:15ff.). This experience of meeting changes the life of one, and conversion becomes mission (Acts 9:5, 11; etc.).

- it means making a break: abandoning former values and customs (Acts 6:14; 16:20f.; Gal 4:9). This is the radicality of conversion.

- finally, it means fullness: the converted finds the proper values (culturally, religiously) "purified and elevated in the church" (*AG* 9, 11).

What is the part of the missionary in this process of conversion? The missionary has the role of mediator through the proclamation of the gospel (Mark 6:12; John 17:20). Mediation is necessary in God's design of salvation. It does not mean proselytizing, forcing one to convert (*AG* 13b). The attitude of the missionary is to offer peace to all (Luke 10:3ff.; Matt 10:16), and with peace proclaim conversion in Christ. This brings with it a sense of humility and admiration for the work of God in non-Christians, and respect for the rhythm of God and humanity (López-Gay 1988, 28).

Conclusion

To conclude this chapter, we indicate again that most of the missiological themes in the concept of mission are taken up today with more vigor in various aspects of the so-called new ways of mission: e.g., evangelization, inculturation, ecumenism, interreligious dialogue, human promotion, etc. (see Colzani 1996, 55ff.). Furthermore, it is a well-known fact that in the postconciliar period, in spite of the crisis in missiology, there is great support and hope for Christian mission (*RM* 2). Some have described it as the springtime of Christianity even as we grapple with the negative tendencies. The period has battled with two dominant questions: the shift in ecclesiology with its progressive emphasis on mission and its actualizing of the universal communication that brings to the whole world a unique transformation. There is also a tendency to provide a Trinitarian and economic reading of mission and to consider it from a unifying perspective of a salvific dynamism in the force of which the divine life reaches all and is open to all creatures. To this must be added the progressive profile of a missiological tendency that has led to a profound evangelization and humanization. It must be noted, therefore, that a precise determination of the relationship between the kingdom, church, and history is an object of theological discussion today. The result of this is that those who want the determination of the missionary activity want also the mission of the church. But unfortunately, their positions are not presented with one voice and shared mode (see Colzani 1996, 57-59).

Therefore, in all of these contexts, it is important that one equips oneself ecclesially and theologically with knowledge of the themes that have come from the major interventions of the magisterium (especially, *Ad Gentes* and *Ecclesiam Suam*; *Populorum Progressio* and *Evangelii Nuntiandi*; *Redemptor Hominis* and *Postquam Apostoli*; *Slavorum Apostoli* and *Redemptoris Missio*; *Tertio Millennio Adveniente* and postsynodal exhortations [i.e., documents released by the holy father based on the continental synods that discussed fundamental missiological issues in relation to Africa, America, Oceania, Asia, and Europe]). Be that as it may, the results of these continental synods and also of recent missiological congresses confirm our basic argument in this study, namely, that dialogue with contexts (contextual theologies) is the emerging trend in mission studies.

Moreover, in the midst of all this, an interesting phenomenon is emerging in the contemporary missiology. Today, missiological discussion is being restructured around the mystery and lordship of Christ (Christology and eschatology). And this fact is also most vividly seen in the emergent contextual theologies. In fact, a careful study of the writings of Third World theologians reveals that, of all the theological themes, Christology has received their greatest attention. It is the focal point from which theologians address various theological and missiological themes. This is a promising development, and is still open to further study. Moreover, in the Christian religion, the person of Jesus Christ is at the center or rather is the determining factor of theological evaluation. This fact should apply as well to mission studies. Likewise, today humanity is also receiving a central place in missiological reflection as well as in other theological discussions. For the human being is the reason for God's salvific work in Christ. In the light of this, it has been observed, and rightly too, that modern man appears to be more religious, as he looks for the meaning of life, of events, while remaining open to the truth, to the Absolute. As this phenomenon brings new facts to missiology, the church is challenged to continue with renewed vigor her missionary work.

2

MISSION AND THE GROWTH OF MISSIOLOGY IN THEOLOGICAL EDUCATION

In the preceding chapter we saw how the shift in modern theology has placed missiological studies at the center of attention: evangelization, Christology, religious pluralism, contextual theology, inculturation, interreligious dialogue, human promotion, globalization, etc. As already indicated, however, this new development does not mean that missiology has been accorded its rightful place in theological education. Though already established as a discipline in its own right, missiology is still struggling with its identity and purpose in theological education. So missiology's problem in theological education still lingers on. Missiology has never gotten the space it required in theological education.

The present chapter will discuss the growth of missiology as a science of its own in theological education. It will present a brief history and evolution of missiology, its missionary role and place in theological education. Thereafter, the chapter will highlight the functions of missiology in the missionary activity of the church as well as the new challenges facing the discipline in the field of theology.

The Term "Missiology"

Mission studies as a distinct branch in theological education has been known by other titles before its present name, "missiology" (see Jongeneel 1995, 15ff.). For instance, Gustav Warneck (1834-1910), the pioneer Protestant missiologist, called it *Missionslehre* ("theory" or "doctrine of mission"), which is still used to describe the course of missiological study at Free University in Amsterdam. Warneck also entitled his three-volume book *Missionslehre* (see Verkuyl 1987, 1). The Catholic pioneer missiologist Josef Schmidlin (1876-1944), who died in one of Hitler's concentration camps,

41

called it *Missionswissenschaft* ("mission science"), which is also the name given to the University of Münster school of missiology—"department of mission science." Subsequent authors inevitably build on Warneck's and Schmidlin's perspectives.

In recent decades, the term "missiology" has been the favored name for the discipline. It retains the originally Greek and Latin meaning of the word—the academic study of mission (mission studies). It is an academic study of the missionary dimension of the Christian faith, the Great Commission (Matt 28:18-20). It is a theological discipline that engages in a systematic and scientific study or elaboration of the fact that the church is missionary by nature (*AG* 2). Furthermore, it examines scientifically and critically the activities through which the church does her mission—the work of evangelization and of planting the church itself among various cultures and peoples (*AG* 6, 9). In a more technical sense, missiology is a branch of theology that studies the salvation activities of the Father, Son, and Holy Spirit throughout the world geared toward bringing the kingdom of God into existence. It studies the church's divine mandate to bring the gospel message to the ends of the earth. In dependence on the Holy Spirit and word and deed the church has the obligation to bring the gospel and God's saving plan to all humanity (see Verkuyl 1987, 5).

The significant thing about missiology is that it is often defined in the context of the question, What is mission? instead of the question, What is missiology in and of itself? About this, more will be said later. In this situation missiology is a theological discipline that tries to prove how "all generations of the earth" are objects of God's salvific plan of salvation in Jesus Christ (Camps et al. 1988, 19). It tries to show that this dimension of the Christian faith is not an option. Instead, as the Vatican II decree on mission, *Ad Gentes*, states, "The Church on earth is by its very nature missionary," and it is the intrinsic nature and mission of the church to proclaim the message of salvation in Christ to the ends of the earth (art. 2). To neglect this mission is for the church to deny its very raison d'être. But this does not mean that missiology as a theological discipline is a neutral or disinterested enterprise; rather, it seeks to look at the world from the perspective of commitment to the Christian faith. Such an approach implies as well a critical subjection of every manifestation of the church's missionary activity to rigorous analysis and appraisal, precisely for the sake of the Christian mission itself (Bosch 1991, 9).

We have to distinguish between "mission" (singular) and "missions" (plural), since missiology is defined in the context of these terms. The first refers primarily to the *missio Dei* (God's mission), that is, the divine intervention in favor of all humanity of all times and of the whole world (*AG* 2). It is God's self-revelation as the one who loves the world, God's involvement in and with the world, and in which the church—the sacrament and instrument of bringing about realization of God's plan of salvation among all humanity—is privileged to participate. *Missio Dei* enunciates the good news that God is a God-for-people.

The word "missions" (*missiones ecclesiae*, the missionary ventures of the church) refers to those particular undertakings by which the heralds of the gospel are sent by the church and go forth into the whole world to carry out the task of preaching (evangelization) and planting the church among peoples or groups who do not yet believe in Christ (*AG* 6). In the words of David Bosch, "missions" refer to particular forms, related to specific times, places, or needs, of participation in the *missio Dei* (see Bosch 1991, 10; Davis 1966, 33; Hoekendijk 1967, 346; Rütti 1972, 232).

Missiology, however, is concerned not only with missio *ad extra* but also with missio *ad intra*. Its field of operation is the entire spectrum of the Christian mission—the three concrete situations in which the church carries out its various evangelizing activities: (1) mission *ad gentes*, (2) pastoral care, (3) new evangelization, etc. (see *RM* 33; Bellagamba 1993, 40ff.).

Development of Missiology as a Theological Discipline

Early Studies of Missiology

Mission studies (missiology) as a theological discipline is of recent origin (see Müller 1987, 11). Though theology itself, as reflection on faith, was born out of finding itself in new circumstances, often because of mission, it did not consider it a necessity to develop a discipline of systematic reflections on mission until recently. This may be an oversight in theological studies. In the early centuries of Christianity, theology was generated largely by the emergency situation in which the missionizing church found itself. Because of this situation, it is impossible to read the New Testament without taking into account that most of it was written within a missionary context; this is also true of patristic writings (see Kähler 1971, 189). In other words, mission was the "mother of theology." However, as Europe became christianized and Christianity became the established religion in the Roman Empire and beyond, theology lost its missionary dimension (see Bosch 1991, 489).

There are some exceptions to this situation, however. The great Franciscan scholar, poet, philosopher, and missionary Raimon Lull (died 1315) undertook a scientific analysis of mission in various forms. Lull urged the church to establish schools for studying those languages spoken by the peoples to whom the gospel had yet to be proclaimed. His chief interest was Arabic, and in 1276 he personally founded a seminary on Majorca for missionaries for the study of the *idiomata diversa*. At his urging the Council of Vienne (1311) established chairs for the study of these languages in Rome, Bologna, Paris, Oxford, and Salamanca. They did not exist for long, however. After a lengthy period a great awareness came in 1627 when the *Collegium Urbanum de Propaganda Fide* was founded in Rome. It had a profound impact on the many students who went there to study.

There were also Protestant mission theorists as far back as the Dutch colonial mission of the early seventeenth century. In 1622 the East India Trading Company requested the theological faculty of Leiden University to sketch a plan for a proposed seminary for pastors who were planning to serve in India and who could thus concurrently work for the "conversion of the heathen." The East India Company abolished the seminary in 1633, saying that the results did not seem worth the heavy costs to the company. A similar attempt was by A. H. Francke's *Collegium Orientale Theologicum* in Halle, founded in 1702. This, along with Leibnitz's *Akademie der Wissenschaften* in Berlin, was a training center for theological candidates to "propagate the faith through knowledge" (*propagatio fidei scientias*). The impact on missiology, however, was very slight. J. Flatt gave a course of lectures on mission in the University of Tübingen as far back as 1800. Moreover, in 1832, at the beginning of the modern renewed efforts in mission studies, J. T. L. Danz, the Jena church historian (who coined the expression "apostolics"), mentioned the concept "study of missions." But these efforts were not immediately pursued as one would have expected (see Myklebust 1955/57, 76).

Other efforts were also made. In 1864, Karl Graul (1814-1864), director of the Leipzig Mission, made an initial try to introduce to Europe the scientific study of missions. In that year he delivered a speech that qualified him as a private teacher at Erlangen; in it he made a plea for including missiology in the *universitas litterarum*. Among other things, he said: "This discipline must gradually come to the point where she holds her head up high; she has a right to ask for a place in the house of the most royal of all science, namely, theology." This was the first knock on the door of the theological faculties. Graul's call was realized when C. H. Plath (1829-1901), inspector of the Berlin and Goss Mission, began to lecture in missiology at the famous Humboldt University of Berlin. Plath taught privately at first (1867) and later became honorary professor, that is, one who is not an official member of the faculty (see Verkuyl 1987, 11ff.).

The year Platt began as private teacher in Berlin (1867), Alexander Duff (1806-1878) assumed his task as missiologist at the New College in Edinburgh with the delivery of his inaugural address entitled "Evangelistic Theology." But it was a long journey before the Duff era. It could be said that the event that led to his new position began as early as 1811 with the resolution adopted at the General Assembly of the Presbyterian Church in the United States of America to establish a theological seminary for the training of missionaries. This resolution was not implemented until 1836 when Charles Breckenridge was appointed as the first professor to teach, specifically, "Missionary Instruction" at Princeton Theological Seminary in New Jersey. When Breckenridge withdrew as a professor in 1839 the idea was again dropped. Then came the effort in 1867 in Presbyterian New College, Edinburgh, which culminated in the appointment of Alexander Duff to the chair of "evangelistic theology." Duff's chair is the first of its kind. With Duff, "missiology" was taught as an independent subject in its own right. Hence, Duff is often referred to as "the first professor of missions in Christendom." Duff himself had been a missionary of the Church of Scotland in India for three decades. Thus, his appointment was controversial, not because his qualifications were questioned but because it was doubtful whether a competent successor could later be found for such an "abnormal" subject. As a matter of fact, Duff's professorship, having been demoted to a lectureship, was totally abolished in 1909 (see Myklebust 1955/57, 147ff.; Müller 1987, 11).

The Study of Missiology in the Contemporary Era

After these initial attempts, efforts were intensified once more to introduce missiology as a theological discipline in its own right. In the meantime, missiology had grown beyond the "experimental" character that Duff had to struggle with, and had found its permanent position in many theological faculties and universities. It was, however, mainly because of the indefatigable efforts of Gustav Warneck, who taught at the University of Halle (1896-1910), and those of Josef Schmidlin, the founder of the first chair of missiology at a Catholic institution in 1910, at the University of Münster, that missiology was established as a discipline in its own right: "not just a guest but as having the right of domicile in theology" (Bosch 1991, 491). The precedents of Warneck and Schmidlin were soon followed elsewhere, particularly because of tremendous impact and demand from missionary congregations, societies, and conferences such as the 1910 World Missionary Conference of Edinburgh. Pressures came also from students (particularly in the United States), and in some instances even from governments, as happened in Germany (see Bosch 1991, 492). In the course of time, some chairs of missiology were converted into chairs for world Christianity, comparative theology, ecumenical theology, and the like. The Catholic Church, however, was ahead of the other churches. Indeed, after the Catholic chair of missiology at Münster, Germany, in 1910, a faculty of missiology was established at Rome's Gregorian University (in 1923), Urban University (1933), at the Catholic University of Louvain, and at St. Paul's University, Ottawa, Canada. Missionary congregations and institutes had before this maintained the publication of scientific journals and monographs on mission.

Meanwhile, it suffices to say that some cogent factors were responsible for the slowness of the development of mission studies as an academic branch of its own. In the entire premodern period, theology was understood primarily in two senses (see Farley 1983, 31). First, it was a science of and knowledge of God and things related to God. Second, it was the term for a discipline, a self-conscious scholarly enterprise. Furthermore, for many centuries there was only *one* discipline of theology, without subdivisions. There were, of course, distinctions, but they all referred back to the first concept of theology: the knowledge of God and the things of God (see Farley 1983, 77).

Another reason for the slow development of missiology was the impact of the Enlightenment. The subdivisions of theology in this epoch were still not broad enough to include mission studies as a distinct discipline in its own right. When progress should have been made in this era, theology came to be subdivided first into only two general areas: theology as the practical know-how necessary for clerical work, and theology as one technical and scholarly enterprise among others (theology as *practice* and as *theory*). From here, theology evolved gradually into what Farley calls the "fourfold pattern": the disciplines of the Bible (text), church history (history), systematic theology (truth), and practical theology (application). Each of these had its parallels in the secular sciences. Practical theology became a mechanism to keep the church going, and the other disciplines were examples of pure science. The two elements were held together by what Farley calls the "clergy paradigm." Mission was something completely on the periphery (and this was most noticeable in Protestantism; see Jongeneel 1989, 117-47) and did not evoke any theological interest worth mentioning.

Models in the Growth of Missiology as a Theological Discipline

As noted earlier, things began changing when missionary enterprise expanded and the reality of mission and the existence of young churches in mission territories more and more impressed themselves upon "Christian" Europe. It then became necessary to begin scientific reflections on mission. It took not only various historical stages but also models (strategies) for this to be achieved. The following models can be identified: (1) incorporation (of mission studies) into existing disciplines; (2) the introduction of missiology as an independent theological discipline; (3) integration (incorporating mission studies into the entire field of theology); (4) missiology as a "comparative theology"; and (5) the stage of defining the object of missiology and efforts to articulate the functions of missiology.

Incorporating missiology into existing theological disciplines. When the necessity of mission studies started gaining support, the first attempt was to find ways and means of incorporating it (the missionary idea) within the existing theological disciplines. The most natural solution was to append the study of mission to one of the existing disciplines, usually practical theology. In this respect, Friedrich Schleiermacher was the pioneering spirit (see Myklebust 1955/57, 84-89). He appended missiology to practical theology and thus created a model that is still followed in some circles. Karl Rahner, for example, defines practical theology as the "theological, normative discipline of the self-realization of the church in all its dimensions" (Rahner 1966, 50). In this view, then, missiology (being one of these dimensions) becomes the study of the self-realization of the church in missionary situations, and practical theology proper is understood as the study of the self-realization of the existing church. This implies, in the opinion of Ludwig Rütti, that the object of missiology's theological reflection is therefore essentially the same as that of practical theology. André Seumois (according to Thomas Kramm) differentiates mission from those areas in which the church is already "constituted normally"; practical theology has to do with the *pastorate* of the church, missiology with the church's *apostolate,* but in such a way that the apostolate is clearly tending toward the pastorate (see Kramm 1979, 47-51).

Missiology as an independent theological discipline. A second strategy was to advocate the introduction of missiology as a theological discipline in its own right. This was pursued in the usual "fourfold pattern" (a problem encountered by other "new" theological disciplines as well, notably, theological ethics, ecumenical studies, and the science of religion), but nevertheless this strategy gained ground rapidly. Professors appointed to teach missiology were also allowed to continue with other subjects. For instance, when in 1836 Charles Breckenridge was appointed to teach missionary instruction at Princeton Theological Seminary he was, at the same time, professor of pastoral theology. Not so, however, with Alexander Duff's chair of evangelistic theology (as it was then called), established in Edinburgh in 1867; here missiology was taught as an independent subject. And with Gustav Warneck (at the University of Halle) and Josef Schmidlin (at the University of Münster), missiology became fully established as an independent theological discipline.

This entire development, however, turned out to be, at best, a mixed blessing. It gave no guarantee that missiology now had a legal domicile in theology. Chairs were established not because theology was understood to be intrinsically missionary but because of pressure from missionary societies (particularly in the United States), from students, or in some instances from a government (as happened in the case of the chair at Münster which, at least in part, came into being because the German Ministry of Culture urged the theological faculty to attend in its lectures to the "colonial system" and particularly to missions in the German protectorates). In fact, Schmidlin's first major publication after he took up the chair in Münster was entitled *Die Katholischen Missionen in den deutschen Schutzgebieten* (1913). The result of this was that missiology continued to be viewed as a subject not strictly within the domain of theology. Thus an alternative strategy was sought: the integration of the new subject into the existing disciplines of theology (see Müller 1989, 69).

Integrating missiology into the field of theology. A third stage was marked by the effort to integrate missiology into the entire field of theology. When it was becoming evident that the teaching of missiology as a separate subject may be abandoned (as happened mainly in Britain), other theological disciplines were expected to incorporate mission studies into the entire field of theology. Some of the factors that led to this have been pointed out above. For example, when missiology was first established as a subject in its own right, it was partly as a result of the prompting of the government to attend to the "colonial need." Thus, despite its entire earlier development, missiology was still seen as theological "department of foreign affairs," dealing with the exotic but at the same time peripheral. The development of missiology thus far was no guarantee that it had legal domicile in theology. Chairs were established not because theology was understood to be intrinsically missionary but because of pressures from interest groups. Other theologians continued to regard their missiological colleagues with aloofness, if not condescension, particularly since they frequently happened to be retired missionaries who had worked in far-away countries, mission lands (see Sundkler 1968, 114). As a consequence, it meant that other teachers regarded themselves as being absolved of any responsibility to reflect on the missionary nature of theology (see Mitterhöfer 1974, 65).

All this was further compounded when missiologists began to design their own encyclopedia of theology, naturally modeled on the fourfold pattern (see Linz 1964, 44; Rütti 1974, 292). In this effort, "missionary foundation" paralleled the biblical subjects; "missions theory" paralleled systematic theology; "missions history" had its counterpart in church history; and "missionary practice" in practical theology. For the rest, missiology continued to exist in splendid isolation. By duplicating the entire field of theology, it confirmed its image as a dispensable addendum; it was a science *of* the missionary, *for* the missionary (see Bosch 1991, 492).

In this situation, it appeared that the best thing to do was to abandon the teaching of missiology as a separate subject and to encourage other theological disciplines to incorporate missionary dimension into their various fields. This solution sounds good, but it has several serious deficiencies, as illustrated by Kenneth Cracknell and Christopher Lamb in their study (1986). One of the serious deficiencies in this model is that teachers of other subjects usually are not sufficiently aware of the innate missionary dimension of all theology. Furthermore, teachers may not have the knowledge and patience to pay proper attention to developments in mission and to the missionary dimension of their vocation (see Myklebust 1961, 330-35).

Missiology as comparative theology. In the meantime, missiology has been accorded recognition as a theological discipline in its own right. But no one should be under the delusion that the basic problem of this discipline is resolved; critical assessment and self-criticism were still necessary (valid also for our time). None of the three models—incorporation into an existing discipline, independence, or integration—could be said to be acceptable to all. One has to add that, at least in theory, the third model was theologically the soundest (see Cracknell and Lamb 1986, 26). But there was still the problem of distancing the new discipline from the government's ulterior motives and from unnecessary control of the sponsoring institutions and organizations. This concern has been highlighted in recent time by Ludwig Rütti and J. C. Hoekendijk (as we shall see later). The concern here is whether one could justify distinguishing missiology as such from other theological disciplines and absolve it completely from the control of the sponsoring institutions or the church. This was not an easy task because missiology, like the other existing theological disciplines, must work in harmony and serve the mission of the church. But there was a need to cut through this Gordian knot if missiology was to continue its distinct mission while serving the church in company with the other theological disciplines. To resolve this impasse a middle position was sought for missiology. This can be seen in the work of the Catholic theologian Adolf Exeler (see Exeler 1978, 199-211).

According to Exeler there is only one logical course of action, namely, to discard the old missiology totally and substitute something new. As an alternative he suggests "comparative theology." He assigns the following tasks to this discipline: the promotion of understanding that the faith and its modes of expression are culturally conditioned; intercultural and international theological dialogue; and interdisciplinary working procedures, even beyond the perimeters of theology.

But is Exeler's "comparative theology" not really the same model as the "integration of missiology into different theological subjects"? This model had not been achieved in the missiology of the old style, and its relevance to the comparative methods used in other fields of scholarship had not been established. Exeler intends in this methodology to overcome the Eurocentric captivity of theology, to substitute partnership for paternalism, and to give a proper status to the intercultural theological dialogue already under way. Like other contemporaries, Exeler felt that the very success of the more recent mission resulted in a grave crisis not only for mission itself but also for missiology. The assumptions under which both began had radically changed. Paternalism, condescension, treating people as objects and the Western claim to universalism—all these concomitant symptoms of a mission infected by colonial thinking, says Exeler, are untenable for various reasons, for instance, because of the emergence of independent mission churches. For these reasons traditional missiology is no longer justified. The so-called young churches do not regard themselves as objects but rather as subjects of their existence as communities sent into the world. Why should Western missiologists dictate to them how a missionary church is to be realized in their special context? And even if missiologists did not dictate to them but merely confined themselves to a descriptive account of the "sent" character of these churches, they would not be immune to the danger of still asserting their outdated absolutist claims (see Müller 1987, 13). Exeler claims, therefore, that comparative theology is the only way out.

Nevertheless, for at least two reasons, it is doubtful whether Exeler's alternative suggestion could solve the problem of missiology as a theological discipline. First, comparative theology, indispensable as it may be, would inevitably result in driving this redefined missiology into a theological bottleneck not commensurate with the all-embracing, integral character of the universal mission of the Christian faith. The missionary commission, which has its source in the *missio Dei*, cannot appear only in the specifically theological sphere but also embraces liturgy, prayer, proclamation, and communication of the faith in all its forms. All of this, of course, needs thorough theological reflection, especially in the cultural context, but must not be confined to it. Besides, Exeler's theory seems paradoxical insofar as he takes with one hand what he gives with the other. In plain language, this theory harbors the danger of submitting a mission about to be freed from the paternalism of the West to subservience to a theology in which, despite its best intentions to the contrary, Western dominance would still reassert itself.

Second, another paradoxical consequence inherent in Exeler's theory is that the Western churches as a result of this narrow view of missiology might feel relieved of their responsibility by delegating the complicated business of comparative theology to a few theological experts. This means, in practice, that the Western churches would not be forced to take their partnership in mission seriously enough, with all the consequences this would have for their missionary praxis. As a matter of fact, however, the main problem today is to shake the churches out of their insularity and complacency and awaken them to an understanding of their charism of "being sent" to renew their whole existence. It would be presumptuous to ask missiology to shoulder this responsibility alone. But, considering the urgency of the missionary duty, it would also be dangerous to develop a missiological model that was not principally geared to this task (see Müller 1987, 15).

The Object of Missiology

The basic problem under discussion concerns the object of missiology (see Bosch 1991, 492). Indeed, none of the models discussed above resolved this problem. The issue, of course, was not with what *missiology* is but with what *mission* is (as we tried to show above), that is, what is the object of missiology? There were attempts made to answer this question. First, there was a question whether missiology can regard the missionary work of the church as such to be what it studies, possibly even to the extreme of understanding itself as the "science of the missionary and for the missionary" (as discussed above). In this case missiology could concern itself with mission history, missionary geography and statistics, the morphology and phenomenology of mission, and, of course, with exploration and further development of missionary method. Karl Graul, who offered this suggestion about a century and a half ago, thought that in this way missiology would "lift itself from the twilight of sentimental piety to the broad daylight of faithful scholarship" (see Myklebust 1955/57, 94ff.). Recently, this suggestion has been followed and carried out in a systematic form. This attempt is associated in the Protestant sphere particularly with the person and work of the Dutch missiologist J. C. Hoekendijk and, in Catholic circles, with Ludwig Rütti and Johann Baptist Metz (see Hoekendijk 1967, 297ff.; Rütti 1972, passim). While they may place the accents differently, the purpose and elaboration of their programs largely coincide. They hold that missiology should not and cannot be concerned with missionary activity in the sense of canvassing for new members for the church nor with institutional transmission of the faith. The object of missiology is, rather, a praxis of mission in which the world sets the agenda and the Christian message is primarily understood as a message of promise related to the world, history, and society, independent of any intermediary of tradition or hierarchy (see Müller 1987, 12-13).

This model sounds good, but it is doubtful whether it would be more than a theory of a certain established praxis that may not necessarily be of interest to the other theological disciplines. Strictly speaking, it suggests that missiology could do without any specifically Christian framework. The model takes its bearings from *shalom,* the call to peace in the broadest sense of the term, the peace through which all aspects of human life acquire their promised fullness. Rütti, who developed this concept more consistently than Hoekendijk, advances a "political hermeneutic" that must be realized in social and political action in contrast to the traditional missionary practice and its theological implications. This theory received mostly negative responses from missionary societies and many institutions. It was also viewed by theologians as placing the role and task of missiology in a second, wider sense. Thus, this model compounded the problem instead of solving it.

Furthermore, we should be wary of the very one-sided argumentation of the supporters of this theory. For example, Rütti (a great advocate of this theory) condemns as an obsolete "ecclesiological expansive" model Karl Rahner's conventional idea of missiology as a science of the missionary "self-realization of the church" (see Rahner 1966, 49ff.). Rahner's definition, at any rate, preserves the reference to the concrete praxis of mission and its modalities which is indispensable for missiology. This relationship is critical, and this is so not only because the world provides the agenda but because of the properly understood function of witness "out of faith towards faith," which has been a constituent element of the universal mission of the church from the beginning. This heritage must be preserved—a responsibility that many missiologists (not excluding Rütti and Hoekendijk) have stressed. We have to disagree with Rütti, however, in the way he tries to justify his views and to impose them on a new theology of mission. The apostles knew that the task of mission could only be determined as responsibility for and transmission of the faith "within the horizon of the world." But they would hardly have agreed that mission is a "worldly matter," taking its own pathway according to the current agenda of the world, legitimized in the last analysis only as an "excentric program" of a worldly reign of God and essentially reduced to "human relations" as the decisive reference conforming it to the world. According to Rütti's statement of intent, there can no longer be any question of a missiology that "develops the essence and necessity of mission from Biblical and dogmatic sources." Rather, he says, missiology is globally committed to an "experimental theology" that reacts to every new historical situation and, thus, is supposed to point the way for all theology to the unqualified affirmation of the world (see Rütti 1972, 12). With different arguments Hoekendijk too described missiology as experimental theology (see Hoedemaker 1977, 9).

Missiologists and scholars of the other theological disciplines had to react to such a claim. Karl Müller sums up the reaction of many when he notes that Rütti's position has the church (the mystery of the body of Christ veiled in history and the tabernacle of God among men) pushed aside in this confrontation with the radical exodus into the world and into the coming *shalom* (see Müller 1987, 16). By this he wanted to emphasize, together with Manfred Linz, that it is one thing for missiology to concern itself with the "gathering and sending of the church" as "a subject to all theology." It is an entirely different matter if, as a consequence, missiology is said to have the right and duty to meddle continuously in the work of other theological disciplines (see Linz 1974, 35). For the moment, the possibilities of missiology are more realistically assessed when one asks whether missiology possesses "the institutional compactness and energy" to satisfy itself once again with its position and thus, at the same time, its responsibility in the company of theological disciplines (see Kramm 1979, 69). Recent tendencies point at this same direction when they described the task of missiology as necessarily "controversial, contextual, and confrontational." This implies that missiology, at any rate, could no longer retreat from a position between the battle lines into introspective complacency (see Müller 1987, 16). Vatican II was to attend to this problem in an unprecedented manner.

Challenges and Functions of Missiology

Another important stage (which is still a major preoccupation) is the discussion of the tasks of missiology. Several attempts have been made to draw conclusions concerning the position of missiology—its functions among the theological disciplines—in the form of short propositions. A brief reference to these will help us take some steps beyond the dilemma and ambivalence mentioned in the preceding discussions.

Missiology according to David J. Bosch has a twofold task: the first with respect to theology and the second with respect to missionary praxis (1991, 496-98). This can be elucidated in a better way following the treatment of the subject by Karl Müller, who proposed that the function of missiology was to relate its studies to Christian faith, to the various theological disciplines, and to missionary praxis (see Müller 1987, 16).

As regards the first (the faith commitment), missiology as a theological discipline must make the missionary dimension of the faith its most important object and the main measuring rod of its work: *mission as God's own concern* set in motion by him alone, and brought to fulfillment by him alone in the eschatological kingdom. This dimension means that God wills the salvation of the world, and it is he who brings about salvation by making his son *Kyrios*, "Lord." This constitutes also the missionary "intention": this means that God brings about the salvation of the world in his Son by having the gracious lordship of Christ witnessed to, proclaimed, and thus realized by human beings (see Gensichen 1971, 80). It is absolutely necessary for missiology not to allow itself to be exclusively preoccupied by one side of this mutual relation but to attend, as it were, constantly between dimension and intention. Missiology should avoid being a theory confined to specialists to the exclusion of its faith commitment, or worse still, not attending to the concrete situation or reality of the faithful.

In this regard also, missiology as a theological discipline must pursue the dimensional reference to the *missio Dei* throughout *the domain of theology*, and this far beyond the limits of the operational mission in the traditional sense. Thus it can no longer lay claim to the missionary factor as a kind of *disciplina arcana* reserved for itself alone. At the same time, it cannot "attempt to convert all theology into missiology" and present itself as the authoritative discipline of integration without ever being able to realize this claim. Only in partnership with the other theological disciplines can missiology hope to find its proper place. This means in practice that as a theological discipline missiology must realize its *dependence on the other theological disciplines* and avail itself of their help. For example, missiology must allow itself to be enriched by biblical scholarship, church history, systematic theology, pastoral theology, liturgy, and so forth. The missiologist should by no means claim to be an expert in exegesis, church history, or systematic theology. The important thing is that missiology strives for partnership among the disciplines, and this has to be tried out, above all, in interdisciplinary functions. Only in this way will missiology have the ability to question other disciplines whether and how they can accommodate their special reference to the missionary dimension and intention.

This brings us to the second critical responsibility of missiology within the context of theological disciplines. In this respect also, missiology performs a critical function by continuously challenging theology to be *theologia viatorum*, that is, in its reflecting on the faith, theology is to accompany the gospel on its journey through the nations and through the times (Schoonhoven Jansen 1974a, 14; Mitterhöfer 1974, 101). In this role,

> missiology acts as a gadfly in the house of theology, creating unrest and resisting complacency, opposing every ecclesiastical impulse to self-preservation, every desire to stay what we are, every inclination toward provincialism and parochialism, every fragmentation of humanity into regional or ideological blocs, every exploitation of some sectors of humanity by the powerful, every religious, ideological or cultural imperialism, and every exaltation of the self-sufficiency of the individual over other people or over other parts of creation. (Bosch 1991, 496; see Linz 1964, 42; Gort 1980a, 60)

Indeed, missiology's task in every age is to investigate scientifically and critically the presuppositions, motives, structures, methods, patterns of cooperation, and leadership which the church brings to her mandate. In addition, missiology must examine every other type of human activity that combats the various evils to see if it fits the criteria and goals of God's kingdom, which has both already come and is yet coming (see Verkuyl 1987, 5).

The third major task of missiology is to make missionary praxis a subject of its scientific endeavors—not from the safe distance of an onlooker but in a spirit of coresponsibility and of service to the church of Christ (see Barth 1957, 112ff.). Missiological reflection is, therefore, a vital element in Christian mission. It helps to strengthen and purify it (see Castro 1978, 87). Mission is an *intersubjective* reality in which missiologists, missionaries, and the people among whom they labor are all partners. This reality of the missionary praxis stands in creative tension with mission's origins, with the biblical text, and with the history of the church's missionary involvement. None of these should see themselves as opponents or competitors in the missionary task. Rather, "faith and concrete-historical mission, theory and praxis determine each other and are dependent on each other" (Rütti 1974, 240). But in this crucial task, the primary function of missiology is to keep a critical eye on the work and operation of the church's mission, whether this be appreciated by the institutional mission or not. In this respect also, among the theological disciplines, missiology has the task of developing new aspects of worldwide Christian responsibility in which the other subjects also participate. There are some current themes that provide excellent examples of this. They are quite often not sufficiently realized in conventional theology and in theological formation, although more and more interest is being shown in them at the grassroots level of the church. They include the following:

- emergent contextual theologies of the Third World

- ecumenical, interfaith, and intercultural dialogue, and dialogue with secular ideologies

- the church's responsibility for development on a world scale and response to the challenges of globalization

- utilization of the means of mass communication and new technologies in the apostolate

- issues arising out of contemporary emphases on healing and reconciliation and healing ministries and charisms.

Drawing up such a list does not mean that missiology is expected to make all these (or any of them) a monopoly of its own. But missiologists should see that such issues get proper recognition in the other theological disciplines.

Conclusion

The goal of this chapter has been to explore the origins and relevance of missiology in theological education and research for the promotion of Christian mission. The chapter has shown that missiology is a theological discipline that reflects on the faith in relation to the missionary activity of the church. As such, missiology must in its function always challenge other branches of theology to be at the service of the evangelizing mission of the church. In addition, missiology must recognize always that all peoples are subjects in God's saving plan. Today, people do not want to be considered as objects of compassion in mission. Thus, missiology has the task of constantly examining its own terminology and that of other branches of theology in relation to mission and the people being evangelized. One aspect of this role of missiology is the traditional way of perceiving the people of the so-called mission lands. Today missiology is challenged to examine and rethink the terminology used with reference to mission. Clearly such language—often an attempt to attract financial donors for the traditional missions of the church in general and for specific missionary congregations—tends to highlight a bizarre image of the people of the so-called mission land and makes the recipients of mission look like abject objects of charity (Africa seems to have suffered most from this stereotype).

As a theological discipline, missiology is a process of communication and proclamation. As such, it has, in the first place, a frontline role in the proclamation of salvation and restoration of human dignity in Jesus Christ. This means that learning a theological language appropriate to rendering this insight should be important in mission studies. And because missiological reflections must accompany the three concrete situations in which the church carries out her mission today—mission *ad gentes*, pastoral care, and new evangelization (*RM* 33)—one of the central tasks of missiology is to articulate the theological foundations of the church's missionary activity and to examine carefully the various ways in which the church exercises her mission. Finally, and in keeping with the basic argument of the present study, missiology must take the lead in the effort to promote dialogue in theological studies. In addition to promoting studies of its traditional subjects, missiology must also encourage the ongoing dialogue between the dominant theology of the North Atlantic and the emergent theologies of the Third World. To engage in a dialogue of this kind, missiology must enter into specific studies and develop its own methods of reflection and research into areas such as evangelization, ecumenism, inculturation, interreligious dialogue, human promotion and liberation, and so forth. These themes, which have been described as "new means of mission," receive special attention and an indepth approach in theological writings that are emerging in various cultural zones of the globe. Missiology has the task of examining the theological languages of these contextual theologies and of promoting dialogue between them and previously dominant themes of traditional theology. It is on these principles (among others) that missiology must find its distinct role in theological education.

This remains a hazardous undertaking. Every branch of theology—including missiology—remains fragmentary, fragile, and preliminary in our rapidly changing era. In other words, missiology proves itself a theological discipline also insofar as it remains *missiologia semper reformanda.* Only in this way can missiology become not only an *ancilla theologiae* ("handmaiden of theology"), but also an *ancilla Dei mundi* ("handmaiden of God's world"; see Scherer 1971, 153).

Part Two

HISTORICAL PERSPECTIVES

3

MISSION AS CONVERSION

The establishment of missiology as an independent theological discipline came with great challenges to the pioneers of the subject. The authors encountered, first, the problem of defining precisely the concept and goal of Christian mission as the main subject matter of the "new" discipline. At the same time, they were engaged in discussions about missionary approaches to other cultures and religions. Thus, the pioneer authors started by writing theories and histories of Christian mission. For example, Gustav Warneck, a pioneer Protestant missiologist, entitled his two first major works *Evangelische Missionslehre* (Protestant/Evangelical Mission Theory) and *Abriss einer Geschichte der Protestantischen Missionen von Reformation bis die Gegenwart* (Protestant Mission History from the Reformation to the Present; see Anderson et al. 1994, 373-82). Josef Schmidlin, the Catholic pioneer missiologist, followed the same pattern. He entitled two of his major works *Katholische Missionsgeschichte* (Catholic Mission History) and *Katholische Missionslehre im Grundriss* (Catholic Mission Theory; see Anderson et al. 1994, 402-9). In these volumes the authors proposed theories about the concept and goal of mission and argued for the teaching of missiology in theological faculties.

The basic issues in this task concern the concept and goal of the Christian mission as well as the requisite missionary approach to other cultures and religions. The latter questions are dealt with in more sophisticated ways today as a result of studies of culture and the theology of religions. But the growth of these disciplines has also led to greater problems of relativism in some forms of contemporary missiology. Nevertheless, the pioneers emphasized the quest of the goal of mission, which was defined only as saving souls or implanting the church. They wrote in a situation in which missiology was envisioned as a science of and for the missionary, as a practical subject that responded to the question, How do we execute our task? (see Bosch 1991, 492).

The discussion is best seen today in the context of debates on the nature of Christian mission and questions concerning our attitude toward other cultures and religions. In this context, then, we are confronted with the problem of how to bring missiology to bear on questions concerning what is at the very heart of the church's mission and theological education. Approaches and attempts at solutions among Catholic and Protestant scholars show different emphases, yet all are confronted with the same problem. It is interesting to note that both the pioneer Catholic and Protestant missiologists started with reflections on the issue of conversion as the goal of mission. This was the first attempt to articulate in vigorous theological terms the goal of mission and the subject matter of missiology in theological education. Gustav Warneck and Josef Schmidlin were the leading authors in Protestant and Catholic circles respectively. In what follows, we shall attempt to present briefly ideas of some of the pioneer authors of the missionary theory of conversion as the goal of mission.

Catholic Authors and Schools of Thought on Mission as Conversion

In Catholic discussions, conversion as the goal of mission is associated with the Münster school of missiology. The basic argument of the Münster school is that the primary goal of mission is the conversion of non-Christian individuals and that mission is aimed at the salvation of souls (*salus animarum*). The systematic working out of this theory can be traced back to the German missiologist Josef Schmidlin, the founder of the Münster school. Thus, to understand the conversion model we shall examine here the positions of Josef Schmidlin, Thomas Ohm (a successor of Schmidlin at Münster), and Karl Müller (a modern interpreter of the conversion model). The contributions or criticisms of some other authors on the subject will also be alluded to.

Josef Schmidlin (1876-1944)

The beginnings of Catholic missiology go back to the formidable figure of Josef Schmidlin (See Rzepkowski 1985, 104). Schmidlin was born on May 29, 1876, in Klein-Landau in Sundgau, Alsace (when it was part of Germany). He earned his doctorate in philosophy and theology at Strassburg in 1906 and qualified as a professor in church history. While professor of dogmatic theology and patrology in Münster, he was given a lectureship in missiology in 1910; in 1914 this position was raised to a chair of missiology, the first of its kind in any Catholic university. Thereafter, Schmidlin concerned himself mainly with missiology, especially mission history; he is recognized as the father of Catholic missiology (see G. Anderson 1998, 599).

Schmidlin's missiological lectures led to the publication of substantial works in missiology, many of which became standards in the field and are still significant. In his missiology he borrowed extensively from Gustav War-neck, but not without examining Warneck's ideas critically, even polemi-cally, and asserting his own personal ideas and convictions. Missiology was fostered by his initiatives in founding the International Institute for Scientific Missiological Research, the *Zeitschrift für Missionswissenschaft* (Journal for Missiological Studies), *Missionswissenschaftliche Abhandlungen und Texte* (Missiological Treatises and Texts), and *Missionswissenschaftliche Studien* (Missiological Studies). He fostered interest in the missionary cause among students by founding university mission groups and by organizing mission conferences for diocesan clergy, which led to the founding of mis-sion associations for priests. He organized mission study weeks for teachers, missionaries on leave, and religious communities, and promoted the idea of a German missionary society for the diocesan clergy.

Among his major publications are *Einführung in die Missionswissenschaft* (Introduction to Missiology, 2nd ed., 1925), *Katholische Missionslehre im Grundriss* (Catholic Mission Theory, 1923; Eng. 1933), and *Zeitschrift für Missionswissenschaft*, which he founded in 1919 and which published 165 of his own major articles.

Schmidlin was preoccupied with providing a biblical foundation to mis-sion (see Müller 1987, 36). In the 1917 edition of *Einführung in die Mission-swissenschaft*, he derives his vision of the mission of the church from the Johannine text, "As you have sent me, so I have sent you" (17:18). From here, Schmidlin distinguishes a twofold task for the church: (1) to proclaim and spread the Christian faith and the Christian gospel and so, of necessity, to propagate itself; and (2) to preserve and strengthen this faith and this church (see Schmidlin 1917, 46-47).

His recourse to Scripture and the church fathers furnished proof for mis-sionary activity. Missionary activity is rooted in the certainty that God is the origin of mission (Matt 28:18-20). After providing the scriptural evidence Schmidlin goes on to cite the church fathers, theologians, and the magis-terium of the church. He observes: "Every ecclesiastical epoch, whether pres-ent or past, confirms the statement that the obligatory character of the pagan missions is established by the teaching of the Bible and Tradition—by the command of God and of His Church" (Schmidlin 1931, 74). He also empha-sizes the "natural basis for mission." According to him,

> In the eyes of unbelievers and pagans the chief justification of the Chris-tian missions lies in the fact that, as the representatives and preachers of a superior and absolute religion, they bring to the pagan religious blessings which he had not before enjoyed—the true God and a bliss-giving redemption. (Ibid., 105)

Schmidlin then adds that mission also has certain "cultural objects and tasks," which, although "secondary missionary motives," are nevertheless grounded "in the very nature of the missions, and make the latter a cultural factor and civilizing agent of the first rank" (106).

Schmidlin was confronted with the task of defining the term "mission." He realizes that the word can have different meanings. So, he distinguishes between mission in the narrower sense, which he defines as "that ecclesiastical activity whose aim it is to plant and spread the Christian religion and church, and then to preserve it," and mission in the wider sense as "the totality of all ecclesiastical organizations which serve the spread of the faith" (Schmidlin 1917, 48). Schmidlin feels also that there is reason to regard certain Catholics as the "object" of mission, by which he means "especially those who outwardly count as church members but who, because of lack of faith or sin, are dead or estranged members, who stand in need of conversion anew" (Schmidlin 1917, 51). In his later book on mission theory, therefore, Schmidlin extends the missionary activity of the church to all, "to those who belong to her [the church's] communion and already share in her faith, so that they may preserve it and live according to its dictates, and to all others who still stand in the darkness of error and outside the fold, that they may be converted and join her communion" (Schmidlin 1931, 38).

Schmidlin acknowledges the use of mission in the wider sense by the Roman Congregation for the Propagation of the Faith, the Code of Canon Law, and also by other reputable Catholic authors, particularly as defined by T. Grentrup: *Est illa pars ministerii ecclesiastici, quae plantationem et consolidationem fidei catholicae in acatholicis operatur* ("[mission] is that element of ecclesiastical ministry which accomplishes the establishment of the Catholic faith among non-Catholics"; Grentrup 1913, 265). Nevertheless, Schmidlin himself chooses to emphasize a narrower interpretation and, in terms that sound strange in our more irenic times, writes:

> Missions in the narrower sense (also called foreign missions) are thus missions among non-Christians—that is among those who are outside the Christian faith and the Christian religion. Consequently, in a descending line, the term is applied: (1) to missions among pagans, whether polytheistic fetish worshippers or pantheistic votaries of Brahma or Buddha (pagan missions proper); (2) missions among Mohammedans . . . ; and (3) missions among Jews. The last two types of mission are included in the broader conception of pagan missions although the Mohammedans and Jews profess a monotheistic religion. (1931, 36)

In following pages Schmidlin singles out the preeminence of the religious character of mission, which does not exclude

> cultural, intellectual, moral, social, charitable, and even scientific objects of various kinds; and they do so because, on the one hand, these are subordinate parts of the missionary program, and on the other,

serve as important means and levers for the attainment of the religious and moral aims of the missions. (43)

He then describes mission as

the commission which issued from God the Father, in the fullness of time, and was given to His Apostles and His Church by Christ Himself, on the conclusion of His life on earth—a commission to go forth and preach the Gospel to all peoples. This divine command assigned a double task or mission to the Church—first, to preach and spread the Christian faith, and secondly, to preserve and confirm it. (44-45)

From this perspective, according to Karl Müller's study, Schmidlin took the step of distinguishing different stages in missionary work: (1) the proclamation of the gospel of the Christian faith among the "heathen"; (2) the internal conversion and the incorporation of the former nonbeliever into the church by the reception of baptism; and (3) the organization of the church from the simple formation of communities to the establishment of the full hierarchy (*plantatio ecclesiae*). The mission church becomes an established church when a people as a whole have accepted the faith and the church has become self-sufficient regarding personnel and finances (1987, 37).

As for the goal of mission, Schmidlin writes that for practical and historical reasons, mission aims at the conversion of the non-Christian individual, "the spreading of the faith among non-Christians," and he considers the "confession of Christian teaching" (with the simultaneous reception of baptism) and the "grafting into the church" to be two aspects of the one mission, a "twofold function found inseparable in the aim of the Catholic mission" (1917, 56). Later, in his *Catholic Mission Theory*, he distinguishes more clearly between the individual and social aims of mission, but he still holds firmly that

This question has no acute aspect for the Catholic missions, and may be answered simply by stipulating personal conversions *and* a general Christianization. Both must be striven for and combined, not necessarily simultaneously, but to a certain extent as successive developments. On the one hand, the missions must seek to convert individuals, to form them into communities, and then through these communities to renew whole nations in Christ. Neither of these objects may be neglected or relinquished, neither fostered at the expense of the other, but each must supplement and support the other. (1931, 258)

In fact, for Schmidlin, "conversion" means the profession of Christian teaching, on the one hand, and baptism in the name of the Trinity, on the other (1917, 55).

Schmidlin's theory has been criticized. In recent years, his theory that the goal of mission is the conversion of souls has been considered weak. The theory is said to be based on a type of dualistic anthropology that runs the risk of disregarding the concrete, historical dimension of integral salvation brought by Christ. It is also argued that Schmidlin's theory leads to the rejection of the cultural and religious traditions of non-Christian peoples. His critics argue that the work of redemption is not opposed to the work of creation. Moreover, grace, they say, does not destroy nature but perfects it (see Gutiérrez in Echegaray 1984, ix; Mushete in Gibellini 1994, 13-14).

Whatever the defects of his theory of the goals of mission, in his personal life Schmidlin was exemplary during the Hitler period. Refusing to give the Hitler salute, he was forcibly retired from the university in 1934. He finished his life as an inmate in one of Hitler's concentration camps in Alsace. Schmidlin's pioneering effort as the first Catholic missiologist itself is noteworthy. He was the inspiration behind the Münster school of missiology, with its emphasis on proclamation and salvation. As we shall see, the Louvain school, which developed an alternate theory during World War II, regarded planting the church to be the goal of mission. Only at Vatican II was the controversial question tackled and finally settled.

It must be added that, through Schmidlin's effort, the idea of having the theme of mission handled at the university level also caught on elsewhere. Thus in Munich missiological questions were treated by Königer in 1911 and by Aufhauser in 1912; in Bamberg by Königer in 1912; in Hamburg by Schmidlin, Friedrich Schwager, and R. Streit from 1911 to 1913; in Würzburg by Alfred Weber and D. Zahn in 1915. A lectureship in mission history and comparative religion was set up in Munich in 1919 with Professor Aufhauser given the chair. After World War I, the missiological movement passed on to other places too, especially Rome. Thus, Thomas Ohm, Schmidlin's successor in missiology on the faculty of Münster, was not exaggerating when he said, "It is impossible to think of missiology and mission history without Schmidlin. For a long time he was mistrusted or even rejected in many missiological circles. But he won through all the same. Catholic missiology gained a secure place in the curriculum of universities and developed into an independent, well-defined, clear-sighted and true science. It has, thanks to Schmidlin's exertions, reached a position that commends attention" (1962, 7).

Thomas Ohm (1892-1962)

After World War II, Schmidlin's chair of missiology at Münster faculty was given to Thomas Ohm, a Benedictine of the Abbey of St. Ottilien. Ohm attempted to fill in weaknesses in Schmidlin's theory of the goal of mission as the conversion of individuals. A German from Westerholt, ordained a priest in 1920, Ohm earned his doctorate in theology in Munich in 1923. He taught at the University of Salzburg and then at Würzburg. Dismissed in

1941 by the Nazis, he had time to prepare important works on non-Christian religions during the war. In 1946 he was called to the University of Münster as successor to Schmidlin. There he founded a new mission institute, reorganized the *Zeitschrift für Missionswissenschaft*, and revived the International Institute for Missiological Research, which under his guidance held national mission study weeks in Münster (1953), Würzburg (1956), Bonn (1958), and Vienna (1961). He was an inspiring teacher, leading many of his students to academic degrees. One of them, Johannes Schütte, a veteran of missionary work in China, became superior general of the Divine Word missionaries in 1958 and, probably more than any other individual, was responsible for the Vatican II decree on mission, *Ad Gentes*. Ohm himself became a member of the Roman Mission Commission preparing the document on mission in 1960 and worked to ensure that adequate, up-to-date ideas would be included in it. He died, however, three years before *Ad Gentes* was accepted by the council. One of his books, *Asia Looks at Western Christianity* (New York: Herder & Herder, 1959), was translated into English; it was one of the first books by a Catholic missiologist to publicly criticize Western Christianity from an Asian perspective. His major work, *Machet zu Jüngern alle Völker: Theorie der Mission* (Make Disciples of All Nations: Mission Theory) was published in 1962.

The first task Ohm took on was to clarify the meaning of the term "mission." He noted that in recent years there had been a remarkable escalation in the use of the term among Christians, a fact that went hand-in-hand with a significant broadening of the concept in certain circles. Indeed until the 1950s, he said, mission, even if not used univocally by all, had a fairly circumscribed set of meanings. He summarized them as (1) the sending of missionaries to a designated territory; (2) the activities undertaken by such missionaries; (3) the geographical area where the missionaries were active; (4) the agency that dispatched the missionaries; (5) the non-Christian world or "mission field"; (6) the center from which the missionaries operated on the "mission field" (see Ohm 1962, 52ff.). In a slightly different context "mission" could also refer to (7) a local congregation without a resident minister and still dependent on the support of an older, established church; or (8) a series of special services intended to deepen or spread the Christian faith, usually in a nominally Christian environment (see Bosch 1991, 1).

Karl Müller, in a more specifically theological synopsis, made a synthesis of Ohm's views of the traditional ways in which the word mission has been used as (1) the propagation of the faith; (2) the expansion of the reign of God; (3) the conversion of the heathen; and (4) the founding of new churches (1987, 31-34). Ohm, however, insisted that all these connotations, familiar as they may seem, were of fairly recent origin. Until the sixteenth century, he showed, the term was used exclusively with reference to the doctrine of the Trinity, that is, of the sending of the Son by the Father and of the Holy Spirit by the Father and the Son. According to Ohm, the Jesuits were the first to use it in terms of the spread of the Christian faith among non-Christians and other people (including among Protestants) who were not members of the Catholic Church (see Ohm 1962, 37-39). Thus, the new use of the word was associated closely with the colonial expansion of the Western world into what has more recently become known as the Third World. In this situation, the term "mission" presupposes a sender, a person or persons sent by the sender, those to whom one is sent, and an assignment. The terminology thus presumes that the one who sends has the authority to do so and that ultimately the real sender is God, who has indisputable authority to decree that people be sent to execute his will. In practice, however, the authority was understood to be vested in the church or in a mission society, or even in a Christian potentate (see Rütti 1972, 228). It was part of Ohm's entire approach to view mission in terms of expansion, occupation of fields, the conquest of other religions, and the like (see Bosch 1991, 2). Thus Ohm's thesis is rooted in conventional interpretations of mission that are today gradually being modified, at least in some circles.

A major contribution of Ohm is his attempt to view mission in terms of the authentic Old Testament tradition and context into which Jesus of Nazareth was born. These, he recognized, paved the way for the universal understanding of the mission of Christ. Before Ohm, it was customary for Christians, particularly in missionary circles, to view Jesus in purely idealistic terms as if mission were completely unique to the Christian testament. In the course of time, so that argument went, all this-worldly, national, social, and historical aspects of Old Testament faith were superseded and held significance solely as the manner in which God prepared for Christianity as the universal religion for all humanity. In his *magnum opus*, Ohm argues that this universal tendency, which was always, even if only latently, present in the Old Testament, reached fulfillment in the life and teaching of Jesus. Nevertheless, according to Ohm, the center of Jesus' teaching was his message about God's reign, which he interprets as being of "a purely religious, supranational, other-worldly, predominantly spiritual and inward nature" (1962, 247). It was something infinitely "higher" than the Old Testament and was no longer tied to the people of Israel.

Though this view is not accepted today in its entirety, at least Ohm attempted to cut the Gordian knot and began to recover a concept of mission informed by the historical Jesus as a Jewish person, formed by the traditions of his people. Precisely from this perspective, the historical Jesus becomes crucial as we begin to rediscover him and the context in which he lived and labored, through the eyes of faith of the four evangelists and the many layers of the theology of early Christian communities (*Gemeindetheologie*). Today scholars show a greater confidence in the importance of the earthly Jesus than was customary even a few decades ago (Burchard 1980, 13-27; Hengel 1983, 29). Consequently, the "practice of Jesus" recorded in Scripture has become the focus of much contemporary theologizing. Jesus, as Echegaray puts it, inspired the early Christian communities to prolong the logic of their own life and ministry in a creative way amid historical circumstances that were in many respects new and different (see Echegaray 1984, xv-xvi). They handled the traditions about him with creative but responsible freedom, retaining those traditions while at the same time adapting them (see Bosch 1991, 20-21).

Another area in which Ohm amplified and applied the principle of the conversion model is in his interpretation of the theory of missionary accommodation and adaptation. The problem for him was how to transcend heated debates in which some maintained that the Western church should not be transported to Asia or Africa. All peoples, the argument goes, have a right to express their religious and Christian experience in their own way. They have a right to have their own leaders and to develop their potential. But, Ohm observed, this right should not be made into an absolute. Christianity in particular should be a sign that universal human and Christian solidarity is stronger than cultural particularity, nationalism, or individualism. Christianity is essentially a matter of give and take in which all must be prepared to participate. We must certainly have indigenous local churches, but never in an exclusive sense; we are always called to self-transcendence (see Müller 1987, 152).

In that context, Ohm spoke of a threefold process of adaptation: accommodation, assimilation, and transformation (1962, 700). His thesis is that accommodation and adaptation are more than a help for establishing contact. All three aspects are important: *accommodation*, which is possible because our common nature gives us a natural disposition for contact; *assimilation*, because the church is able to absorb the riches of others, in fact needs the other for its eschatological fulfillment; and *transformation*, because everything in the world which is good, true, and beautiful "somehow or other can be raised to a higher level and thus serve salvation" (1962, 702).

Adaptation and accommodation are as old as the church itself. Since diversity is inherent in God's plan for creation, mission must take it into account; and since it is from God himself, it must, in principle, harmonize with the christianizing process. Nothing that is essentially good should be destroyed; it should rather be developed and cultivated. The reign of God does not mean a ban on earthly things, rather that he may be "all in all" (1 Cor 15:28). Thus, Ohm warns that we should not think in a pessimistic way. Adaptation is needed not only for tactical but also for theological reasons (*AG* 22; see Ohm 1962, 696). Since mission is a process of communication, it is first and foremost necessary to take seriously *those to whom the message is addressed*—just as God does. He sent his Son as message and messenger, and through the Holy Spirit he moves human hearts, prepares and arouses them, awakens understanding, and finally leads human beings to the experience brilliantly portrayed in Luke 24:32: "Did not our hearts burn within us as he talked to us on the road and explained the scriptures to us?"

The missionary addresses his message to real people of good will and under-standing in whom God has been active all their lives through their con-sciences and the religious traditions in which they grew up. They may not yet be sufficiently aware of the fulfillment in Christ, but deep down in their hearts they are receptive. This is what Ohm meant when he said that Chris-tianity is accommodation, assimilation, transformation. But not only that. Christianity, he was clear, also entails "contradiction." Thus, Ohm insists that Christianity demands "struggle against nature" (1962, 711). Taking up that theme, Vatican II speaks of the "corruption of the human heart" (*GS* 11) and of hope and anxiety; hunger and extreme need; illiteracy, social, eco-nomic, racial, and ideological tensions; and the threat of war that the gospel meets and alleviates (*GS* 4).

In his theory of accommodation and adaptation, Ohm tried to corrobo-rate a natural foundation for mission by pointing out the inner relationship between nature and grace. He believed that

> nature and grace are related in so far as they both have the same author. The giver of grace is also the creator of nature. Since God is both he can dispose of the latter freely according to his will and wisdom and con-sequently, if he wishes, can enable even the created spirit to act with power far beyond its nature. But this presupposes in the created spirit the ability to obey the divine movement that lifts him above his nature. Does it have such an ability? The answer to this question must be, yes. Human nature is receptive to grace. (Müller 1987, 65)

Karl Rahner has similar reflections about the "supernatural existential," a question that we have not discussed (Rahner 1966, 5:115-34). Similarly, Andreas Bsteh arrives at the following position through investigating the matter as treated by the church fathers of the second century. Bsteh asserts,

> Thus all in all there is good reason to hold that, arguing from the way the Fathers of the second century understood the faith, Christ's work of salvation not only [in] *potentia* but also [in] *actu* embraces all of humanity; in other words, that Christ's saving action *eo ipso* and directly effects the whole sinful human race in an internal and real way. (1966, 185)

Nevertheless, the shortcomings in Ohm's thesis have come under serious attacks in recent times, especially from Third World theologians. For instance, Gustavo Gutiérrez points out that such an accommodation or adap-tation theory succumbs to "the temptation of *concordism*, which equates the social groups and forces within first-century Palestine with those of our time" (Gutierrez 1988, xi). Yet, even where the sociocultural gap between today's communities and those of the first Christians is narrow, it is there, and it should be respected. The approach called for requires an interaction between the self-definition of early Christian authors and actors and the self-definition of today's believers who wish to be inspired and guided by those early witnesses (Bosch 1991, 23). More recent representatives of the Münster school, including Joseph Glazik, Karl Müller, and Giancarlo Collet (see Verkuyl 1987, 187), have addressed and attempted to overcome these shortcomings in the theories of conversion and accommodation/adaptation models. Of these, the contribution of Karl Müller is outstanding.

Karl Müller (1918-2001)

Another major Catholic interpreter of the conversion model is Karl Müller, SVD. Müller was born in Blankenberg in East Prussia (today an area of Poland called Gologóra). He obtained his doctorate in missiology from the Gregorian University in Rome in 1952 and was a professor of missiology at the Divine Word Missionaries' seminary at Sankt Augustin (near Bonn), Germany. In 1962 he received a doctorate in theology from the University of Münster. He spent several years as mission secretary for the Society of the Divine Word in Rome, all the while continuing as director of the SVD Missiological Institute at Sankt Augustin. He returned in 1983 to Sankt Augustin as professor of missiology, as well as director of the Anthrops Institute from then until 1986. He remained on-site director of the Missiological Institute until he retired in 1992. He died in 2001. Of Müller's many works, several are particularly notable: *Geschichte der Katholischen Kirche in Togo* (1958); *Mission Theology: An Introduction* (1987); the *Lexikon missionstheologischer Grundbegriffe*, edited with Theo Sundermeier (1987; translated and published in an enlarged English edition as *Dictionary of Mission: Theology, History, Perspectives*, by Stephen B. Bevans and Richard Blies in 1997; see G. Anderson 1998: 480-81).

The aspect of Müller's contribution that concerns us here is his introduction of the concept of "integral" salvation to the conversion theory debate (see Müller 1987: 82). Aware of the many criticisms that had been leveled against the Münster school because of the latter's one-sided emphasis on salvation (*salus animarum*), Müller acknowledges that

> The concepts "salvation of souls" and "care of souls" [in German, *Seelsorge*, meaning "pastoral ministry"] . . . are no longer in favor because, for one thing, they can lead to dichotomy of the human person, and secondly do not incorporate other problems such as poverty, hunger, suppression, exploitation, the armaments race, war, manipulation etc. which weigh on humanity today, especially in the Third World. (1987, 82)

Considering all this, Müller asserts that "Today 'integral salvation' is the preferred term, that is, salvation that embraces man in his full reality" (1987,

82). This is in line with the new thinking in missionary circles today, and elsewhere as well, where the mediating of "comprehensive," "integral," "total," or "universal" salvation is increasingly identified as the purpose of mission, in this way overcoming the inherent dualism in the traditional and more recent models. In this sense, of course, it is tautological to add any adjective to the noun "salvation"; salvation is, in the nature of the case, comprehensive and integral or it is not salvation (see Bosch 1991, 532).

Today, according to Müller, missionary practice emphasizes that we should find a way *beyond* every schizophrenic position and minister to people in their *total* need, that we should involve individual as well as society, soul *and* body, present *and* future in our ministry of salvation. Müller adds that never before in history has people's social distress been as extensive as it is today. But never before have Christians been in a better position than they are today to do something about this need. Poverty, misery, sickness, criminality, and social chaos have assumed unheard-of proportions. On an unprecedented scale people have become the victims of other people, exemplifying the old Latin adage *homo homini lupus* ("man is a wolf to his fellow human beings"). Moreover, marginalized groups in many countries of the world lack every form of active or even passive participation in society; inter-human relationships are disintegrating; people are in the grip of a pattern of life from which they cannot possibly wrench themselves free; marginality characterizes every aspect of their existence. To introduce change, as Christians, into all this, according to Müller, is to mediate salvation, following the teaching of Vatican II (*GS* 1). Precisely because our concern is salvation, we may no longer regard ourselves or others as prisoners of an omnipotent fate; in its mission the church constitutes a resistance movement against every manifestation of fatalism and quietism (see Müller in Waldenfels 1978, 90).

Commenting on this, David Bosch adds that, since we may never overrate our own or others' capabilities, we have to ask critical questions with respect to all current theories of human self-redemption. Final salvation will not be wrought by human hands, not even by *Christian* hands. The Christian's eschatological vision of salvation will not be realized in history. For this reason Christians should never identify any project with the fullness of the reign of God (see Bosch 1991, 400). We therefore hold on to the transcendent character of salvation also, and to the need to call people to faith in God through Christ. Salvation does not come except along the route of repentance and personal faith commitment.

Müller, however, limits the human aspect of integral salvation to basic human needs, and he praises the works of charitable organizations such as the German Misereor and Bread for the World. He alluded to the biblical references to charitable works and said that just as Jesus cared for the disadvantaged and sent out the apostles to expel demons and heal the sick, so did missionaries help people in all kinds of ways, even to the laying down of their lives. Furthermore, since mission concentrated on schools, the aim was definitely not only to bring about conversions but also to train people for life and to help them live in a fashion worthy of human beings in a changing world. Although making development an explicit concern of mission, according to Müller, is a recent phenomenon, it presented hardly any problem for Catholics because the way had been prepared through the Thomistic doctrine of the unfolding of the person through membership in the growing family of God and had been spoken of in church documents such as *Gaudium et Spes* (*GS* 25, 41) and the encyclical *Populorum Progressio* of Paul VI (see Müller 1987, 83).

Without going into the controversy that led to Müller's augmentation of the theory of salvation of individuals, it suffices to say that the main criticism centers on the near-total neglect of the prophetic role of missionaries toward their sponsoring institutions and nations, which often carried on practices and supported structures that caused impoverishment. The strength of Müller's thesis lies in his emphasis on the integral character of salvation, which, he was clear, demands that the scope of mission be more comprehensive than has traditionally been the case. Salvation is as coherent, broad, and deep as the needs and exigencies of human existence. Mission, therefore, means, in the words of Jerald Gort, being involved in the ongoing dialogue between God, who offers his salvation, and the world, which—enmeshed in all kinds of evil—craves that salvation. "Mission means being sent to proclaim in deed and word that Christ died and rose for the life of the world, that he lives to transform human lives (Rom 8:2) and to overcome death" (*International Review of Mission* 71 [1982]: 458-77). From the tension between the "already" and the "not yet" of the reign of God, from the tension between the salvation *indicative* (salvation is already a reality!) and the salvation *subjunctive* (comprehensive salvation is yet to come) there emerges the salvation *imperative:* Get involved in the ministry of salvation! (see Gort in Camps et al. 1988, 209-14).

In addition, those who know that God will one day wipe away all tears will not accept with resignation the tears of those who suffer and are oppressed *now*. Anyone who knows that one day there will be no more disease can and must actively anticipate the conquest of disease in individuals and society *now*. And anyone who believes that the enemy of God and humans will be vanquished will already oppose him *now* in his machinations in family and society. For all of this has to do with salvation (see Bosch 1991, 400).

Protestant Authors and Schools of Thought on Mission as Conversion

In the preceding section we discussed pioneer authors of Catholic mission theology who saw the goal of mission as conversion. In the present section we shall see their counterparts in the Protestant circle. As we noted in the former section, the problem centers on the validity and aim of the Christian mission. On the Protestant side, the discussion took a more radical turn. Mission belongs to the essence of Christianity and the churches, as burning belongs to fire. It is, however, a gift and also a task. Wherever the church preached the gospel and lived by it, it was missionary. It obeyed the commission to go into the world of nations. But this Protestant approach resulted from the new awakening of interest in mission among Protestants themselves. The early attitude in Protestant circles in this respect was not so clear. In fact, the churches of the Protestant Reformation adopted the view that the missionary commission given by Jesus had been fulfilled by the apostles (Rom 10:18) and that it was no longer incumbent upon the church as a whole. This view led the founders of the Protestant Christianity, such as Martin Luther and John Calvin, to give little or no consideration toward developing mission theology. However, the awakening that led to the development of a theology of mission (just as in Catholic circles) coincided with the expansion of Western domination and apparently sprang from the same origin. This influenced missionary work in many ways but also harmed it (see Sundermeier in Müller et al. 1997, 429).

From the time of its inception, Protestant mission theology has concentrated more on giving a rationale or justification for missionary proclamation. Missionary practice set the standard, and later missiology provided the legitimization. In this respect, Gisbertus Voetius, an early seventeenth-century Reformation theologian and the first Protestant to have developed a comprehensive theology of mission, is of crucial importance (see Bosch 1991, 256). However, from the nineteenth century onward, Protestant missionary efforts began to be exposed to a whole series of creative agencies that were confessionally stamped by theological tendencies and Christian forms of faith. The decisive discussion is still on the fact that Christianity is a world religion and that its missions are "world missions." All these theological streams converged and found their culmination in the missiological treatise of Gustav Warneck.

Warneck himself, under the spell of the nineteenth century, combined pure research with practice in his writings, which are a genuine reflection of contemporary missionary processes. Protestant missiologists regard him as the father of missiology. The "Warneck Era," rooted in the nineteenth century, was carried on into the twentieth by other Protestant missiologists not only in Germany but also in Anglo-Saxon countries and, of course, in Catholic circles (see Rzepkowski 1985, 100). Since then a number of missiological schools of thought have emerged from the writings of Protestant authors.

It may serve a good purpose to mention once more that the development of mission theory in Protestant circles in general, and in the Evangelical camp in particular, has its inspiration in the Pietist theologians, especially of the seventeenth century and onward (see Müller 1987, 30). Missiologists concerned themselves intensely with the concepts and theory of mission. The Protestant Pietist theologians speak of mission as the spreading of kingdom of Christ throughout the whole world, of the extension of the kingdom of God and the promotion of the glory of God and Christ. For the Pietists, "God does not wait until the heathen come and seek his grace but rather brings it to them" (quoted in Müller 1987, 31). In fact, the primary concern of the pioneer Protestant missiologists was the conversion of the "heathen" and the work of instructing the "heathen."

This trend in the development of Protestant mission theology belongs to the missionary theory that conversion is the goal of mission. The first serious attempt to work out the theology of this trend, as we have said, is the work of the Dutch missiologist Gisbertus Voetius. But the systematic efforts to define mission around that model began with Gustav Warneck. We turn now to examining the thought of Voetius and Warneck as pioneer advocates of conversion as the goal of mission.

Gisbertus Voetius (1589-1676)

Gisbertus Voetius, Dutch Reformed Church theologian, was born in Heusden, North Brabant, Netherlands. He studied theology at Leiden, served as a Reformed minister in Vlijmen and in Heusden (1610-1634), and was the founder of Utrecht University, where he served as professor of Semitic languages and theology (1634-1676). His first engagement with mission issues occurred at the national synod of Dordrecht (1618-1619), where he dealt with the question of whether baptism could be administered to children from non-Christian backgrounds living with Dutch families in the East Indies. In 1643, he wrote a treatise on religious freedom. His theology of mission is found in *Selectae Disputationes Theologicae* (5 vols., 1648-1669) and in *Politica Ecclesiastica* (3 vols., 1663-1676; see G. Anderson 1998, 708).

Voetius saw the goals of mission in this order: conversion of the heathen, planting of the church, honor of God (see Müller 1987, 31). This formulation of the threefold goal of mission has become widely known and is still unparalleled. The immediate aim is *conversio gentilium* ("conversion of gentiles," i.e., nonbelievers, heretics, and schismatics). This is subordinate to the second and more distant goal, *plantatio ecclesiae* ("planting of the church"). The supreme and ultimate aim of mission, however, and the one to which the other two are subservient, is *gloria et manifestatio gratiae divinae* ("the glory and manifestation of divine grace"). In addition, Voetius sees mission as aiming at bringing together churches that are on the brink of collapse or that have been scattered through persecutions, seeking the renewal of churches that have retrogressed theologically, as helping unify churches separated from one another, as supporting oppressed and impoverished churches, and as striving toward the liberation of churches experiencing opposition from the authorities (see Jongeneel 1989, 133, 147; Bosch 1991, 257).

Voetius emphasized that missions are grounded in both the hidden and the revealed will of God. Inspired by the Protestant distaste for the teaching authority of the Catholic Church, Voetius taught that only apostles and assemblies such as synods are agents of mission; only they have the right to establish missions; it is not the right of the pope, nor of princes and magistrates, nor of companies to do so. Mission churches, he maintained, should not be subordinated to the sending churches in Europe. The "older" and the "younger" church stood in a relationship of equals (see Jongeneel 1989, 126ff., 136ff.).

In addition to being influenced by Pietism, Voetius's idea is also rooted in the Puritan understanding of mission (see Bosch 1991, 257). For the Puritans, God predestines individuals to salvation (and others to perdition). Some Puritans regarded themselves as God's elect, sent to plant and cultivate a garden in the wilderness of North America, where they were to advance God's kingdom by the displacement of the native population. This fundamentalist interpretation of the doctrine of predestination can be found time and again in Calvinist groups. For instance, in South Africa, the white Afrikaner churches, particularly the Dutch Reformed churches, whose members benefited from the apartheid system, developed a kind of Puritan theology of mission to justify the subjugation of blacks to the rule of the white minority. They argued that racial segregation was the will of God, because God created different races. Thus racial integration was against the will of God. In fact, in South Africa this theology hardened into a political dogma, which found its religious mythology in the Voortrekers' understanding of themselves as the elect of God, set apart to possess the promised land by dispossessing the black Africans. It had its ecclesiastical outgrowth in the separate racial units that constituted the Dutch Reformed Church in the then apartheid South Africa. The supporters of the apartheid system maintained that God gave the white minority a special vocation to civilize and christianize the other races in South Africa. As a consequence these churches banned interracial marriages. This is one of the unhappy sides of the missionary expansion into Africa. This missionary endeavor was too often characterized by the curious paradox that, while preaching the equality of all before God, it nonetheless elevated white Christians into superior beings, thereby tainting Christianity with racism (Parratt 1995, 156). For the Dutch Reformed in southern Africa, however, the ultimate goal of mission remained, as it did for Voetius, the glory of God. The Christian's entire life stood as a sign to magnify God's name and to acknowledge his sovereignty over everything.

"Constrained by Jesus' love," however, the Puritans understood the love of Jesus in a twofold manner: his love as experienced by the believer and his love for unredeemed humanity. This constitutes the most important point of similarity between Pietism and Puritanism (see Bosch 1991, 258); and on it also lies the strength of Voetius's theology of mission, the ability to systematize currents in the Protestant missionary thought of his day. For as in Puritanism, in Pietism there is emphasis on a warm and devout union with Christ. In Pietism, concepts such as repentance, conversion, new birth, and sanctification received new meaning. Pietism also emphasized discipline and subjective experience of the individual, and played down the place of sound doctrine and ecclesiastical authority. It was also very prescriptive about the way in which individuals should become true believers. The movement opposed the idea of group conversion but emphasized individual decisions.

Those were the currents in Protestantism that Voetius tried to bring together and provide with a theological and missionary outlook, and there was growth in interest in his thinking after 1800 (see G. Anderson 1998, 708). Today his views on mission appear, on the one hand, hopelessly outdated and, on the other, surprisingly modern (see Jongeneel 1989, 146ff.; Bosch 1991, 253). Voetius's emphasis on the individual rather than the group is both the strength and weakness of his missiology. This emphasis emerges, for example, in his treatment of the role of the church and ecclesiastical authority in mission. Mission was, for him, not an activity of the church sanctioned by ecclesiastical authority, but an activity of apostles and synods. From a Catholic view, certainly, and from that of many Protestants today, it seems that Voetius forgets that what he refers to as "ecclesiastical authority" is indeed exercised by present-day successors of the apostles. Furthermore, if the church and only the church could be the legitimate bearer of mission, as Voetius seems to agree, it follows, then, that the leaders of the church and, in particular, again from a Catholic point of view, the pope and bishops have a central role to play in directing and carrying out the concrete mission and missions of the church. In fact, it is inconceivable to think of the church as the agent of mission without acknowledging the indispensable role of the pope, bishops, religious orders, and congregations in the work of evangelization and church implantation. That said, it is also a fact that Catholic religious orders long functioned as de facto independent bodies in mission and that the Congregation for Propagation of the Faith exercised only nominal authority over them. One of the singular facts of mission in both Catholic and Protestant churches is the *voluntary* nature of the process whereby missionaries were drawn into missionary societies that functioned as a virtual parachurch organization.

Gustav Warneck (1834-1910)

Gustav Warneck, the pioneer of missiology as an academic discipline in universities and independent higher educational institutions, was born and raised in a humble German craftsman's family near Halle. He began his theological studies at Halle University (now Martin-Luther Universität) in 1855 and received a Ph.D. degree from the University of Halle in 1883. After serving several years as a pastor, Warneck went on to become an internationally renowned professor of mission at Halle (1897-1908), holding the first chair of its kind in Germany (see G. Anderson 1998, 718).

Hans Kasdorf lists nearly four hundred titles of Warneck's publications (see Kasdorf 1976 cited in Anderson et al. 1994, 373-82); notable are the following: *Evangelische Missionslehre* (Protestant Mission Theory, 5 vols., 1883-1905); *Abriss einer Geschichte der protestantischen Missionen von der Reformation auf die Gegenwart* (Protestant Mission History since the Reformation Era, 1913). In those works one notes the tendency in Protestant circles to concentrate on providing a rationale or justification for mission, which is designed to serve as an apologetic both for the broad foundations of mission and to make a case for the study of mission as a genuine field among the classical theological disciplines (see Sundermeier in Müller et al. 1997, 430).

Warneck's five-volume *Evangelische Missionslehre* was his *magnum opus*. The volumes are divided into three major parts, each dealing in great detail with the many dimensions of mission philosophy and principles. In part one of his work, Warneck attempts to build a broad foundation for his concept of mission from dogmatic, ethical, biblical, ecclesiological, historical, and ethnological perspectives. These branches of theology demonstrate for him the reason why Christianity must be involved in mission and why the church must have a missionary dimension. His thesis is that God has chosen to make himself known through Christianity as the full and final revelation of God for the complete and universal salvation of humankind.

In part two Warneck discusses the role of mission societies and agencies, maintaining that as a result of the developments in church life, the existence of mission societies is legitimate. The last part treats the mission field of the world in all its complex geographic and religious diversities. The Great Commission, says Warneck, rests upon all Christians to evangelize all non-Christians by making disciples of peoples, not just of individuals. His key concept is *Volkschristianisierung* ("the Christianization of [entire] peoples"; see Kasdorf in Anderson et al. 1994, 380).

In fact, for Warneck the religions of the world wait for Christianity to replace them. As someone steeped in the European idea that Western culture represented a decisive advance in civilization, Christianity was at the disposal of the modern world as its spiritual basis because of its flexibility and adaptability. "[Christianity] is, therefore, certain to become the general religion of humanity" (Warneck 1892-1905, 1:96). For Warneck, because Christianity is not form or law but spirit and life, it can pervade the whole of human personal and social life and take on popular, civic, social, and cultural forms (Warneck 1892-1905, 1:292). Warneck, nevertheless, rejects the identification of "Europeanization" with "Christianization," because Christianity's universal dimension means that it is not reducible to a single culture. Christianity is for humanity and humanity for Christianity (see Warneck 1892-1905, 1:319; Sundermeier in Müller et al. 1997, 430). The proclamation of the saving message is a natural inference from the absoluteness of Christianity. Warneck wrote:

> We are confronted here with the inescapable conclusion: if truth and redemption can be found *only* in Jesus Christ and if both are destined to be the common possession of all, then Christianity *must be* the world religion and world mission must be its central task grounded in its very nature (Rom 10:11-17). (Warneck 1892-1905, 1:94; see Rzepkowski 1985, 100)

Like Voetius, Warneck is indebted to the Pietist heritage for his ideas of mission, but he has also learned from the denominational conflicts of the nineteenth century that there cannot be mission without the church. The mission of the church must be spared denominational wrangling as far as possible. His definition of mission, which has been widely disseminated, is, therefore, very open and states: "By Christian mission we understand the entire activity of Christendom that is directed to the planting and organization of the church of Christ among non-Christians" (1892-1905, 1:1). The subject of mission is Christianity. Therefore, the instruments of mission are individual Christians, especially those who are committed and called. Mission requires a special vocation through the Holy Spirit and a sending by the church. Mission aims at the conversion and baptism of non-Christian individuals and at the planting of churches. According to Warneck, when the church is founded in a non-Christian environment, mission has achieved its aim (see Sundermeier in Müller et al. 1997, 430).

Warneck developed his theory within the framework of what has come to be known in our time as the history of salvation model (which we will discuss below), according to which God not only works in nature but is also present in history, which is recognized as the sphere of divine activity. Warneck interprets this to mean, among other things, that nations have a prescribed place in history, as well as a special destiny. They come into being through God's revelation. Mission, therefore, must apply itself to the conversion of nations and to the building of national churches. The roots of his theology in the German Reformation and its path to self-understanding over against the universal claims of Catholicism and within the process of nation-building in the nineteenth century are unmistakable. He writes in the age when Bismarck had made Germany the foremost nation in Europe and as it was beginning its colonial adventures.

It is significant here that Warneck's experience of German nationalism triumphing over regional identities is projected onto distant peoples. The existence of denominational churches, which sprang up as a result of Protestantism, led Warneck to see the founding of national churches as a goal of mission. From a contemporary point of view, this is a major weakness in Warneck's theology of mission. If one seeks to build churches after one's own national model (here we are not talking of inculturation and church communion), then the universality of the church, which for Catholics is symbolized and realized in the chair of Peter as the center of universal ecclesial communion, is thrown overboard. What we see today in the disunited world Christian movement, borne at least in part out of the wounds of the Reformation, carries with it the need for a renewed attention to the prayer of Jesus for unity in the church (see John 17: 21). Nevertheless, Warneck's major contribution lay in his ability to bring together the different strands of the missionary movement in Protestantism and to work for the teaching of missiology as a separate theological discipline in the Protestant world.

The Orthodox Theology of Mission as Divinization

We cannot conclude this chapter without saying a few words about missiology among the Orthodox. Until recently, Orthodox missiology did not attain complete development as a documented body of theological thought. Nevertheless, it has had a rich history of practical mission work, symbolized best perhaps by the apostolic work set in motion by Saints Cyril (ca. 827-869) and Methodius (ca. 815-885), whose work was praised so roundly by John Paul II in his encyclical *Slavorum Apostoli*. Since Orthodox theology takes its rise from a Trinitarian perspective (in contradistinction to the more usual Christocentric perspective of the West), we will discuss the missiological thought of Orthodox theologians from this standpoint.

First, the Orthodox consider salvation to be the ultimate *thēosis* ("divinization") of the human person wherein we reach the fullness of life intended for us by God. The church (*ekklēsia*), characterized by communion (*koinōnia*) of human beings with one another and with God, is the place where salvation is actualized on earth. Synergy (*synergismon*), a communion in the principle of the energy of cosmic and human life, characterizes the relationship between God and the free human being in salvation. Orthodox theology accentuates the interior character of salvation, though, to some moderns, it does so at the expense of the universality of God's grace and its universal availability and a sense that God is present and active, too, in what we call the "secular" world.

Whatever truth there is to the critique of Orthodoxy by some Western theologians, much of the renewal in Trinitarian theology in the modern era, which most see as an important retrieval of essential elements in the Christian tradition, owes its inspiration to Orthodox theology. Orthodox theologians argue that the doctrine of the Trinity is not something removed from day-to-day life; it is something that has a living, practical importance for every Christian. The mutual openness of Father and Son, Son and Spirit, Spirit and Father serve as a model of mutuality in relationships and also point to the fact that vital relationships are constitutive of personal identity and to the necessity of including an a priori appreciation for diversity in every true community. All these vital truths and the practices that flow from them, Orthodox teaching insists, are rooted in Trinitarian reality and existence. Orthodox theologians understand Trinity as an *ec-static* communion of persons, one in which God is always involved in the world, always inviting all members of creation to share in the triune life of communion-in-mission. Such an understanding of God as Trinity is the basis of the Orthodox theology of mission (Bevans and Schroeder 2004, 294). According to famous Orthodox theologians such as Yannoulatos, behind this Trinitarian approach there is a theme of "mission-unity," in the concept of *doxa* (glory of God) and missions. The Orthodox also speak of missionary *kenō-sis* (self-abnegating), carried on without obtrusive proselytism, and the epiphanic or manifestational nature of mission. Characteristic, too, is an acknowledgment of the unitary and universal character of the Logos as the origin and end of creation that give mission its focus. Stressed too is the relationship between what is carried on in missions and the eschatological fulfillment of the cosmos. And all these dimensions are brought together in mission as a liturgy after the liturgy. From these various themes, we select mission as *doxa* for further elaboration.

For Orthodox theologians, mission as *doxa* means that mission is an activity through which the glory of God is revealed and communicated. This occurred at the first moment in Israel and in a definitive form in Christ. Today it occurs in the life of the church. Finally, it will be realized fully in the parousia ("coming" and "presence") of the kingdom. A great advocate of this theme is Anastasios Yannoulatos (see Yannoulatos 1965, 281-97), who returns again and again to the doctrine of the Trinity and speaks of it as a loving communion of persons, wherein to be church means to share in that dynamic life of love. By sharing in the life of the risen Christ, living the Father's will moved by the Holy Spirit, he says, *we* have a decisive word to speak and role to play in shaping the course of humankind.

James J. Stamoolis presents what could be called a classical Orthodox mission theology in which he defines the church not as "an institution" but as "a new life with Christ and Christ, guided by the Holy Spirit." Relying heavily on an earlier work by M. A. Siotis, Stamoolis points out two important aspects of this definition in relation to mission. First, he understands church as constituted not by structures (hierarchy) but by activity. Second, this activity is characterized by an extension of God's *activity* in the world, although the church's activity cannot be equated with the *missio Dei* as such, for God's mission is carried on outside of and independently of the church. But to be in the church is to share in that mission by virtue of one's participation in the life of Christ, and to be guided, like him, by the Holy Spirit. This is why, for Orthodox theologians, the church *as such* is mission (Stamoolis 1986, 103).

Furthermore, authors following this line place the term "glory" (Hebrew, *kabod*; Greek, *doxa*) at the center of their reflection. The glory of God is not a static concept, but dynamic and therefore missionary. It is the blazing manifestation of the salvific power (love and light) of God. The glorification of God in its subjective aspect is the response of the man that is converted, in whom is manifested this power of God. Thus, the definition of a missionary: "I glorified you on earth, having accomplished the work which you have given me to do" (John 17:4). Mission is not a conquest but a doxology, because through it, Christ, present in the church, continues to render glory to the Father in the Spirit. Thus, Orthodox theologians exhort that we should not isolate the soteriological or liberation aspect from mission. For the Orthodox, soteriology means liberation.

Before the creation of the world, the Word (the preexistent Logos) was full of glory. This glory is the fruit of the Father's love and becomes important in Johannine theology: "And now, Father, glorify me and those you have given me because you loved me before the foundation of the world" (John 17:5, 24; see also 1:14; 11:49; 12:41; and passim). Creation manifests the glory of God, as the psalmist says (Ps 19:1-4). Creatures also manifest the wonders of the power of God. This "glory" was obscured by sin (Rom 1:23ff.). The whole history of salvation is united at the manifestation of the glory of Yahweh (Exod 14:4f.; 15:1-2; 16:7). The glory was manifested at the moment of the Sinai covenant (Exod 24:16-17).

In the same manner, the glory lived in the Tabernacle from where it is salvifically communicated to the people (Exod 25:8ff.; 40:34; Luke 1:35). Thereafter, in the Temple shall live the glory of God (Ps 26:8; 1 Kgs 9:10). Also in the Tabernacle shall the glory of God continue to live (Lev 9:22-23; Num 16:19). The Old Testament speaks of the glory of God in messianic times. This shall be the glory that shall be manifested to all peoples and nations (Isa 66:1; 60:1-2; 35:1-2). When the Messiah comes he will manifest this glory to all (Isa 40:5; 49:3; Pss 96:3; 97:7; 102:16-17).

The New Testament says "the Word became flesh, he lived among us and we saw his glory, the glory that he has from the Father as only Son of the Father" (John 1:14). The emphasis is on the verb *skenein*, "to live, to dwell." This verb is used to render the Hebrew word *shekina* or presence of God in his Tabernacle or in his Temple. At his birth the angels have begun the song of glory (Luke 2:1). The whole ministry of Christ was to glorify the Father (John 17); with his first miracle, Christ himself manifested the glory (John 2:11). At the same time, the Father was manifesting his glory in the Son (John 13:32; 7:39; Acts 3:13). Finally, Christ will return in glory (Mark 8:38; Titus 2:13). Christ showed his apostles, together with his missionaries, his glory (John 17:22). The missionaries preach the gospel of glory (2 Thess 3:1; 2 Cor 4:4; 4:6; 3:6, 8). Today, glory-salvation is in the church (Eph 3:21; Rev 21:23, 26); participation in the divine life is participation in glory (Rom 5:2; 8:30; 6:4; 1:6, 12-19; 3:16), which follows a continuing conversion (2 Cor 3:18; Col 3:4). When nonbelievers are converted, the church glorifies God (Acts

11:18; 13:14). All creation is awaiting participation in this glory (Rom 8:19). The new Jerusalem becomes the glory (Rev 21:3). The Spirit is sent to help in this work of glorification (John 16:14). The missionary transmits the glory, as did Moses (2 Cor 3:17ff.; 8:23; see also Voulgarakis 1965, 298-307).

In general, Orthodox theologians give central place to liturgy. The liturgy of the Eucharist is very important to an Orthodox understanding of mission. Liturgy is always the entrance into the presence of the triune God and always ends with the community being sent forth in God's name to transform the world in God's image. Mission is thus conceived as "the liturgy after the liturgy," the natural consequence of entering into the divine presence in worship (Bria 1978, 86-90). It is the source of Christian witness because at liturgy believers open themselves to the Spirit through communion in the Lord's body and blood. The Eucharist transforms the church into what it is, "transforms it into mission" (Bevans and Schroeder 2004, 295).

Conclusion

To conclude this chapter, it is important to note that the missionary model of conversion of individuals as the aim of mission has persisted and been brought into the missiology of Vatican II, where it has been deepened and supplemented by being joined to the council's teaching on the aim of mission as evangelization and planting of the church (*AG* 6). In other words, the term "conversion" is still valid, and it refers not just to missionary activity that seeks the salvation of individuals but includes all the traditional concepts of mission as preaching or proclamation of the gospel. In this new understanding, conversion is still recognized as an aspect of evangelization, and the word evangelization itself assumes a broader meaning. All missionary activities centered on planting the church, human promotion, struggle for justice and peace, interreligious dialogue, and so forth are an integral part of evangelization.

This means that the present inclusive accent on evangelization as the goal of mission retains the specific meanings and dimensions of the various aspects of mission that go with it. In the process of conversion, mission is seen to have the role of mediation through the proclamation of the gospel (Mark 6:12; John 17:20). And this mediation is salvific. It does not entail intrusive proselytizing or acting in ways that force conversion on others (*AG* 13). Rather, it is an offer of peace to all—an opportunity for people to experience the peace of Christ in a new way through hearing and responding to the proclamation of the gospel and the invitation to convert (i.e., "turn," *epistrephein*, Acts 14:15) to Christ. This understanding of conversion recognizes that missionary proclamation and the evangelizing activity of the church are the means for the Spirit to bring about conversion to Christ. As important as the work of the church is, its role is to mediate and serve as God's invitation-bearer in the name of Christ before the world.

4

MISSION AS CHURCH PLANTING AND CHURCH GROWTH

Alongside the model of mission as conversion is the theory of "church planting" (among Catholic authors), and "church growth" (among Evangelical
Protestant authors). The two theories, however, differ, but since both center
their attention on understanding mission under the rubric of establishing the
church, we will discuss them together in this chapter. This may help us to see
both their differences and commonalities.

Catholic Mission Theology of Church Planting

In addition to the Münster school, which we have been characterizing as
focused on the many dimensions of conversion, is the Louvain school. The
basic thesis of the Louvain school is that the goal of mission is the "planting"
of the church, and so it is also called the "plantation theory" (*plantatio ecclesiae*). The chief exponents of this theory are the Belgian Jesuit Pierre Charles,
Joseph Masson (Louvain), and André Seumois (Rome).

Pierre Charles (1883-1954)

Pierre Charles was born in Brussels on July 3, 1883, became a Jesuit on Sep-
tember 23, 1899, and was ordained to the priesthood on August 24, 1910.
He served as a professor of theology at Louvain from 1914-1954, where his
special interest lay in missiology. He also wrote widely on ethnology and the
history of religions as they bore upon missional issues. He served as professor
of missiology at the Gregorian University in Rome from 1932 to 1938.
Father Charles was a prolific writer. Apart from the many mission journals
that he launched and directed personally for the promotion of missionary
work in Belgium and France, he wrote articles on different aspects of missi-

ology and published the *Dossiers* on missionary activity beginning in 1916, and started the Xaveriana series in 1923. In his *Les Dossiers de l'action missionnaire*, a manual of missiology, he outlined his theology of mission. He was the secretary of Semaines de Missiologie from 1925 to 1953. He died at Louvain on February 11, 1954 (see Anderson et al. 1994, 410-15).

Charles founded the Louvain school of missiology, which maintained that the aim of missionary activity should be the planting or formation of a church (with its own hierarchy, indigenous clergy, and sacraments) in non-Christian countries. It broke away from the German school of missiology founded by Josef Schmidlin at Münster in 1919, which viewed the aim of missions as the conversion of individuals. The theological foundation of Charles's thesis is God's desire for the salvation of everyone not individually but as members of the church. His influence was definitive in Catholic missiology up to and including Vatican II (see *AG* 6; Anderson 1998, 127).

Charles began by defining the object of mission. According to him, the formal object of mission is "the establishment of the visible church in those countries where it is not yet established" (P. Charles 1939, 59). Furthermore, for him missionary activity ought to be directed not only to non-Christians but to any groups among whom the visible church was not established. Mission, in his view, is a developing church that is growing toward maturity. In terms of the motivation for mission, it is carried out not simply because of obedience to the mandate of Christ (the "Great Commission") or out of concern for the salvation of individuals. Rather, the ultimate justification for mission is the nature of the church itself, which will achieve its full identity as the body of Christ and manifest God's plan for humanity when it embraces the whole world. Thus, concern for saving souls is an imperfect motivation for mission. The one and only complete raison d'être of mission is rather the establishment of the visible church (P. Charles 1938, 37).

Thus, like Schmidlin, Charles understood mission primarily as an activity carried on by a missionary working outside his or her native land, and a mission territory is a place where the church is not yet visibly established. Unlike Schmidlin, Charles does not see mission primarily as converting non-Christian individuals or saving souls. Instead, the primary goal of mission is to plant the church where it is not yet visibly established, and to nurture it and all its necessary organs by erecting a local hierarchy and native clergy, and by making the sacraments, the means of salvation, accessible to an entire region or people. Wherever such a visible church is absent, theologically speaking, that is a mission land. Thus the aim of missionary activity is to establish an "adult church," a tangible society with its own structures, rooted in the soil of a given land, complete with the necessary socioeconomic and material wherewithal for teaching Christian doctrine and celebrating the sacraments (P. Charles 1954/56, 15-32). Charles insists on his position that the real criterion whether a country is a mission land is the presence or absence of the visible church with all necessary structures. The purpose of mission is thus to plant the visible church wherever it is not yet planted, that is, to bring the means of salvation (faith and the sacraments) within the reach of all souls of good will. In many countries this task is completed. Here mission as such no longer exists. Nevertheless, there are many souls to be converted and all souls here must still be saved. (P. Charles 1938, 65)

Charles took exception to the then prevalent notion that reduced the church to being a *means* of saving souls (an "instrumentalist" vision of the nature of church). For him church is more than that because it is "the divine form of the world, the one point of contact where the whole work of the Creator returns to its Savior; it is less because belonging to the church is by no means sufficient for salvation." Thus he asserts: "The special task of mission is to extend the boundaries of the visible church, to complete this work of growth, to strew the whole world with prayers and adoration, to win back for the Savior his whole inheritance" (ibid., 84-87).

Charles's proposal of the goal of mission as planting of the church is linked to his theory of the proper adaptation of the church in local cultures. He argues that a successful planting of the church entails genuine adaptation, since no mere conversion of individuals suffices. The people to be evangelized are members of cultures, and these cultures have lasting influence on them. From childhood to death the individual undergoes a cultural process of maturation in which perons adapt to the discipline of the social group. By the time the person attains adulthood, the local culture becomes a "second nature" or habitual manner of envisioning the world and the human being's place in it in an "inculturation" process—a term used by Charles in an anthropological sense as descriptive of a universal process that takes place in concretely different ways in diverse cultures (P. Charles 1954/56, 20). Thus the isolation of neophytes in Christian villages or mission posts to protect them from unchristian influences of their native culture is counterproductive in the missiology of Pierre Charles. Instead, the Christian message should be shaped to penetrate a given culture and transform it from within, like yeast in dough. Only in this way, he believes, will negative aspects of a given culture be transformed and resistance to Christian conversion be overcome or weakened (ibid., 20-27).

In planting the church in what Charles calls a mission land, the missionary does not, in other words, encounter a vacuum that is to be filled with Christian truths. On the contrary, the missioner encounters a culture, an organized system of life, with beliefs, customs, social systems, juridical conceptions, artistic taste, and so on. Missioners adapt to this sociocultural ambient not as a tactical ploy to win the favor of the people but in order to become effective ambassadors of a people before God, and conversion is the process whereby a people becomes more pleasing to God (P. Charles 1938, 169-70).

For Charles, adaptation is not merely a missionary's way of being or acting. It is the fundamental attitude of the Catholic mission toward indigenous institutions and is an important theological issue. The incarnation of the Word is the ideal model for adaptation. To save humankind and to restore human nature to its full dignity and to attain its full potential, the Word of God became flesh in human history. And as the church fathers used to say, by assuming our nature Christ saved that which he had become with us. In a similar manner, the missionary seeks to identify himself with the people he sets out to evangelize and to become a mediator of grace for them, so as to introduce a Christian soul into the people and to enable them to participate in a new richness (P. Charles 1954/56, 120-21). Besides the incarnation of the Word, Charles gives other theological reasons for adaptation. One of these is the continuity between creation and the work of redemption. The church was willed by God to be the means of God's revelation of the divine intent for the world, and its coming was prepared by divine providence. He draws on patristic insights that see the work of the creator as not opposed to the work of the redeemer but being completed by Christ. Indeed, whatever is good in creation, and especially in the cultures of the people, contributes in some way to the work of redemption and consequently to the mission of the church (P. Charles 1938, 170).

Charles also admits that the theory of adaptation has suffered distortions in practice in instances like the rites controversies in the Far East in the seventeenth century and under the domination of mission by a European cultural outlook and the "missionary romanticism" in the nineteenth century (ibid., 171-72) that idolized the exoticism of mission life and its voyages and was marked by a romantic interest in the civilization of "savages" that dehumanized the peoples of Africa, Asia, and Oceania. This had the affect of making mission a heroic adventure in pursuit of the salvation of souls in near and in distant countries. To win support and finance their cause, missionaries painted bizarre pictures of the pitiful moral state of the "savages . . . to demonstrate their urgent need of salvation" from eternal damnation (ibid., 379-82). Having to rely on a negative image of the people among whom they worked, missionaries did not give due consideration in evangelization to people's cultural values. Nevertheless, Charles insists that adaptation was the general policy of the church in the past. He refers particularly to two church documents which, according to him, constitute the charter for missionary adaptation: the letter of Gregory the Great to Mellitus in 601 (see *Patrologia Latina*, ed. J. P. Migne [Paris, 1844-1855], 77, 1215, and 1187), and the *Instructio de Propaganda Fide* in 1659 (*Collectanea Propaganda Fide* [1907], 1:42 n. 135; see P. Charles 1938, 171-72).

In conclusion, it can be said that for Charles, there is a connection between adaptation and the planting of the church in a particular region. Authentic planting of an adult church requires the necessary adaptation to the cultures of the people. This includes providing the new church with the necessities for its mission, especially a local clergy, to ensure the stability and maturity of the church. Adaptation is neither a concession nor a mere tactic the missionary uses to win the favor of the people; it is a fundamental theological issue that finds its justification and foundation in the incarnation. Moreover, Charles saw a continuity between the work of creation and the work of redemption. Whatever is recognized as good in creation and in local cultures, including the religions of the people, is to be considered a first step toward God and a providential preparation for the Christian faith and the church. Such values must therefore be appropriated in order to enrich the patrimony of the church. Today such ideas are taken for granted, but at the time Charles was expressing them before Vatican II, they constituted a major development in the theological valuation of local cultures and their religious traditions.

The most zealous champions of the church planting theory (after Pierre Charles) are Joseph Masson and André Seumois. We shall consider briefly the positions of the two authors.

Joseph Masson (1908-)

Joseph Armand Masson, SJ, is the successor of Pierre Charles at the Louvain school of missiology. Masson was born in Montegnée, Belgium, and was ordained a priest in the Jesuit order in 1938. He obtained a doctorate at the Oriental Institute in Louvain in 1943 and worked as a chaplain and missiologist in Louvain and Namur. He was professor of mission theology, missionography, and Buddhism at the Gregorian University, Rome, from 1958 to 1978. His main interests are mission theology and world religions, especially Buddhism. From 1946 onward, as collaborator and successor of Pierre Charles, he was responsible for the Louvain Missiological Week. During Vatican II he was J. M. Sevrin's theologian and in this position helped to influence the missionary decree *Ad Gentes* in accordance with the ideas of the Louvain school. At his suggestion, the phrase "preaching the gospel" was supplemented by "and implanting the church," a meaningful compromise about the aim of missionary activity. He was consultor to the Congregation for the Evangelization of Peoples and the Pontifical Council for Interreligious Dialogue. He has published more than two hundred articles, some for the collection *Unam Sanctum*, and written commentaries on the conciliar decrees *Ad Gentes* and *Nostra Aetate*.

Among the more important of Masson's books are *Missions Belges sous l'Ancien Régime* (1947), *L'attività missionaria della chiesa* (text of and commentary on *Ad Gentes* [1966]), *La missione contiuna: Inizia un'epoca nuova nell'evangelizazzione del mondo* (1975), *Le Bouddhisme, chemin de libération* (2nd ed., 1975; 1992), *Père de nos pères* (1988), and *Mystique d'Asie* (1992). A noteworthy aspect of Masson's contribution to the debate is his idea of *indigenization*. Masson argues (particularly in his book *Vers L'église indigène*) that mission should aim at establishing indigenous churches. In fact, this may be regarded as Masson's version of the church planting theory. He asserts that it was the model that was used in the apostolic era. He notes also that the work of the Roman Congregation for the Propagation of the Faith and missionary societies is geared toward this goal (see 1966a, 37ff.). His idea of indigenization emphasizes mainly the training of local clergy and formation of local churches as they have taken shape historically in the West. According to Masson, mission must aim at indigenization because only in this way can Christian doctrine, worship, pastoral practices, and art be brought to bear on a local people's culture and religious tradition. This notion of indigenization is also inherent in Masson's concept of *Catholicisme inculturé* (inculturated Catholicism). He introduced this expression into missiological circles in 1962, and this led to the use of new missiological terminology revolving around the word "inculturation." Masson's ideas on inculturation, however, have been linked with his concept of indigenization and been criticized (see Ukpong 1987, 161-68). In fairness, he was interested in showing how indigenization must not be understood as movement toward nationalism (see 1966a, 43ff.), but should be understood in the context of its faithfulness to the catholicity of the church. This, he says, does not demand uniformity, but rather points to the modern understanding of unity in diversity in cultural expressions.

The term "indigenization" has attracted much criticism in recent times. For instance, Arij Roest Crollius rejects it for having a pejorative connotation (see 1978, 725 n. 8). But Justin Ukpong cautions that the term need not be understood in a pejorative or static sense for it is not so much the word used as the meaning that grows up around it that is important (1987, 164). He believes that it is possible for indigenization to have a dynamic and good meaning, for example, as he defines the term:

> As the name implies, indigenization aims at making Christianity an indigenous religion of the society concerned. It seeks to create dialogue between the indigenous thought system and European Christian thought system for the purpose of mutual understanding, interpretation and transformation. (Ibid., 165)

Ukpong continues, the term

> Indigenization . . . focuses basically on creating endogenous channels of communicating the Christian message cross-culturally, and is thus concerned with the search for alternative models of Christian expression within the local culture. Its goal is to make Christianity part and parcel of the people's worldview. It employs ethnographic and anthropological methods in its analysis of society. (Ibid.)

In any case, the scope of indigenization regards the way in which religiocultural aspects of the society can be carried over into facets of Christian life such as theology, liturgy, forms of ministry, catechesis, pastoral practice, and spiritual formation. Masson's theory of indigenization arose out of the tension between Catholic Christianity and local cultures during the earliest days of Christianity in modern mission situations. In those early days, the way of life of the local people was often indiscriminately condemned as unsuitable for Christians. Too little attempt was made to research the indigenous people's thought systems for the purpose of more effective communication of the Christian message. The point to be stressed here is that, in practice, indigenization looked forward to the gradual replacement of foreign missionaries with local personnel in order to give a local face to ecclesiastical structures so that the church may appear less foreign. During the struggles for political independence in the 1960s and down to the present, the church was accused of collaboration with Western colonialism. Thus, the indigenization agenda was proposed to show that the church was at home in those mission territories and that Christianity was truly the local people's religion (see Oborji 1998, 92).

In the last few years the need to enter into intercultural dialogue for the purpose of effective evangelization became intensified. What we have increasingly become aware of is the fact that the culture of the missionary was only *a* culture and in no way superior to African, Asian, and Oceanic cultures. And it is precisely here that the strength of Masson's theory of indigenization lies. He stressed the fact that the indigenous people need not lose their identity on becoming Christians and that the people's thought systems should not normally be replaced by another. They will not so much be modified by the novelty of Christian faith as used in the conversion of all things to Christ and put under his lordship. But they will retain their identity, just as the human person retains his identity in spite of growth and change. Christianity and its bearers must therefore dialogue with peoples of all cultures (see Masson 1975, 15).

André Seumois (1917-2000)

André Seumois, OMI, a Belgian, studied missiology at the Pontifical Urbaniana University (then Propaganda Fide Athenaeum) in Rome, obtaining a doctorate in 1948. He was appointed professor of missiology at the newly established Institute of Missionary Sciences at the University of Ottawa, where he taught from 1948 to 1951. In 1952 he was appointed visiting professor for the course on introduction to missiology at the Scientific Missionary Institute of the Propaganda Fide Athenaeum, and in the following year, he was put in charge of the program. In 1969 he became professor of missiology at Urban University, Rome, where he taught until he retired in 1987 (see G. Anderson 1998, 612-13).

Seumois has published widely in the area of mission studies; among his publications are *Vers une définition de l'activité missionnaire* (1948); *L'intro-duction de la missiologie* (1952); *La Papauté et les missions au cours des six premier siècles: Mèthodologie antique et orientations modernes* (1953); *L'Anima dell'apostolato missionario* (1958); *Apostolat: Structure théologique* (1961); *Oecuménisme missionnaire* (1970); *Théologie missionnaire*, 5 vols. (1973-1981); and *Teologia missionaria* (1993). In 1987 a festschrift for Father Seumois was published entitled *Chiesa e inculturazione nella missione.*

Seumois's contributions to the debate are well documented in his *magnum opus*, the five-volume *Théologie missionnaire*. In vol. 1 Seumois discusses the scope and limits of the missionary function of the church, and in vol. 2 we find his treatment of the church planting theory. Volume 3 discusses salvation in Christ vis-à-vis the non-Christian religions; vol. 4 is dedicated to missionary church and sociocultural features. Finally, in vol. 5, Seumois examines the dynamism of the missionary role of the people of God (the church). Of primary interest to us here is vol. 2, where he examines the theology of church planting.

The main thesis of Seumois is that the idea of *implantatio ecclesiae,* when it is properly grasped, is consistent with the whole concept of the church universal. When the church is established in a new cultural area, it makes present and brings with it the prophetic-mission dimensions of both the Old and New Testaments. It enlarges the tenure and demeanor of the people and makes them part of the universal church and conscious agents in God's universal salvific plan. Yet even as a new church is part of the church universal, as a newly evangelized region, it retains its own national and cultural expressions and brings this particularity to participate and share in the whole heritage of the universal church, which is now implanted in the area. Therefore, the theory of church planting is, in reality, the way in which the universal church becomes concrete and catholic in a given area (see Seumois 1973, 7-8).

Seumois returns to the structures that make the planting of the church possible, or rather the characteristics of a truly "planted" church. He contends that there are organisms that characterize the universal institution-alization of the church: establishment of ecclesiastical administrative machin-ery for the Catholic community; taking possession of its proper territory for the ministry of the sacraments; and, in general, instituting the ecclesial medi-ation of the means of salvation. Church is planted when the newly formed Catholic community assumes full responsibility for pastoral action in its ter-ritory, endowed with apostolic zeal, self-sufficiency in resources for its par-ticular needs, and stability for harmonious development of the community and the whole people within the area. For Seumois, the church is planted when a diocese has been established in stability with its proper resident bishop and clergy and becomes a community sufficiently equipped to carry on the church's evangelizing mission in that area by executing the full range of pastoral, liturgical, and sacramental ministries. In other words, the church reaches maturity when the local community has the means necessary to function in that territory and make present to the people the mystery of the universal church as visible sacrament and salvific act of Christ (see Seumois 1973/81, 58-59).

Seumois's thesis centers on descriptions of the founding of a particular church (diocese). Thus, he goes on to indicate the importance of communion with the *le Président de l'*"*agapé*" *universelle* (the pope) in the concretization of *plantatio ecclesiae*. He writes that the notion of church implantation refers to establishing an integral relationship of the local church to the successor of Peter, the center of world Catholic communion. This is the basis on which he differentiates mission areas from areas in which the church is already "constituted normally." On the one hand, we have to continue with the pastoral activity of the already planted church, and, on the other, we must contend with the church's apostolate *ad extra* (outwardly directed activity) in such a way that the apostolate is directed to deepening pastoral life. Seumois employs these terms to depict what is inherent in the Latin word *missio*, a word employed in Trinitarian theology to denote the sending of the Son by the Father and the sending of the Holy Spirit by the Father and the Son. Seumois asserts that the church, in addition to seeing her missionary endeavor in that perspective, has in the last fifteen centuries also used other terms to refer to what we subsequently came to call "mission": such expressions as "propagation of the faith"; "preaching the gospel"; "apostolic proclamation"; "promulgation of the gospel"; "augmenting the faith"; "expanding the church"; "planting the church"; "propagation of the reign of Christ"; and "illuminating the nations" (1974, 18).

Seumois responds to and sometimes even attacks representatives of the conversion theory such as Ohm and Glazik (see Müller 1987, 44), who accused plantation theorists of an "ecclesiocentric" euphoria. According to Seumois, such critiques of ecclesiocentric missiology have their origin in Calvinist tendencies propagated in recent years by the Dutch missiologist Johannes C. Hoekendijk. Seumois asserts that the criticism of Hoekendijk that, for Catholics, "mission is from the church for the church" and that it serves mainly ecclesiastical interests cannot be used properly to interpret the aim of mission as planting of the church. Seumois adds that even Schmidlin, the pioneer Catholic missiologist, and T. Grentrup spoke of juridical foundation of missionary activity. Seumois says that the notion of mission as planting of the church is classical and traditional (1974, 61). Seumois wrote later that the gaps between conversion theory and that of planting the church have today been bridged by a more solidly based synthesis of the concept of mission. E. Loffeld, of the Louvain school, shares similar sentiments (see Müller 1987, 38). It could be said that the dividing line between the Münster school and the Louvain school is the issue of the goal of mission as the salvation of souls. As Karl Müller pointed out, "Although Schmidlin hardly ever mentioned the matter of the salvation of the heathen and never in an exclusive sense, this point became the special characteristic of the Münster school as opposed to the Louvain school" (1987, 76). Already René Lange (who could be described as the mentor of Pierre Charles as far as the plantation theory is concerned) had contested the idea that the necessity of mission should be deduced from the salvation of souls. His argument is based on the fact that souls could also be saved outside the visible church. Thus, like Charles, he saw the reason for mission in the catholicity of the church independent from the question of salvation (see Lange 1924, 33). At Vatican Council II, as already noted, a compromise was sought between the two positions, as can be read in *AG* 6: "The special end of this missionary activity is the evangelization and the implanting of the Church among peoples or groups in which it has not yet taken root."

Catholics and Protestants on "Young" and "Mature" Churches

One of the problems that arose at the beginning of the twentieth century, and to which Evangelical Protestant missiologists offered important contributions, centers on defining mission in relation to the newly founded local churches in so-called mission lands. Let us begin with an overview of the Catholic perspective on these matters.

For Catholics, the issue of local and universal is handled within discussions of the problem of enunciating the relationship between local autonomy and worldwide communion in the universal church. In that context Catholics have long differentiated between "mission-sending churches" and the newly founded "missions" or "emerging local churches" in the Third World. Catholics emphasize the universality of the church, the necessity of communion among all parts of the church, and coresponsibility of all Christians for mission. Mission is theologically conceived as participating in the one mission that Jesus Christ commissioned the apostles to carry on, with Peter as the primate of the church founded by Christ. Thus, the church is a sign and the sacrament of his saving ministry in the world, and its visible unity is both signified and effected by the communion of the bishops, who are the successors of the apostles, with the pope at the center of the communion, the one entrusted with the office of overseeing this mission for which the church has been commissioned.

On the Protestant side, at least superficially, the "three-selfs" formula (self-government, self-support, and self-propagating) has been used as the guiding principle for articulating the relationship between those who are sent to found a church and the church that results from their labors. In reality, as is too often the case among Catholics, young churches are looked down upon and are regarded as immature and dependent on the wisdom, experience, and help of the older churches or mission societies (Bosch 1991, 378-79). But among Protestants, awareness of the situation and judgment that such attitudes are deficient began to surface at the Jerusalem (1928) and Tambaran (1938) meetings of the International Missionary Council (IMC), where the younger churches were spoken of as "equals." The Whitby Conference (1947) coined the phrase "Partnership in Obedience" in an attempt to give expression to the conviction that it is theologically preposterous to distinguish between autonomous and dependent churches. The Ghana Conference of the IMC (1958) concluded "that the distinction between older and younger churches, whatever may have been its usefulness in earlier years, is no longer valid or helpful" (Orchard 1958, 12). Thus, even if all this practice still falls short of theory, there is no doubt that Protestant churches recognized relatively early that time for rethinking the relationship among churches throughout the world had arrived: Mission could no longer be viewed as a one-way street; from the North (or West) to the South (or Third World), every church, everywhere, came to be understood as a center of mission (see Sundermeier 1986, 65; Bosch 1991, 379).

One of the strongest attacks against prevailing dependency structures in missionary and ecclesial self-understanding came from Roland Allen. In his classic book *Missionary Methods: St Paul's or Ours?* Allen alerted his readers to the glaring differences between Paul's missionary methods and those of contemporary mission agencies. According to Allen, the basic difference is that Paul had founded "churches" while modern missionaries founded "missions" in the sense of *dependent* organizations. When Paul wrote the first of his letters to the church in Thessalonica, where he had spent a mere five months or so, he wrote not as if to a mission he was still directing but to a *church*. Furthermore, at no point did the sending church, Antioch, have juridical authority over the fledgling Christian communities in Ephesus, Corinth, and elsewhere. Paul's success, Allen suggests, was due to the fact that he trusted both the Lord and the people to whom he had gone. In both these respects, modern missionaries are blatantly different from Paul (1956, 90, 107-90).

This awareness coincided with the rediscovery of the local church as the primary agent of mission; it led also to a fundamentally new interpretation of the purpose of mission and the role of missionaries and mission agencies. On the Catholic side, the general attitude is that in the midst of these new circumstances and relationships there is still need for the formation of experts or, rather, trained missionaries. However, the missionaries are to recognize that their task pertains to the *whole* church, and they are to appreciate that they are sent as ambassadors of one local church to another local church (where such a local church already exists), as witnesses of solidarity and partnership and as expressions of mutual encounter, exchange, and enrichment (see *AG* 26).

Donald A. McGavran and
the Theology of Church Growth

As matters developed in Protestant missiological circles, this new awareness of the missionary nature of the local church initiated debates on the goal of mission in the midst of emerging circumstances. For, despite the changed circumstances, it was discovered that many of the old approaches and attitudes lived on, some virtually unchallenged. Traditional sending agencies—both societies and denominational bodies—continued life as usual. It appeared as if nothing had changed, especially among the so-called historical Protestant churches (e.g., Lutherans, Methodists, and Presbyterians). Moreover, there were new concerns for numerical church growth in both the North and the Third World. In that context, some missiologists started to propose church growth as a major and irreplaceable goal of mission. The church-growth model is associated with the works and person of Donald A. McGavran. This is only partly true, however, since McGavran developed his ideas collaboratively with Alan Tippett and Ralph Winter. Winter and Peter C. Wagner, in turn, developed a number of ideas that went beyond McGavran's own thinking (see Wagner 1979). Since McGavran is the seminal mind behind the church growth tradition, we limit our discussion of the model to his contributions, but the writings of the others merit serious study. Although it is not true that Fuller Theological Seminary's School of Intercultural Studies is dominated by church-growth thought, Fuller remains a very important center for missiological research, one that pays special attention to empirical research in anthropological, linguistic, and social studies in its theological and missiological reflection.

Donald Anderson McGavran, popularly known as an American church-growth missiologist, was born in Damoh, India, where his parents were serving as missionaries. He studied at Butler University and Yale Divinity School and obtained his doctorate from Columbia University. He served the Christian Church (Disciples of Christ) as an educator, evangelist, church planter, and mission executive in India. In 1965, he became founding dean of Fuller Theological Seminary's School of World Mission (now known as the School of Intercultural Studies), where he contributed to a renaissance in Evangelical Protestant mission studies, and particularly to the development of the church-growth strategy for mission (see G. Anderson 1998, 449). His major publications include *The Bridges of God* (1955); *How Churches Grow* (1959); *Ethnic Realities and the Church: Lessons from India* (1979); *Momentous Decisions in Missions Today* (1984); and *Understanding Church Growth* (1970, 1980, and 1990). A festschrift in his honor, edited by A. R. Tippett, *God, Man, and Church Growth*, was published in 1973.

Stimulated by J. Wascom Pickett's research into India's "mass movements" of people into the Christian faith, McGavran began asking, "Why do some churches grow and others do not?" This question led him to twenty years of field research in various churches and cultures. As he became immersed in this research, McGavran began to develop the church-growth model and to identify four questions posed by it: (1) What are the *causes* of church growth? (2) What are the *barriers* to church growth? (3) What are the factors that can make the Christian faith a *movement* among some populations? (4) What *principles* of church growth are reproducible in other locales?

McGavran's key insight came from the perception that Christianity spreads most naturally and contagiously within what he called "homogeneous population units," and specifically within kinship and friendship networks. He advised the churches to use these insights to reach nonbelievers and, *mutatis mutandis*, to nurture passive or nominal believers into a more vital sense of the wider Christian brotherhood and to work to increase it. He believes that good missionary strategy takes full account of existing social relationships and works for the conversion and transfer to Christianity of the whole "homogeneous unit." This could be a tribe, an urban middle class, a caste, an extended family, subgroups, and so forth. A homogeneous group of people is any group whose members self-consciously belong together. McGavran gives the highest priority to building up the churches in areas that are receptive to the gospel. According to McGavran, multiplying churches and encouraging the growth of churches should be the primary concern of missionaries. Any other work (e.g., diaconal assistance and developmental projects) are secondary or even tertiary, for in his view, the spiritual is more important than the physical, and the soul more important than the body. Diaconal programs and projects must serve only one end—church growth. If they do not, he says, they must be terminated (see McGavran 1980, 24; Verkuyl 1987, 67ff.).

Furthermore, McGavran believes that the numerical approach is essential to understanding church growth, because the church "is made up of countable people" (McGavran 1980, 93). In fact, a basic theme of McGavran is that one must begin by winning vast numbers of disciples. Only then can a people "learn all that Jesus commanded." Jesus' two commands in Matthew 28 become for McGavran two phases of a single strategy: "Make them my disciples and teach them to obey everything I have commanded you." McGavran defines church growth as "the sum of many baptized believers," and declares that "the student of church growth . . . cares little whether a church is credible; he asks how much it has grown" (McGavran 1980, 147, 159). And if that criterion seems simplistic, McGavran responds that, although it appears to be, in fact, the vitality of a growing church is a sign of God's blessing. McGavran believes that mission is essentially apostolic, so that evangelism and church planting are indispensable and perennial expressions of mission, though he recognizes that postcolonial approaches are now required. McGavran reflects on the abuses of mission's colonial period and asks that the mistakes of the past never be repeated. Still he disagrees with some Third World theologians who called for a moratorium on sending missionaries and who announced the end of the missionary era in the 1960s. Instead, McGavran challenges mission agencies to change because he believes that, despite the worries of Third World theologians, postcolonial approaches to mission are possible and desirable and that the need for "foreign missionaries" cannot be ruled out in principle. Thus he declares, "we stand in the sunrise of missions!"

Mining another vein, McGavran challenges the "mission-station" paradigm that became dominant in the nineteenth century and still prevails today. In that model, the mission is confined to and identified with the mission compound's services and institutions. This arrests the development of wider mission. His view is that mission stations are merely a stage that leads to the indigenization of leadership and the wider expansion of the national church. He regarded as naive the missionary strategy of individual conversion, which regarded only one-by-one conversions as valid. He opts for what he describes as "group conversions" and "people movements" within peoples who have a group identity and make important decisions together. It is from this context that he calls for deployment of mission personnel to receptive populations while they are receptive. McGavran adds that, contrary to prevailing Evangelical myths, people do not usually become Christians when a stranger bears witness to them; indeed, most Christian strangers (including most missionaries) make few converts. Most people become Christians when reached by a Christian relative or friend in their intimate social network; these social networks of living Christians, especially those of new Christians, provide "the bridges of God" to undiscipled people.

McGavran's church-growth model of mission has attracted some criticisms. For instance, his emphasis on evangelism for conversion is criticized for paying little or no attention to the need for dialogue, better relations, and practical collaboration with people who follow other religions. Some criticize McGavran's use of field data, statistics, graphs, and behavioral science insights, judging his approach to be insufficiently biblical, theological, or spiritual. His homogeneous-unit model is criticized on the basis that it makes it difficult for the churches to transcend humanity's divisions and model reconciliation (see Hunter III in Anderson et al. 1994, 520). It is also argued that McGavran's model signifies a departure from engagement with the pressing social issues that can oppress a given community and keep it from attaining its full human potential. The church-growth model, say some, makes an explosion in the number of converts look like a retreat into escapism and makes a mockery of elements of social concern that are clearly rooted in the mission of both Israel and Jesus. Moreover, as the work of Rodney Stark shows convincingly, church growth in the first five centuries was clearly the result of a church that knew how to teach doctrine and exercise a vital role in alleviating human misery (Stark 1997). In the view of Paul VI's *Evangelii Nuntiandi*, mission, while aiming to make more disciples for the Lord Jesus, also needs to take into account the demands of the social areas of the gospel: a gospel proclamation without demands for justice, peace, and equity is incomplete (see *EN* 23; see Bosch 1991, 382).

Conclusion

Seen from the point of view of the Catholic magisterium the two perspectives we have been discussing—conversion of individuals and planting new churches—are two aspects of the church's one mission. Both are prominent in the doctrine of Vatican Council II. The former has been broadened with the modern emphasis on the integral dimension of salvation and the recognition of cultural diversity, and both are joined to the practice of interreligious dialogue and respect for the need for inculturation (see Oborji 1998, 73). However, with regard to church formation as the goal of mission, it is important not to confuse the theory of church planting with that of church growth. While church planting is based on understanding the church as the universal sacrament and means of salvation in Christ, the church-growth thought is dominated by a view of the church as primarily a voluntary congregation of believers for the purposes of prayer, Bible reading, and decisions about faith and evangelism. All these are good in themselves, but emphasizing these aspects runs the risk of reducing the church's nature to only some of its important functions. *Lumen Gentium* chapter 1, in particular, sees the church as a much deeper and more complex entity.

This is not to say, however, that the argument that mission must aim at inviting people into the church is unimportant. Without a vital membership, how can it be a sign of Christian presence in a given locale? And an important positive element in the church-growth model of mission is the recognition of the need to attend to culture and to learn how social groups function. Sociology, anthropology, and other empirical studies have been too long neglected in planning evangelization efforts. Vatican II highlights the fact that evangelization begins with sowing of the seed of the word of God. The word grows in and through the local people and culture, taking the nutrients from that soil. From reverence for the local soil, evangelizing efforts help a church evolve that is both in communion with the universal church and inculturated. A people that is thus respected and dialogued with will bring new insights into the gospel into the universal church and have new spiritualities and ways of celebrating the gifts received in accepting the gospel. Thus, church planting is much more than the act of transplanting an older church from a foreign land into a new place.

Similarly, church growth should go beyond the mere concern to win converts to the faith. It must, above all, include the effort to introduce them into
a church that has the means for sustaining the faith of the neophytes and
that makes them feel that they are full members of the larger community of
the universal church-family. A numerical growth that aims only at mass conversion and cares little about how the mystical bonds of faith bring new converts into a vital relationship with brothers and sisters worldwide is too
superficial to be the realization of Christ's mission in the full biblical sense.

5

MISSION AS ADAPTATION AND INCULTURATION

We begin this chapter with a caution. Third World Christians, including Catholics, tend to be cautious about discussions of mission when they turn to questions of adaptation and inculturation. At a fundamental level, they have witnessed a long history of missionaries from the Euro-American cultural zone using this language in ways that—even if unintentionally—have had the effect of denigrating the cultures of the so-called global South. In beginning our analysis of adaptation and inculturation, it is important to note that the conversion and church-planting models we discussed in chapter 4 are seen to be aspects of a discredited form of adaptation theory by contemporary authors. This view is prevalent in the writings of Third World theologians (see Mushete 1994, 13-15). As a result of the complex aftermath of colonialism, adaptation has been described by some Third World theologians as a missionary theory employed to give warrants for exporting Euro-American cultural versions of Christianity into the rest of the world, as if the peoples outside the Euro-American cultural orbit have no worthy cultures of their own in which the transcendent aspects of Christian faith can be anchored (see Bosch 1991, 228).

One major contention of these critics of adaptation is that, even when the importance of culture in evangelization was paid attention to, the missionaries engaged local cultures only in a kind of reconnaissance in which they looked for points of contact, for example, when they were translating catechisms into a Melanesian language. Local cultural values, this critique states, served only as functional stepping stones in evangelization, and a deeper dialogue between local people and missioners was short-circuited. Mission theorists, according to this school of thought, conceived of adaptation as a means of searching for elements in the people's culture for comparison and contrast with those of the missionary. In this view of the matter, missionaries did not, for example, think of Xhosa language, proverbs, songs, poetry, and stories as the locus of insights into matters such as forgiveness and the mystery of life that could enrich the universal church's understanding of the fundamental mysteries of faith.

Accordingly, it must be asked if adaptation language and models run the risk of making practitioners seek superficial parallels between aspects of the local people's traditional religion and similar aspects in Christian doctrine, while missing deeper meanings that are available only from serious study of and dialogue with the other as someone who is an equal. Thus, critics may commend the adaptation model for paying attention to the values in local traditions while being wary lest the attention degenerate into a search for stepping stones across a large cultural gap and betray a mindset that does not recognize the entire culture as a coherent whole of rationally organized elements. Furthermore, critics say that, in the final analysis, the adaptation model aimed at translating a Christianity developed elsewhere into the so-called mission lands, as if the people of the mission land were condemned to receive finished products and had not the ability to produce something new or original for themselves (see Oborji 1998, 89).

However, as already noted in the first chapter, adaptation in its classical meaning refers to the efforts to employ the cultural and religious worldview of the people in the work of evangelization. Accordingly, it discovers elements in the traditional religion and culture that could serve as *preparatio evangelica* and therefore might be purified for the mission of the church in the area. This effort is as old as Christianity itself. Catholic and Protestant missiologists were all confronted with this need, because it is an essential part of the entire "translation dynamic" in Christian faith from its very beginning. In the contexts of Catholic missionary efforts since the mid-twentieth century, there has been a lively debate on missionary adaptation and, more recently, on the term "inculturation." In Protestant circles, we see many of the same things discussed as issues of communication and translation, which have typically paved the way for the current debate on contextualization and mission.

Adaptation in Catholic Missiology

As we have noted above, advocates of conversion and church-planting models are sometimes grouped together as adaptationists. Here, however, we will be discussing other authors who must be regarded as the seminal writers on and advocates of the adaptation theory. These are the authors who have written extensively on the role of cultures in evangelization (or in the new terminology, "inculturation"). Among them are Angelo Santos Hernández and Louis Luzbetak. For purposes of clarity we call them (here) advocates of the adaptation model, because they are its most prominent figures, though in both cases, their writings treat the full range of missiological issues.

Angel Santos Hernández (1915-)

Angel Santos Hernández, a Spanish-born Jesuit, received his ecclesiastical formation at the University of Madrid, where he obtained a licentiate in philosophy and sacred theology, and a doctorate in classical history in 1942. He studied also at the Gregorian University in Rome, from which he obtained a doctorate in missiology in 1949. He served as the librarian and professor of missiology (*misionología* as it is called in Spanish) at the Pontifical University of Comillas and as a professor of missiology at the Gregorian University, Rome.

Hernández is very informed on principles of modern idioms and as a librarian at the University of Comillas, he compiled an impressive bibliography on mission studies, published in twelve volumes under the title *Bibliografía Misional* (1965). The most-cited and discussed ideas emanating from him concern his thoughts about the adaptation theory, which he later published in a book titled *Adaptación Misionera* (1958). Other notable publications by Santos Hernández are *Salvacion y Paganismo: o El Problema Teologico de la Salvación de los Infieles* (1960); *Misionología: Problemas Introductorios y Ciencias Auxiliares* (1961); *Iglesia de Oriente: Repertorio Bibliográfico* (2 vols., 1963); *Las Misiones Bajo El Patronato Portugues* (1977); *Teología Sistemática de la Mision* (1991); and *Los Jesuitas en América* (1992).

In *Adaptación Misionera*, Hernández maintains that the goal of the missionary apostolate is the salvation of souls through the establishment of the visible church in the mission lands. Therefore, the church must direct its evangelization not only to individuals, but to the whole people, to their mind, law, and national character, taking into account (that is, "adapt to") a people's inclinations and fundamental attitudes in matters of religion, social life, morals, and culture (see Hernández 1958, 584-85). Hernández distinguishes between two types of adaptation. There is *subjective* adaptation, by which the missionary adapts himself and his method of preaching to the mentality of those with whom he works to present the gospel in a language they can understand. However, since he considers the main aim of missionary activity to be that of "christianizing" the entire culture of a people, mere subjective adaptation is not enough and *objective* adaptation is also required. This he sees as the task of the entire Christian community, which acts under the inspiration of the Holy Spirit as it seeks to assimilate local cultures into Christianity. It is a difficult but necessary task, because it requires a certain death on the part of the culture so that its elements may acquire new life in the Mystical Body (ibid., 586-88). Hernández insists that adaptation is an essential demand of mission, flowing from the very nature of the church. Being universal like the Christian faith that it proclaims, the church is proper to all nations and cultures. Besides, grace does not destroy nature but perfects it; in a similar way, the church does not destroy racial differences or civilizations, but perfects them by adopting and elevating them (ibid., 18-19).

Hernández asserts that the incarnation provides the justification and a model for missionary adaptation. In the incarnation the Word of God assumes all that was assumable in human nature, except sin and other human defects contrary to the dignity of Christ and his work of redemption. The work of evangelization carried out by the church is a continuation of the incarnation, and, therefore, Christianity must assume that whatever is good in the different races and cultures is compatible with the essential message of the gospel.

Hernández further distinguishes between cultural, religious, and philosophical adaptation. Cultural adaptation consists of "baptizing" and perfecting cultural practices that are compatible with Christianity, just as the church appropriated and transformed Greco-Roman cultural practices, or as Thomas Aquinas "baptized" the philosophy of Aristotle (ibid., 72-73). Religious adaptation aims at penetrating the religious spirit of the people, using traditional beliefs as a starting point. Philosophical adaptation, for its part, seeks to present the Christian message in the philosophical categories of a people. To illustrate what he calls religious and philosophical adaptation, Hernández refers to Bantu philosophy (which was first articulated by Placide Tempels in his book *La Philosophie Bantoe* [1945]) as an example of using a suitable stepping stone for presenting Christianity to the Bantu of Africa (ibid., 232-44). The Bantu, like other Christians, ought to understand Christ in their own categories of thought, so that they can establish a personal contact with Christ. Consequently, he says, the missionary apostolate is to be adapted to the mindset of a local culture, using its philosophical categories, symbols, and symbolisms to present Christ; thus Christ will speak to this people through the media of their sociocultural experience (ibid., 240).

As for the process of adaptation itself, Hernández distinguishes between the essential and the external form and clothing of Christianity. The essential elements of Christianity include what is derived from revelation, namely, the deposit of faith, moral law, the essential sacramental rites, and the fundamental features of the structure and the law of the church. The external form comprises such things as canon law, scholastic philosophy, the cultic forms from Roman tradition, and the use of Latin as the liturgical and theological language. These are of ecclesiastical origin. External clothing refers to the external appearance of the church: the attitude of the missionary in relation to the people of the missions, the methods of Christian instruction, diverse social works, institutions of charity, extraliturgical ceremonies and popular devotions, art and architecture of the church. Of these, the essential elements of the church can neither be tied to any race or nation nor be subject to adaptation. The external appearance of the church can be modified because it does not have metaphysical or universal value. Even the external form may be adapted. However, the church cannot abandon scholastic philosophy because its dogmas are defined in scholastic philosophical categories. There-fore, in adaptation the local philosophy of the people is used only to prepare people's minds for the proper reception of Christianity and its dogmas (ibid., 589-91).

Hernández adds that for a successful adaptation, certain conditions must be met. The first of these conditions is an adequate knowledge of the culture. The participation of the indigenous clergy and hierarchy in the adaptation process is therefore necessary, because the latter have better knowledge of the culture of their own people (ibid., 592). Second, adaptation has to be a collective task, because the Christian faith is a faith of the community. It aims at transforming the entire culture with the gospel. The third condition is genuineness. There must exist customs and cultural practices that can be reconciled with the Christian faith. Fourth, there must be real assimilation; that is, a complete purification of the values and expressions taken from the non-Christian religion. Fifth, every adaptation must accommodate itself functionally to the Christian religion and must be based on the tradition of the church. And sixth, genuine adaptation should conform to the cultural characteristics of the generation that is to be converted. It should therefore look to the future in order to avoid cultural archeologism (ibid., 594-95).

According to Hernández, if these conditions are met, adaptation could have some advantages for both Christianity and the recipient cultures. First, besides being an efficacious means by which Christianity encounters the non-Christian world, adaptation brings about the enrichment of both Christianity and the local cultures. But for Hernández, this enrichment of Christianity by the nations concerns only the formal expressions; for while the latter are subject to growth and diverse cultural expressions, the essentials of Christianity remain unchanged for all times. The second advantage of adaptation is that Christianity is assimilated by the new converts and so penetrates deeply into their lives and souls. Third, it manifests the true universal character of the church of Christ. And fourth, respect for other national cultures, according to Christian teaching, is an obligation of justice and equity (ibid., 22, 592-93).

In one of his later books, *Teología Sistemática de la Misión* (1991), Hernández traces the evolution of the concept of mission from the early church up to the encyclical *Redemptoris Missio* of Pope John Paul II. Unfortunately, he does not show the difference between inculturation and the missionary adaptation he discussed in the earlier work, nor does he give reasons for the change in terminology from adaptation to inculturation in both theology and church documents after Vatican II. In fact, he gives the impression that inculturation is merely another name for missionary adaptation. For example, with regard to the method of inculturation, he repeats exactly what he had said in his previous book on the necessity of adaptation (1991, 403-15).

Louis J. Luzbetak (1918-2005)

Louis J. Luzbetak, SVD, was born in Joliet, Illinois, and was ordained a priest in 1945. Educated in the United States and Europe, Luzbetak received degrees in theology and canon law from the Gregorian University and a doctorate in anthropology from the University of Fribourg, Switzerland. He did advanced studies in linguistics and religion in Vienna. From 1963 to 1973 Luzbetak served as director of the Center for Applied Research in the Apostolate in Washington, D.C. He taught anthropology, linguistics, and missiology at various schools and in special crosscultural training programs and served on the Vatican's Pontifical Council for Culture.

Luzbetak is best described as both a missionary and an anthropologist. His interest in cultural anthropology began in a dramatic way while doing ethnographic and linguistic field research in New Guinea (1952-56). Over the years, he became increasingly attracted by missiological challenges, especially by the need to articulate adequately the relationship between faith and culture. While uncompromising in matters of faith and doctrine, he was also opposed to all forms of manipulation or pressure in missionary activity, and his foremost concern was the challenge of adaptation. His best-known works in the area are *The Church and Cultures: An Applied Anthropology for the Religious Worker* (1963) and *The Church and Cultures: New Perspectives in Missiological Anthropology* (1988). His books and many articles deal mostly with his favorite theme, the church's need for cultural sensitivity, for which anthropology could provide the necessary help (see Anderson 1998, 416-17).

If Hernández is reluctant to acknowledge a difference between missionary adaptation and inculturation, Luzbetak is not. For him the two are different, representing different perspectives in the theology of mission. In his book *The Church and Cultures: An Applied Anthropology for the Religious Worker,* Luzbetak spoke highly in favor of missionary adaptation. And in his later work, *The Church and Cultures: New Perspectives in Missiological Anthropology*, reflecting new developments in the church's understanding of her mission since Vatican II, Luzbetak distances himself from adaptation in favor of the language of inculturation. We shall examine below his conception of missionary adaptation and the reasons he gives for this shift of emphasis from adaptation to inculturation.

Missionary adaptation, according to Luzbetak, is "the respectful, prudent, scientifically and theologically sound adjustment of the church to the native culture in attitude, outward behavior, and practical apostolic approach" (1963, 341). It is the adjustment of the mission subject (the older churches) to the cultural requirements of the mission object (the new churches) (Luzbetak 1967).

Like the other authors discussed above, Luzbetak maintains that missionary adaptation was the policy of the church from the beginning. Down through the ages the church adopted practices and customs from the cultures of the European peoples evangelized. During the age of discoveries and colonization, however, the wisdom gained in ancient and medieval experience was almost invariably disregarded. It was reintroduced in more recent times, with encouragement from popes Benedict XV to John XXIII. For Luzbetak, the mission of the church is to continue in time Christ's mission for the salvation of souls and the socioeconomic betterment of peoples. This task necessarily involves the transformation of cultures, because it is impossible to effect changes in the religion and morality of people without changing their culture. But to transform the local culture while at the same time respecting the people and adopting their values requires adaptation (1963, 342).

The theological justification for adaptation lies in the natural goodness of human nature. Although it is wounded by sin, he insists, human nature still retains a naturally Christian propensity. Illumined by divine light and nurtured by divine grace, human nature can be raised to genuine virtue and supernatural activity. Moreover, there is much in the mentality and ways of non-Christians that is both neutral and good in the natural order. The missionary, he maintains, should adapt such naturally good and true beliefs, values, and practices to Christian living without compromising Christian truths because the natural goodness of humanity can be supernaturalized and christianized (1967, 121).

For Luzbetak, missionary adaptation is not a mere pedagogical tactic because it is founded on vital theological grounds. First, one of the basic rights of a people and an individual is the right to maintain national distinctness and culture. Therefore, the first principle of appropriate accommodation on the part of the church is to be just to a given people and to respect their cultural identity. Second, the supranational nature of the church demands missionary adaptation so that the church may be at home everywhere. For Luzbetak, there was never any question but that a universal church was a church that could not bow to attempts to remake the church to support nationalism. World War II's lessons of the evils of national socialism and the domination of Luzbetak's parents' native Slovakia by Russian communism, he often said, were seared in his memory. Third, he saw adaptation as necessary for missionary effectiveness. The most effective crosscultural communication is the one accommodated to the sociocultural structure and the basic psychology of the people to whom one wishes to communicate. This requires immersion in the local culture of the people so as to direct social change from within and thus avoid serious disorganization. Moreover, effective communication of the Christian message aims not only to inform non-Christians about the true religion but to show them how to live it. Therefore, the missionary should preach the gospel in a way relevant to the time and place (1963, 342-45).

The object of missionary adaptation, according to Luzbetak, is the entire local culture, understood anthropologically as the total inventory of life, a people's socially shared system of coping with the physical, social, and ideational environment. Therefore, adaptation cannot be limited only to particular areas because culture is a total structure in which the various elements are interlocked into a system (345-47).

Adaptation as portrayed in Luzbetak's writings entails a two-way movement between the church and the local culture. The church accommodates itself to the local culture as much as this is possible without compromising its doctrine. The local culture, though, must adjust itself to Christian norms in all essential aspects of life. As regards the adaptation of faith, Luzbetak suggests that a distinction be made between the *essentials* for the unity of faith and the *accidentals* of the church. The deposit of faith must be preserved in its entirety and purity. However, the purely human aspects of the shape of the church and canon law are in many ways accidental to the church's essence. These accidentals contributing to the unity of the church can be adapted to local cultural contexts (1967, 122).

Like other advocates of adaptation, in his first work, Luzbetak follows the "husk-and-kernel" approach, which presumes that there is a body of supracultural truths that the missionary could transpose from one culture by merely modifying the external forms. In 1988, however, he rewrote his book in its entirety to highlight new perspectives that missiological anthropology had developed under the aegis of the Vatican Council II. There are noticeable shifts in the new book. For example, unlike the first, which was addressed to the foreign missionary, the new book is addressed to the local Christian community, because Luzbetak now thinks that the task of incarnating the gospel in local cultures lies "principally" with the local Christian community under the guidance of the Holy Spirit and in communion with the universal church, and not with outsiders, however helpful the latter might be. In other words, the primary agent of inculturation is the local church (1988, 69-72).

The second shift is indicated by his criticism of the very missionary adaptation that he had promoted in the first edition. In practice, according to Luzbetak, missionary adaptation was shallow, affecting only the surface of culture. It tended to be overcautious, paternalistic, and distrustful of the local Christian community, because the sending church determined the type of accommodation, not the new or local church. Despite the beauty of the theory, in practice, he notes, adaptation was insensitive to the aspirations of many local churches, and there was too little effort made to listen to the latter. The whole process was in the hands of outsiders who did not quite understand the cultural language into which they wished to translate Christianity, thus making mission consist mainly of transplanting rather than sowing. Finally, it was assumed that cultural adaptation was a concession on the part of the older churches, meant for the younger churches, rather than a need of every local church (1988, 67-68).

Papal Teachings on Adaptation before Vatican II

The magisterium of the Roman Catholic Church from time immemorial has been concerned with mission and issued decrees and instructions on the subject when necessary. It was equally occupied with the internal matters of the church, especially with the unity of Christian faith, which was often threatened by developments in Europe. At the turn of the twentieth century, however, greater attention than ever was given to questions pertaining to missions. While the missiologists were busy developing theological principles and practical programs for adaptation, papal teaching also began to demonstrate greater openness toward the cultures of the peoples of the missions. Encyclicals were written specifically on the missionary activities of the church, and they took into consideration the diversity of peoples in the church. Here we shall examine briefly some papal documents on mission published before the Second Vatican Council to show the contributions of the popes to the church's evolving understanding of missionary adaptation and its more recent emphasis on inculturation. As we noted in chapter 1, the documents of Vatican II and the postconciliar period represent an updating, extension, and clarification of the church's practice and teaching concerning adaptation and inculturation.

Pope Benedict XV (b. 1854; Pope 1914-1922)

The apostolic letter *Maximum Illud* (November 1919) of Pope Benedict XV was one in a series of encyclicals concerned directly with the mission of the church in the twentieth century. It was addressed to bishops, vicars, and apostolic prefects as heads of missions. Missionary activity had been seriously hampered by the First World War. At the end of the war Pope Benedict called for the resumption of missionary work with greater zeal, to bring the message of eternal salvation to all nations. The document does not actually develop a theory of adaptation. In fact, compared to the current understanding of mission, the aim of mission it proposes is rather narrow. The scope of mission is understood as "salvation of souls," understood as bringing the light of Christ to the innumerable "pagans," who were portrayed as "sitting in darkness and the shadow of death" (see Benedict XV 1919; Hickey 1982, 32-37).

Pope Benedict stressed new elements, which were destined to assume great importance in Catholic mission theology. The first of these was his insistence on the need to form a local clergy, who, he said, constituted the hope of the new churches. Speaking in an age when colonialist ideologies would find his ideas radical, Benedict said that, unlike foreign priests, indigenous priests were in a better position to present the gospel to their own people in a manner that was sensitive to their mentality and aspirations. He insisted that their training should be thorough, so that they could assume leadership among their own people. Implied in this, it should be noted, is the fact that he envisaged a local clergy that would be educated to what we might today call "world standards," to become priests and bishops who would not be second class. Second, Benedict insisted that missionaries should dedicate themselves to the service of the gospel of Christ and not to the extension of the colonial domain of their own nations, lest Christianity be seen as a national religion. Third, a good command of the language of the local population was necessary so as to communicate the gospel message in a manner adaptable to the people, taking into serious consideration their context. To be noted in this regard is the fact that Benedict said this in a context in which colonial administrators wanted them to teach the language of the home countries in order to strengthen bonds with imperial centers. And finally, missionaries were encouraged to study both sacred and secular sciences to acquire basic skills for their apostolate. Such studies were to be made available to indigenous seminarians as well. To attain this goal, he directed that a new faculty for mission studies be instituted in the Pontifical Urban University in Rome and that another institute was to be established in Rome for Oriental studies (see Hickey 1982, 35-39).

Pope Pius XI (b. 1857; Pope 1922-1939)

In his encyclical *Rerum Ecclesiae* (February 28, 1926), Pope Pius XI reiterated the principles outlined in *Maximum Illud*, emphasizing especially the value of the native clergy in volatile situations in mission lands under colonial rule. Should foreign missionaries be expelled, the local clergy, he said, would ensure the future of the church. Therefore, the training of local clergy in seminaries set up in mission lands was to be raised to acceptable standards, so that local priests would be on the same academic level as foreign priests. He also recommended the formation of new active and contemplative religious congregations and orders in mission lands, especially in Asia where contemplation was already known to be an essential value of the cultures. He recommended, in addition, an adequate formation of catechists so that they could adapt the teaching of Christian doctrine to the intellectual level of their students.

Pope Pius XII (b. 1876; Pope 1939-1958)

Among the many contributions made by Pope Pius XII, one of the most important with regard to the church's relations to Southern peoples and world religions was his beginning the process of giving an explicit theological justification for adopting values of non-Christian traditions for Christian use. In his first encyclical, *Summi Pontificatus* (October 20, 1939), he devoted a section to missions in which he outlined the principles of adaptation which were to operate in mission countries. First, he says that the diversity in human cultures and life does not destroy the fundamental unity of the human race but enriches it by the sharing of peculiar gifts and the reciprocal exchange of goods.

In a second major theme, Pius XII says that the church does not depreciate or scorn the peculiar character that each people cherishes as its precious heritage, nor does the church advocate a uniformity that is merely external, superficial, and therefore weak. On the contrary, the church's aim is a supernatural union in an embracing love, deeply felt and practiced, in which whatever good originates from each race is honored and blessed by the church, provided it is not opposed to the unity and common destiny of humanity. And finally, he maintained that pioneer investigations had been undertaken by missionaries of every age to gain deeper insight into the customs and civilizations of diverse peoples in order to put their intellectual and spiritual endowments at the service of the proclamation of the gospel. All the customs of peoples that are not indissolubly bound up with superstition and error are to be preserved and developed.

In his Christmas message of 1945, Pius XII returned to the theme of the catholicity of the church as the foundation of missionary activity. As the mother of all nations and peoples, the church does not belong exclusively to any single people but equally to all. The church is supranational because it is an indivisible and universal whole. The universality of the church is tangible and accessible, based on the mystery of the incarnation (see Pius XII 1945; *AAS* 38 [1946]: 18).

In his encyclical *Evangelii Praecones* (1951), commemorating the twenty-fifth anniversary of *Rerum Ecclesiae* by Pius XI, Pius XII took up again the major mission themes of previous encyclicals, but he also introduced new arguments for missionary adaptation in the light of new developments in the mission lands, such as the need for an increased number of local clergy, creating indigenous bishops, and the role of the laity in evangelization. The main object of mission, he maintained, was not merely to save individual souls but to bring the light of the gospel to all peoples and to form new Christian bodies who would carry on that task. The ultimate goal of missionary endeavor, accordingly, is to establish the church on firm foundations and to place it under its own native hierarchy. Once the local church is reasonably established with its own native bishop and clergy, missionaries are to assume the role of collaborators, serving in an auxiliary capacity (see Pius XII 1951; 1957). The laity, he insisted, should assume new responsibility in such contexts, organizing themselves not only into movements for Catholic action to collaborate with the clergy in the work of evangelization but also by joining associations intended to bring social and political affairs into conformity with the principles and methods of the church. This, he taught, is a right and a duty of the laity both as citizens and as Catholics. In enunciating these principles, he introduced two new elements into the evolving modern understanding of the integral mission of the church—the role of the local church as principal agent for evangelizing its fellow citizens and the role of the laity in both church and society. These themes were further developed by Vatican II.

Furthermore, on the issue of the encounter between the gospel and local cultures, the pope insisted that when the gospel is accepted by the people, it does not destroy whatever is naturally good, honorable, and beautiful in their traditions. On the contrary, the church, like an orchardist, grafts an excellent scion on the wild stock so that more tasty and quality fruit may issue forth and mature. For even though nature is wounded by sin, it still retains something that is naturally Christian (*naturaliter Christianum*), which, if illumined by divine light and nurtured by God's grace, could be raised to genuine virtue and supernatural life.

In his last missionary encyclical, *Fidei Donum* (April 21, 1957), Pius XII did not deal with adaptation as such but with conditions in the missions, especially the situation of the young churches in Africa. The tremendous success in evangelization had not been matched by an increase in the number of apostles, he noted, and there was a shortage of personnel and of the necessary means for the apostolate, particularly in Africa. That was happening at a time when Islam was spreading rapidly and African movements for independence—some of them inspired by atheistic ideologies—were gaining ground. The pope therefore made a passionate appeal to all Catholics, bishops, priests, and laity alike, to accept their missionary responsibilities and to contribute in diverse ways to the work of evangelization and the expansion of the church in Africa.

Pope John XXIII (b. 1881; Pope 1958-1963)

Three years before Vatican II, Pope John XXIII published the encyclical letter *Princeps pastorum* (November 28, 1959), reiterating the major themes developed by his predecessors, especially the role of the local clergy in the church and their proper formation. Particular emphasis is placed on the importance of studies in missiology in seminaries in mission lands. Such studies, he noted, should not only be in strict accord with the sound teaching and tradition of the church but should also aim at sharpening the minds of future priests to make balanced assessments of the cultural traditions of their own peoples, especially in matters of philosophy and theology, and "to discern the special points of contact between those systems and the Christian religion."

With regard to the general attitude of the church to local cultures, the pope repeated the argument already presented by Pius XII; namely, the Catholic Church neither scorns nor rejects anything that is good in the customs of the peoples. On the contrary, it purifies it of all error, and completes and perfects it in the light of Christian wisdom. John XXIII also reintroduced the theme of the role of laity in mission lands, both within the church and in the public sphere, and the formation they need for such an apostolate, adapted to local needs and conditions.

Inculturation in Conciliar and Postconciliar Catholic Mission Theology

As we noted above, Vatican II opened up new perspectives on the value of culture and its impact on the development of the human person. This, in turn, created a deep challenge in mission, one best captured in the question, Is it justifiable—in the interest of uniformity—to transplant a form of Christianity developed in one historical and cultural context to other peoples and cultures around the world? Put as radically as it was in an age that had developed a historical consciousness of the complex processes by which any culture develops, this question challenged the former views of adaptation theology. One specific occasion where adaptation was most pointedly called into question was at the 1974 synod of bishops on evangelization. Here African delegates, in particular, declared "completely out of date the so-called theology of adaptation." The new strategy to be adopted was incarnation of the gospel into local cultures (Caprile 1974, 146).

This development infused a new spirit into many theologians and missiologists as they began to reflect on a more profound process of incarnating the gospel into local cultures. In other words, there was a shift from the culture of the missionary to the culture of those being evangelized. It is a new understanding as well as an effort to express the Christian message in local idioms and with the conceptual tools of those being evangelized. The gospel always encounters a culture in an inculturated form, and between the evangelizer and the evangelized there has to be some form of acculturation if there is to be effective evangelization. Thus, inculturation theologians began to use the results of research terminology of cultural anthropologists (Schineller 1990, 22).

Again, in accordance with the Vatican II mission theology of sowing the good news, inculturation means allowing the word proclaimed to grow and mature, using the soil nutrients of the place where it is being planted. In other words, inculturation implies that Christianity can take root in the new culture only if it assumes those cultural forms. But there is need for a critical symbiosis. The faith criticizes the culture, and the culture enriches the Christian faith. In the process there is interpenetration of both. Christian faith enlightens the local culture, and the basic data of revelation contained in the

Scriptures and tradition are critically reexamined for the purpose of giving them the local cultural expression. Thus, there is integration of faith and culture, and from it is born a new theological expression that is both Christian and culturally sound. In this approach, therefore, inculturation means Christian faith attaining cultural expression (Ukpong 1984, 30).

Thus, inculturation plays a prophetic role to cultures. Cultures need to be open to the gospel and converted to Christ, and the gospel also needs to be opened to the local culture so that it may attain fullness of meaning among the local populace. Again, the fact that Jesus died and rose points to the fact that inculturation involves challenging cultures to a new life. Therefore, inculturation is an ongoing dialogue between faith and culture or cultures. It is the creative and dynamic relationship between the Christian message and culture (Shorter 1988, 11). Moreover, inculturation must be founded on the total mystery of Christ if it is to challenge and transform the culture (Synod of Bishops for Africa 1994, *Message* 9). It must ensure that the gospel message penetrates into and assumes or influences every culture without compromising its identity (Geffré 1987, 236). It must also endeavor to engage the whole culture, with all its values and defects, in order that the gospel values might transform it from within. In this way, inculturation brings about mutual enrichment, which usually occurs when the gospel engages the culture (*RM* 52).

This implies that incarnational theology must guide the process of inculturation. In this way, inculturation assumes its rightful place as one of the ways through which the church lives the principles of autonomy and communion and shares in the diversity of cultures in the universal church-family (*LG* 4, 13; *GS* 53-62). Inculturation implies a dynamic, continuous, ongoing process that goes on as cultures continue to evolve. But it needs to begin with theological reflection on the faith before being translated into liturgical forms. In other words, for meaningful inculturation to take place, theological investigation and reflection are needed (*AG* 22). Theological research helps to develop a new cultural language for the word of God and a new cultural form for the Christianity that will emerge in the process of inculturation. Theological investigation helps to establish the ground rules for inculturation and to clarify the principles, concepts, and symbols to be utilized. Inculturation is not limited to some particular area of Christian life and mission. Rather, it involves all aspects of being a Christian (Schineller 1990, 23). Inculturation, even though it aims at the evangelization of a particular cultural context, must emphasize compatibility with the gospel and communion with the universal church. It is for this reason that John Paul II reminds the bishops of their role as guardians of the "deposit of faith," to take care so as to ensure fidelity and to provide discernment, for a deeply balanced approach to inculturation (*RM* 54). Moreover, no matter how effective inculturation may be, it will never be the same as the first incarnation of the Son of God.

Mission as Communication
in Protestant Missiology

Twentieth-century developments that favored intense discussion concerning contextualization and adaptation of theology continued to lead to the questioning of the validity of the prevailing paradigms of mission. Confronted with the situation of dire poverty in most of the lands traditionally called mission territories, there arose a major concern among the missiologists about how and what method to employ in communicating the gospel to the oppressed and impoverished people of the Third World. Along with this concern there was a growing awareness not only in the West but also among other people of the influence the culture could have on people. People of the Third World began to identify with their native cultures in an unprecedented way. They discovered that they could draw unlimited strength and inspiration from the religions and cultural heritage of their ancestors. Missiologists, and especially theologians in the Third World, began contrasting the present practice with that of the Christians of the New Testament and the church fathers.

The Christian faith never exists except as "translated" into a culture. But with Constantine, when Christianity became the religion of the establishment, the church also became the bearer of culture. Thus Christian missionaries—perhaps inevitably when Europe developed a sense of cultural superiority as its military and technological prowess allowed European colonizers to gain dominance over much of the rest of the world from the sixteenth century on—presupposed that mission was a movement from the civilized to "savages" and from a "superior" culture to "inferior" cultures. For many missionaries, the corollary was that christianization was a process in which non-Western cultures had to be subdued if not eradicated. This attitude affected the missionary enterprise and to some extent compromised the gospel, particularly during the glory days of Western colonialism, which was marked by feelings of cultural superiority and a sense of "manifest destiny" and a *mission civilisatrice*. When the large-scale Western colonial expansion began, Western Christians were not aware that their theology was culturally conditioned. Instead, they assumed that it was supracultural and universally valid. And since Western culture was implicitly regarded as Christian, it was equally self-evident that this culture had to be exported together with the Christian faith. Still, it was soon acknowledged that in order to expedite the conversion process, some adjustments were necessary. The strategy by which these were to be put into effect was variously called adaptation or accommodation (in Catholicism, as demonstrated above) or indigenization (in Protestantism). It was often, however, limited to accidental matters, such as liturgical vestments, nonsacramental rites, art, literature, architecture, and music (see Thauren 1927, 37-46; Bosch 1991, 448).

Contextual theology discusses these issues today under the heading of inculturation, and it handles the problem of development within the context of liberation theology. But prior to this advance, Evangelical Protestant missiologists had developed a theory about the communication of the gospel in the midst of a growing awareness of cultural relativity and the culture-boundedness of European and American missionary methods and goals. In that context, self-critical missiologists identified the communication of the Christian faith as a central problem. Hendrik Kraemer was the first to address the problem of the communication of the Christian faith. He was followed by Eugene A. Nida, among others.

Hendrik Kraemer (1888-1965)

Hendrik Kraemer was a Dutch Reformed lay missiologist. After training in oriental languages at Leiden University, he was sent by the Netherlands Bible Society to serve in Indonesia. In 1937 he became professor of religion in the University of Leiden and in 1948 the first director of the World Council of Churches Ecumenical Institute at Bossey. His thought was very influential on the WCC. His major publications are *The Christian Message in a Non-Christian World* (1938); *Islam as a Religion and Missionary Problem* (1938); *Religion and the Christian Faith* (1956); *World Cultures and World Religions: The Coming Dialogue* (1960); and *Why Christianity of All Religions?* (1962). In these studies, Kraemer argues, *inter alia*, that the Christian revelation is incomparable and *sui generis*, and that cooperation with non-Christian religions is a betrayal of truth.

Addressing the issue of the communication of the Christian faith, Kraemer shows that the real problem is not the methods of proclamation and rhetoric (communication "of") but the definition of the relationship (communication "between people") implied in missionary practice and theory. The immediate problems of missions and of the encounter between Christianity and other systems of life and thought are, for Kraemer, encompassed by a larger and deeper problem. That is the problem of the need of a world in crisis for clear and authentic forms of biblical witness and for an awakening to God's will that is not self-defensive but creative and open to new possibilities. Kraemer claims that one cannot talk about "missions" and "religions" before the particular historical framework in which the missioner comes from and the one in which he or she lives and works come into clear focus. Western secularization is uprooting the religious culture of the "other peoples" of the world (the Third World, we would say today), each with its own specific cultural design and genius, and the resulting sensitivity on both sides is today often characterized as the problem of "the West and the rest" of the world. Problems of nationalism and colonialism, of new ideologies and of racial tensions, are for Kraemer only symptoms that guide us to the deeper layers of what is happening. For the church, the confrontation with this new crisis must coincide with the ever-new confrontation with its own nature and destiny as the agent of revelation of the will of God for human life. It is mission, therefore, that will give new life to the church. For Kraemer, the only real point of contact between the gospel and human life is the missionary presence, from which many new points of contact between God's revelation and human culture can develop.

The paragraph above portrays the background of Kraemer's version of the communication model in which mission is the pouring out of the divine life to which Christ has called Christians to penetrate the deepest and the best of human spirituality, and in so doing to arrive at the deepest truth of the gospel, which always includes its opposition to the foibles of the contemporary world and its ideologies. He insists that, in addition to being a word revealing love, the word "mission" also entails an element of the gospel's "over-against-ness" to many aspects of human life. Thus, mission is the communication to human beings of the powers of renewal inherent in Christianity (see Hoedemaker in Anderson et al. 1994, 511).

Kraemer's position can be regarded as an early version of what emerges later as the communication model. His new definition—communication "between people"—has been criticized on the ground that it merely sought for a way of replacing the former methods of proclamation and rhetoric. This observation is made by Eugene A. Nida.

Eugene A. Nida (1914-)

Eugene Albert Nida, linguist, teacher, and Bible translation theorist, was born in Oklahoma City, in the United States. A pastor of the Northern Baptist Convention, he studied at the University of California at Los Angeles and obtained a doctorate in linguistics and anthropology from the University of Michigan (1943). He taught linguistics to prospective Bible translators at the Summer Institute of Linguistics. He founded *The Bible Translator* (the United Bible Society journal for translators) and became its editor. His lectures and publications covered four primary areas important to Bible translators: analysis of linguistic problems, crosscultural communication of the gospel, translation theory and practice, and the structure of meaning. His major works are *Morphology: The Descriptive Analysis of Words* (1949); *Message and Mission* (1960); *Toward a Science of Translating* (1964); and *Greek-English Lexicon of the New Testament, Based on Semantic Domains* (1988).

In his work *Message and Mission*, Nida notes that the problem of the communication of the Christian faith is not solved by Kraemer's definition of the relationship between people. He asserts that mission and communication models are the same. Just as in the history-of-promise model (which we shall discuss shortly), for Nida there is no existence of Christians for themselves, except in the sense that human beings are receivers of God's message and at the same time its relay stations and transmitters. There is only movement, the act of communication. Being a Christian consists of receiving and passing on the gospel, which means, of course, to those who are not yet Christians. Communication means, then, the missionary going out to non-Christians. How the communication of the faith is carried out is not something that Nida considers. It has no place in his scheme, because in the last resort there is no place for the church in his scheme. Nida analyzes very carefully the anthropological and transcultural problems of communication from one cultural setting to another. The difference between the sender and the receiver of the message is crucial. This difference has its origin ultimately in the infinite difference between the eternal God and humanity. But as God, through the kenosis of the Son, established communication with humanity, so the senders must involve themselves in the limitations of space and the culture of others and even adopt the other's language and culture, without giving up their own identity in any way. It is, therefore, more than a question of translating the words of the Bible into another language. Every culture is a closed value system in itself, the four pillars of which, religion, language, society, and culture, completely determine one's worldview and philosophy. Missionaries translate their message into this other system and link it to its existing thought and knowledge. This process is essential, although the identity of the message must not be endangered. Authoritative revelation is not adjustable (see Nida 1960; discussed by Sundermeier in Müller et al. 1997, 436-37).

Nida is a linguist and a Bible translator by specialization. His model is susceptible to considerable problems of form. It is, therefore, reasonable to combine it with other models and thereby give it substance. Giancarlo Collet, a Catholic missiologist, has attempted to establish a point of contact between such a model and a theology of mission (1984). Collet employs a concept taken from the epistemology of "communicative freedom," to assert that the model could serve as a starting point for a theology of mission. But Collet does not give any recognition to Nida. Even in his recent work in which he made a synthesis of missionary paradigms in their historical order, Collet defines mission as a vital expression of the church; in it lives the Christian vision, open to all human beings. For this, Christian mission, on the one hand, has its foundation in the universal destination of the gospel, and, on the other, has its fulfillment in the witness of the faith, which is realized in the form of communication of the faith itself. Thus, for Collet, the giving witness of Christians is the missionary way in its authentic form (2004, 268ff.). In the same perspective, H. Balz has put forward an important explanation in which he takes note of the fact that mission is a matter not only of rooting the faith but also of defending it (Balz quoted in Sundermeier in Müller et al. 1997, 437). An accessible book that takes Nida's insights to the next level is Charles H. Kraft's *Communication Theory for Christian Wit-*

ness. Kraft's other major works (see bibliography below) offer an excellent perspective on how Evangelical Protestants conceive the role of anthropological studies in missiology when one takes "communicating the gospel message" as the focal image of mission. A comprehensive and balanced view of culture from a Catholic perspective can be found in *The Bible on Culture,* the work of Lucien Legrand, a French biblical scholar who has worked for many years in India. Father Legrand judiciously examines the many layers of Scripture that bear upon the modern notion of culture, which did not exist during the periods in which the Old and New Testaments were written.

Conclusion

To conclude this section of our study, let us draw attention briefly to some of the arguments of the authors and the teachings of the Roman Catholic magisterium discussed above. The first thing to draw attention to is the positive attitude toward local cultures. Cultures are infected by sin but are not totally devoid of good elements that could be appropriated by Christianity. This argument is further strengthened by the continuity between creation and redemption. The natural values of creation and especially of cultures as an aspect of creation find their ultimate fulfillment and perfection in the redemptive work of Christ. The most powerful theological argument for adaptation is the incarnation. As the Word became flesh and transformed humanity from within, so the church must endeavor to insert the gospel into each culture in order to transform and perfect it. With regard to the practical work of adaptation, a distinction should be made between essential and accidental, supernatural and natural elements of Christianity. The accidentals may be adapted and translated into culturally appropriate forms, but the essentials of the gospel remain unchanged.

With regard to the documents of the popes, it can be said that none of them presents a full theology of adaptation. They present certain principles that were used by missionaries and local Christians to justify and carry through the theology of adaptation. For example, there is an insistence on the universality of the church, founded on the mystery of the incarnation, that both requires and enables the church to adopt whatever is good and noble in any human culture. This universality is also the basis for the mission of the church to all nations. Moreover, there is a stress on the natural goodness of human nature. Even though it is wounded by sin, human nature still retains a certain goodness, and therefore can produce good things that can be perfected for Christian use. Catholics, it is clear, are more comfortable with this than some Protestants, but implicit in every theory of adaptation and communication is the notion that there is a healthy point of contact in local cultures and peoples. Also important is the emphasis on the timely formation of local clergy as the necessary foundation of the future local church. The local church, equipped with its own leadership and well-formed laity, assumes responsibility for its own evangelization and for mission elsewhere. In such a situation, the missionary assumes the role of collaborator with the local leadership. These principles were further elaborated within the proper ecclesiological framework at Vatican II.

Finally, the authors of the communication model have shown that faith can exist only when it is *translated* into a culture. The strategy employed in achieving this may not be perfect, but it must neither compromise the gospel nor disregard the cultural ingenuity of the people. A missionary therefore witnesses to the gospel and helps bring it to bear on the cultural heritage of the people being evangelized. The local culture assumes its universal significance when it encounters the gospel and allows itself to be expressed in Christian terms.

6

MISSION AS DIALOGUE
WITH THE RELIGIONS

Before the Vatican II declaration on the relationship of Christianity to other world religions, theological thought, under the influence of developments in the history of religions and comparative religious studies tended to lead Christian theologians to a more adequate understanding and appreciation of values found in other religious traditions. Historical and cultural studies, moreover, made most educated Christians uncomfortable with using the term "non-Christian" to refer to these other religions. The missionary paradigm prior to the conciliar declaration, however, was drawn from the language of early Christians and, in particular, the writings of the church fathers. Thus, missionary writing is rooted in the way the fathers showed a remarkable combination of missionary urgency and confidence about the ultimate fate of non-Christians. The dominant understanding came from the terminology of Justin Martyr (ca. 100-165) on the "seeds of the word" (*logoi spermatikoi*) being found in pagan philosophy (*2 Apology*, chaps. 8, 13) and the presence of the preexistent Word in the world before the coming of Christ (*1 Apology*, chap. 46). If pagan philosophy, according to Justin, had good elements, pagan religion was demonic and the source of many evils (*1 Apology*, chaps. 9, 24-27). A second major position that carried over into traditional church teaching and missiology comes from the dictum of Cyprian of Carthage (ca. 200-258), *extra ecclesiam nulla salus* ("outside the church there is no salvation" (*Letters* 4.4). Though Cyprian's dictum was another way of expressing the uniqueness of Jesus Christ as sole mediator between God and humanity, on the one hand, and the unity of Christ and the church, on the other hand, it came to be taken, often out of context, as a solemn dogma that without faith in Christ and entry into the church pagans would be damned. Moreover, most theologians through history certainly have used Cyprian's famous dictum against non-Christians, even though it was used by him in making a case for the unity of the church and against heretics and schismatics (see Fornberg 1995, 11). In spite of this, the common patristic model that recognized the universal presence of the *logos spermatikos* became the common image governing the conceptual field that looked out on other religions and with which other religions were approached. This model considered the other religions as *praeparatio evangelica* ("preparation for the gospel"), because they and philosophy (which in the classical world was virtually inseparable from what we today call religion) were believed to contain precious *semina verbi* ("seeds of the word"), which can lead a great number of people to be open to the fullness of revelation in Jesus Christ through the proclamation of the gospel. The *logos spermatikos* approach is based on the Gospel of John and on the teaching of the fathers of the church that the Word of God was at work among pagans through the real values in their religions (see the Pontifical Council for Inter-Religious Dialogue, *Bulletin* [1968]: 124).

Some missiologists who were responsible for the teaching of Vatican II on the relation between Christianity and other world religions developed their theories of mission from the perspective of the patristic *logos spermatikos* model. Their approach has been termed the "fulfillment model" (see Müller et al. 1997, 395). This model is based on the belief that the non-Christian religions have found their fulfillment in Christianity. It is assumed that these other religions had served as divinely ordained means of salvation for their adherents until the advent of Christianity and that, with the incarnation of the Son of God, Jesus Christ, they will see themselves as having been perfected in Christianity. Christianity, therefore, in the new dispensation, is the fulfillment of humankind's religious yearnings. It is the ordinary means ordained by God for the salvation of humanity. For an up-to-date sorting out of all these issues, see Paul Knitter's *Introducing Theologies of Religion*, which provides a very helpful introduction to the terminology. He suggests that Christian views on the adequacy of the fulfillment model depend on whether one views Christianity as meant to replace other religions wholly or in part or whether one believes world religions are relatively equal partners in dialogue. While other books by Knitter have been highly controversial, *Introducing Theologies of Religion* has been widely acclaimed for the helpful, even-handed way it lines up the various theologies of religion.

The Fulfillment Theory of Religions

Prominent among theologians of this new outlook are French authors such as Jean Daniélou, Yves Congar, Henri de Lubac, and others. Catholic scholars writing in German on this issue include Karl Rahner, Franz König, and Augustin Bea. Here we discuss some of these theologians and also the Italian Catholic Piero Rossano and several Protestant theologians. These authors have been chosen because they deal with fulfillment theory and inspired the teaching of Vatican II on the relation of the church to other religions.

Jean Daniélou (1905-1974)

Jean Daniélou emerged as a seminal Catholic theologian of mission and religions. He was born at Neuilly-sur-Seine, France, and was ordained a priest in the Jesuit order in 1938. He obtained his doctorate in theology at the Institut Catholique de Paris and at the Sorbonne University in 1944. When studying theology at the Jesuit scholasticate of Fourviére, he developed a passion for the fathers of the church. He became cofounder of the French collection Sources Chrétiennes. He succeeded Jules Lebreton in the chair of history of Christian origins at the Institut Catholique and was appointed editor of the periodical *Études*. Daniélou published widely. His major publications include *The Salvation of the Nations* (1950); *Holy Pagans of the Old Testament* (1957); *The Lord of History: Reflections on the Inner Meaning of History* (1958); *The Advent of Salvation: A Comparative Study of Non-Christian Religions and Christianity* (1962); *Myth and Mystery* (1968); and *Gospel Message and Hellenistic Culture* (1973).

In addition to the books mentioned above, his reflections on the mission of the church in relation to other religions and on issues of dialogue with other traditions are published in part in *Bulletin du Cercle Saint Jean Baptiste* and in *Axes*. As a *peritus* (expert consultant) at Vatican II, he contributed to the council's documents on these issues. He thus was one of the first among pre–Vatican II Catholic theologians to devise a theology of religions and of the church's mission in the context of dialogue. In 1969 Pope Paul VI made him a cardinal, a mark of the great esteem in which he and his work were held.

Daniélou's theological position on religions and Christian mission is characteristic of what we have termed here the "fulfillment theory." He sees other religions as representing humanity's inborn quest for God based on God's cosmic revelation through nature. Christianity, however, is God's personal response to the human quest. Other religions are, moreover, doubly anachronistic in his view because they are superseded first by Judaism and definitively by the Christ-event and Christianity. Whatever positive values can be recognized in them serve as *praeparatio evangelica*, and their role must be clearly distinguished from God's unique and universal intervention in history in Jesus Christ. Christianity is the God-intended means of salvation for all human beings, even though salvation in Jesus Christ is possible outside the boundaries of the visible church.

Daniélou elaborates this position in his work *Holy Pagans of the Old Testament*. After a programmatic introduction which discusses Hebrew 11 and other texts, he deals with a number of "Gentiles" in the Old Testament: Abel, Enoch, Daniel, Noah, Job, Melchizedek, Lot, and the Queen of Sheba. He shows that they were saved despite the fact that not a single one of them knew about Christ, and most of them were even outside the covenant with

Abraham. Daniélou wants to show here that the Bible itself testifies that a conscious faith in Christ is not a necessary prerequisite for salvation. Daniélou shows further that the church fathers also had such an open view of salvation and that a narrower view appeared only with the emerging humanism and Renaissance of the fifteen and sixteenth centuries, and especially when Protestantism and its emphasis on the necessity of individual faith came to the fore.

Daniélou begins by posing two theses: There is no salvation outside Christ and outside the church (which is the body of Christ), and there are people who are saints but who have never heard about Christ. He states:

> That is the unanimous teaching of both Holy Scripture and Tradition. They were not saved by the religions to which they belonged; for Buddha does not save, Zoroaster does not save, nor does Mahomet. If they were saved, then it is because they were saved by Christ who alone saves. . . . Again if they were saved, it is because they already belonged to the church, for there is no salvation outside the church. (Daniélou 1957, 9)

From this position, Daniélou writes that God prepared humanity for Christ not only through the covenant with Abraham but also through a cosmic covenant before Abraham. Abel, Enoch, and Noah are mentioned as persons belonging to the cosmic covenant, and the purpose of Genesis 1-11 is to let us know this cosmic revelation. Heinz Robert Schlette, a disciple of Karl Rahner, considered this cosmic covenant a fundamental sanctioning of all non-Israelite religions (see Schlette 1966, 73). But such a far-reaching conclusion was not drawn either by Daniélou himself or by the other French theologians of the 1950s. Instead, Daniélou accepts the view of Justin Martyr that posits a revelation among the Gentiles through the universal *logos spermatikos*, God's "seminal word," which parallels the revelation given explicitly to the Jews (see Daniélou 1957, 20-22). He points out that Paul considers some pagans to be saints even after Abraham, and that Justin looks upon Socrates and other great figures in the Greco-Roman world as saints. He goes on to conclude that figures like Zoroaster and Buddha can be considered saints, and he refers to the feast of Barlaam and Josaphat in the Catholic calendar, for, as is well known, a legend about Buddha lies behind this feast. His discussion of the development of tradition leads all the way to Thomas Aquinas as a fitting end point in order not to overemphasize the break with neoscholasticism. In sum, Daniélou challenged the limitation of salvation history to Israel and pointed to a wider salvation history that included figures both before Abraham and outside the Israelite people (see Fornberg 1995, 23; Dupuis 1991, 136-37).

Although Daniélou's fulfillment theory represents an important step in the church's reflection on religions and mission, post–Vatican II developments have tended to supersede it (see Anderson 1998, 168-69). The issue today, from a missiological perspective, is not just to demonstrate that these great figures and founders of other great religions are saints but rather how to convince the followers of those religions of the centrality of the Christ-event in salvation and the role of the church in that regard.

Henri de Lubac (1896-1991)

Henri de Lubac, a Jesuit priest and theologian, was born at Cambrai, France, and served in the French army during World War I (1914-1918). He received his philosophical and theological formation in England (1920-1926) and continued his studies in Lyon-Fourvière (1926-1929). He was nominated professor of fundamental and dogmatic theology at the Facultés Catholiques de Lyon in 1929 and of the history of religions in 1939. With Jean Daniélou he became a cofounder of the French collection Sources Chrétiennes. As a theological consultant at Vatican II (1962-1965), he contributed to council documents on religions and the church's mission. Subsequently, he also served as a consultor to the Pontifical Councils for Inter-Religious Dialogue and Non-Believers.

Among his numerous publications are *Le fondement théologique des missions* (1946); *Aspects of Buddhism* (1953); *The Splendour of the Church* (1956); *The Drama of Atheist Humanism* (1963); *Catholicism* (1958); *The Mystery of the Supernatural* (1967); *The Religion of Teilhard de Chardin* (1968); and *The Church, Paradox and Mystery* (1970). De Lubac's approach to the theology of mission has a threefold source: deep familiarity with early Christianity and the fathers of the church, passion for the catholicity and universality of the Christian message, and a will to enter into a sincere dialogue with other traditions on their own terms. His early studies on Buddhism, even if somewhat dated, witness to this openness to others in their differences (see G. Anderson 1998, 413).

At the center of de Lubac's theology of mission is the unity of the plan of God for humankind as this has been realized in the person of Jesus Christ and continues to unfold in history through the mission of the church. This seminal theme, brilliantly illustrated in his book *Catholicism*, was the inspiring axis of his whole theological vision. De Lubac's posture on non-Christian religions comes under the category of what we call here the fulfillment model: In de Lubac's construction of the Christian vision, Jesus Christ alone fulfills human aspirations for union to the divine, since he is personally the God-given answer to humankind's eternal quest for God. To announce him as the one in whom all people of good will may be saved is the church's irreplaceable mission to the world (see de Lubac 1946, 37-54; Anderson 1998, 413).

Critics have labeled de Lubac's theology of religion as a traditionalist's approach, one more helpful for ecumenical dialogue than for dialogue with the religions. There are solid reasons for saying this, because de Lubac was also a great theologian of ecumenical dialogue and believed that unity could occur only when the relationship of Christ and the church were understood. His doctrine of Christ, however, is solidly rooted in both Scripture and tradition, and any theology of religions that is not rooted in these sources runs the risk of a false accommodation that obscures the core of Christian tradition.

Yves J. M. Congar (1904-1995)

Yves Congar, a Dominican, is also a French Catholic theologian. Congar's studies were carried out at the Dominican study house of Le Saulchoir in Belgium, where teachers and pupils had sought refuge from the anticlerical legislation of the Third French Republic. Congar was caught up in Roman condemnations that alleged his teacher Marie-Dominique Chenu (1895-1990) was compromised by "dangerous historicist tendencies." During this period Congar asked to be assigned to the École Biblique in Jerusalem. Later he returned to France where he resumed pastoral and theological ministry in 1955. The negative atmosphere of condemnation of the so-called *théologie nouvelle* was dissipated when John XXIII became pope and named Congar as a consultor to the preparatory commission for Vatican II. At the council, Congar helped write major documents, among them documents on divine revelation, the mystery of the church, and the relationship of the church and the modern world. He was influential as well as in drafting documents on the church's missionary activity and on ecumenism (see Anderson 1998, 148). Notable among Congar's works are *The Wide World My Parish* (1961); *The Mystery of the Temple* (1962); *Power and Poverty in the Church* (1964); *Diversity and Communion* (1984); and *The Word and the Spirit* (1986).

Congar approached the theology of religions and mission from the standpoint of Christian unity and witness. He saw the church and the churches throughout the history of humankind as the sign of the appearance of God's grace in Jesus Christ. All human beings saved in Jesus Christ were in God's providence ordained to participate in the church's sacrament of salvation, at once unique and diverse. In discussing what he terms the "Christology of the captivity epistles," Congar dismisses the views brought forward by the radical exponents of the new theology of religions. He argues that the other religions have a place in the salvific plan of God (see 1 Tim 2:4-6; Rom 1:19; and the well-known sermons in Acts 14 and 17), and it is through them that many people are in communion with God. Nevertheless, they are not "as such, *signs* established by God in the sense in which St. Thomas Aquinas defines Revelation" (Congar 1961, 117-60).

Congar's skepticism about many recent developments in theology is clear when he discusses the use of biblical and patristic texts. He emphasizes that when the Bible speaks positively about Gentiles it is because they are related to salvation history. They are not looked upon positively in their capacity as Gentiles but because they have taken the first step toward Israel or the church; the queen of Sheba and the magi are mentioned as examples. This first step toward salvation is often passed over in silence by modern theologians of religions. Furthermore, Congar differentiates between the theory and the practice of mission. The fact that a sensitive missionary must always be open to dialogue with non-Christians does not mean that other religions can be placed on the same level as Christianity. In Congar's view of God's revelation they are not. In this he sides with Henri de Lubac and considers his views as a *via media* between the negative view of many Protestant theologians and the open view of "several contemporary Catholic theologians, such as E. Cornelis and G. Thils" (quoted in Fornberg 1995, 23-24).

Karl Rahner (1904-1984)

Karl Rahner, born in Freiburg im Breisgau, Germany, was ordained a priest in 1932 in the Society of Jesus. He pursued his doctoral studies in philosophy at the University of Freiburg. Though his dissertation was rejected by his adviser, it was published in 1939 as *Geist in Welt* (Eng., 1968). His doctoral dissertation in theology was accepted at Innsbruck in 1936, and he began teaching there in 1937. In 1964 he succeeded Romano Guardini in the chair of theology at Munich. In 1967 he moved to Münster, where he taught until his retirement in 1971.

His theological essays, in English translation, are collected in Theological Investigations in twenty-three volumes. He co-edited, among other major works, the second edition of *Lexikon für Theologie und Kirche, Sacramentum Mundi*, the Quaestiones Disputatae series, and cofounded the international journal *Concilium*. His theology during and after Vatican II helped show how human history is played out within an invitation to divine grace. In mission history he is important for his proposals about how to see Christianity vis-à-vis other religions. He tried to demonstrate that the grace of Christ was at work implicitly in other religions; his work gave rise to the term "anonymous Christianity" (see Rahner 1974). Ironically, although few liked the term, the genius of his insights in this area is such that many Catholics have tried to claim his authority for their views in theology of religion. In his final years, he developed a more Trinitarian proposal, speaking of the interaction of Christ and the Holy Spirit in the world religions (see Anderson 1998, 556).

Among the most significant aspects of Rahner's theology of religions and mission are his proposals on Christ and other religions, which have recently been studied in an article by Joseph Wong, who discusses Rahner's contribution to the debate on the two currents of inclusive Christology in relation to other religions. While, on the one hand, the exclusive Christology, as an earlier paradigmatic approach to other religions, emphasizes the common Christian belief that understood Christ as the exclusive center of the universe, the inclusive Christology (currently held by the majority of theologians), on the other hand, acknowledges a unique but not exclusive role for Christ and the church in salvation. The inclusive Christology accepts the possibility of salvation for all, though still giving a special place to the role of Christ and the church (see Wong 1994, 612; Bellagamba 1993, 20). The inclusive Christology can be divided into "constitutive" and "normative" aspects. The former (constitutive) views Jesus Christ not only as the decisive and normative revelation of God but also as the one who is constitutive of salvation. The latter (normative Christology) presents Christ not as constitutive but only as normative of salvation for all people. It is a Christocentric view inasmuch as Christ is seen as the fulfillment of human history. He is the decisive and highest revelation of God and of human existence. Salvation, always possible for all humanity even apart from Christ, becomes normatively manifest in him (see Bellagamba 1993, 22).

Within his thought about inclusive Christology, Rahner presents a broader concept of constitutive and normative Christology (see Rahner 1966). In this model of inclusive Christology, Rahner believes that we are faced with two basic principles with regard to the salvation of non-Christians. On the one hand, there is the necessity of faith in God and in Jesus Christ in order to obtain salvation. On the other hand, there is the universal salvific will of God that seriously intends to save all human beings. Rahner resolves these apparently conflicting principles by pointing out the possibility of having implicit faith in Christ. Consequently, Rahner proposes a wider concept of being related to the church by affirming different degrees of relation to it; both the so-called anonymous Christians and those who explicitly profess Christianity would be included in this understanding. The foundation for anonymous Christians is to be sought in the basic structure of humans as spiritual beings and in the design of God at the beginning of creation. Rahner perceives a Christological structure in God's bestowal of grace at the moment of creation, which is aiming at the incarnation as the fullest expression of God's self-communication, and he sees self-transcendence as the most basic characteristic of human beings. Seen as "the uniquely supreme case of the actualization of man's nature in general, the incarnation constitutes the goal of creation and human existence. In this way, Christian revelation can be seen as the explicit statement of the basic revelation of grace which the human person always experiences implicitly in the depths of his being, and perhaps even without realizing it explicitly" (see Wong 1994, 614).

Rahner was next confronted with the function of the extra-Christian religions. Are non-Christians saved in or through their religions? Rahner has four theses in his article on "Christianity and Non-Christian Religions," where he tackled this question. The first thesis states that Christianity claims to be the absolute religion intended by God for all. But this absolute religion comes to human persons in a historical way, that is, when they are existentially and seriously confronted by it (Rahner 1966, 118). The second thesis (121-30) is based on the social aspect of salvation. A human being is called to be a "religious person" in order to attain salvation, but he becomes this religious person in the concrete religion in which he finds himself. Hence, until their followers are seriously confronted by the Christian message, non-Christian religions must be considered as lawful religions leading to salvation. The third thesis recognizes the members of extra-Christian religions as anonymous Christians. Christianity, it is said, makes explicit a previously anonymous state through an inner dynamism (131-33). The fourth thesis (133-34) reflects on the idea of mission in the light of the first three theses.

Rahner's theses, as Wong noted, are meant to clarify and broaden the then standard outlook of the Catholic Church on the followers of non-Christian religions, and implicitly can be used to clarify issues in regard to dialogue and Christian mission (Wong 1994, 616). Most of the issues Rahner tried to resolve here, however, have been developed further and clarified by the conciliar and postconciliar magisterium, especially in Pope John Paul II's *Redemptoris Missio*, as we discussed in chapter 1.

Piero Rossano (1923-1991)

Piero Rossano, a Catholic scholar of interreligious dialogue and theology of religions, was born in Vezza, Alba, in Italy. He was ordained a priest in 1946. He studied at the Pontifical Biblical Institute and obtained a doctorate in theology at the Pontifical Gregorian University, and a second doctorate in classical languages at the University of Turin. Both degrees reflect Rossano's interest in non-Christian religions and cultures. He was one of the founders of the Italian Biblical Association. In 1966 Paul VI appointed him undersecretary and in 1973 secretary of the Pontifical Council for Inter-Religious Dialogue. He held this office until 1982, when John Paul II appointed him auxiliary bishop of the diocese of Rome and rector of the Lateran University.

Rossano published several books and articles in biblical studies and interreligious dialogue. His notable publications include *L'uomo e la religione* (1968); *Il problema teologico delle religioni* (1975); "Christ's Lordship and Religious Pluralism in Roman Catholic Perspective" (in Anderson and Stransky 1981, 20-35); and *Vangelo e cultura* (1985). From 1967 to 1990 Rossano wrote some thirty-five articles in English and French on the theology of religions and dialogue for the *Bulletin Pontificium pro Dialogo inter Religiones* (see Anderson 1998, 578).

Rightly considered a post–Vatican II theologian, Rossano bases his theology of religion on the documents of the council. He analyzes carefully the perennial human religious quest and the plurality of religions "as sociocultural structures with doctrines, moral and ritual elements" (Anderson and Stransky 1981, 20). He bases his evaluation of human religious phenomena on Christ as the perfect image of the perfect human. And he emphasizes that the biblical data include not only God's actions toward Jews and Christians but also his universal actions described by the expression "Wisdom economy."

One of the most appreciable contributions of Rossano while in the Secretariat for Inter-Religious Dialogue was the organization of a number of consultations on dialogue between Christians and adherents of African Traditional Religions (ATR). The difficulty in organizing a formal dialogue with ATR is one of the reasons why the church took up dialogue in Africa at a relatively late stage. In order to overcome the deficit, Rossano organized several sessions in various African countries on dialogue with ATR and, basing himself on *Nostra Aetate*, Rossano proposed that the church's dialogue with ATR should aim at becoming acquainted with creation and the gifts and wealth that God has given to people. He recognized the need to promote the integrity and well-being of the human being in a technological and materialistic world that marginalizes Africa, according to G. T. Spijker (1994, 180). Rossano pointed out the dialogue is directed at knowledge and intercommunication between the partners in conversation, and is an undertaking in which each participant gives the other the opportunity to reveal himself and to exchange ideas for the sake of mutual growth.

In a work that he edited for the Pontifical Council for Inter-Religious Dialogue (Rosanno 1968a), he discusses evaluations of the salvific efficacy of ATR, appealing to the prologue of the Gospel of John and to early church fathers to establish a relation between the God known in ATR and the Christian God. This essential passage taken from the Gospel according to John, he says, should guide our attitudes toward African religions. In his discussion Rosanno makes use of the intuitions of the church fathers on the way that the Word of God was at work among the pagans through the real values in their religion. He goes on to say:

> And if God is at work in the traditional religions, and if man responds to this divine activity, the African religions contain an element of revelation and the help of divine grace, because God, from the beginning of time seeks to make himself known to men, and this response of man to God is religion. (124)

Rossano affirms that ATR is "supernatural revelation" rather than "natural revelation," which the human mind can attain through experience (Rom 1:19), and that redemption was already at work in African religion. Thus, the attitude that the Christian—African or foreigner—is invited to assume toward ATR is an assumption that it has a positive significance in the divine plan of salvation. Elsewhere in the same study, Rossano returns to the ful-fillment theory of religions and maintains that ATR must be viewed as having contributed in the manner of an advent to the preparation of a people of God. African religion has been and still is "pedagogic" to prepare the way for Christ. But Rossano does not stop there. In fact, he affirms that ATR was and still could be *an exceptional way to salvation* for a portion of humanity who have not yet heard the gospel proclamation of salvation in Jesus Christ. Moreover, ATR has been and is still *necessary*, because without it there would be no interlocutor for the Christian Africans that we see today. In the same way, the Old Testament was "pedagogic" for the Jewish Christians of the early church.

Rossano is revered for being one of the foremost postconciliar scholars who has outlined in an exciting and yet doctrinally faithful way new Roman Catholic theological stances toward world religions. Like other authors dis-cussed above, Rossano makes no compromise with the common Christian belief that "the truth is Christ who is the way, the truth and the life" (John 14:6), the center of the universe and of universal history. The Christian, he says, is obliged to justify rationally and historically his act of faith in Christ, the person in whom one finds the fullness of religious life (Rossano in Ander-son and Stransky 1981, 24). And he insists that the problems involved in this new openness and positive appreciation must not be minimized. For despite every attempt at establishing the union and harmonization of reli-gions, he reminds his readers that the Christian "way" is different from the Buddhist "path"; that Hindu "liberation" is not the "submission" of Islam; that the "life" sought in African religious practices is not comparable to that offered by Gnostics or tantric traditions; and that the aim of *bhakti* is not that of Zen; and so on. A reasonable person concludes that systems of such diversity and contrast cannot possibly be considered equally valid and true. Rossano concludes, however, that the religions as such do not appear as antitheses to God's self-communication in Christ but as the providential means, the concrete and historical instruments for furthering the God-human relationship in the Bible, even if many of their elements clearly require purifi-cation and transformation before being assumed or taken up by Christianity (Rossano in Anderson and Stransky 1981, 30).

One common feature of all the Catholic theologians of religions discussed above is their dependence on the view expressed in the Vatican II documents on the relation of the church to other religions. In their writings, one sees immediately the new opening to the recognition of revelation even outside the Christian religion. But this can only be in their relation to the mystery of God revealed fully in Christ and in the way in which other religions are recognized as serving as preparation for acceptance of the fullness of revelation in Christ. This view is vividly evident in the conciliar documents that dealt with the issue. For instance, the Vatican II dogmatic constitution *Dei Verbum* (on divine revelation), while not recognizing any direct revelation in non-Christian religions or in the general experience of humankind, nevertheless widened the concept of revelation to include the pedagogic role of other religions in preparing people for the encounter with the Christ-event (Dulles 1983, 17). Rather, *Dei Verbum* insists that in Christian revelation the deepest truth about God and the salvation of humanity shines forth in Christ, who is at the same time the mediator and the fullness of all revelation (*DV* 2).

The theology of religions of Vatican II, as voiced in the declaration *Nostra Aetate* (1965), widened our understanding of the universal economy of salvation and, although it recognizes the possibility of salvation in other religions, it nonetheless gives the primary place to the Christ-event as the means by which salvation is attained outside the boundaries of Christianity. In the encyclical *Redemptoris Missio*, John Paul II discusses this issue in relation to missionary activity among followers of other religions. The fact that the followers of other religions can receive God's grace and be saved by Christ apart from the ordinary means that he has established does not thereby cancel the call to faith and baptism which God wills for all people. In fact, for John Paul II, followers of other religions are objects of mission and they belong to that class of people with whom God wishes to share the fullness of his revelation and love in Christ. The desire to share the gospel with non-Christians also rests on the fact that God prepares individuals and entire peoples through their own spiritual riches (as seeds of the word), as essential expressions and as a preparation for the gospel (*RM* 55). The document of the Congregation for the Doctrine of the Faith *Dominus Iesus* reconfirms this teaching. In addition, *Dominus Iesus* dismisses as dangerous the theological current that speaks of a limited, incomplete, or imperfect character in the revelation in Jesus Christ, which would be revealed better in a complementary way in other religions. Such a position is in radical contradiction with the Christian faith according to which the full and complete revelation of the salvific mystery of God is given in Jesus Christ. According to the document *Dominus Iesus*, Jesus perfected revelation by fulfilling it through the mystery of his incarnation, death, and resurrection; and finally with the sending of the Spirit of truth, he completed and perfected revelation and confirmed it with divine testimony (*DI* 5). Christianity, in the new dispensation, is therefore the new and definitive covenant put in place by God for the salvation of all peoples. The fact that this truth is spoken in human language does not reduce or abolish the definitiveness and completeness of the revelation of God's salvific ways. Rather, it remains unique, full, and complete, because he who speaks and acts is the incarnate Son of God (*DI* 6).

Protestant Theology of Religions

At its early stages of development Protestant Christianity was not overly concerned with theology of religions and mission, as we noted above. For the Reformers, mission was already accomplished with the apostles. However, with the emergence of Pietism in the eighteenth century and the example of great missionaries like William Carey and others, an explicit Protestant theology of religion and mission began to emerge (Cracknell and Lamb 1986, 12-16). This new development reached a dramatic level in the first half of the twentieth century with several celebrated Protestant mission conferences. The most notable was the World Missionary Conference at Edinburgh in 1910, where the watchword emerged that the world was to be totally evangelized "in our generation." At the Jerusalem mission conference in 1928, liberal theological tendencies began to appear and compete for influence over the missionary movement in a world whose confidence in the superiority of Western civilization had been shattered in World War I. At the Tambaran mission conference in 1938 the influence of Karl Barth's "crisis theology" and Hendrik Kraemer's Barth-influenced missiology led to a kind of line of demarcation being laid down between the religions (among which Christianity was numbered) and Christ, the transcendent Word of God who came among us (Fornberg 1995, 53). Christ was the revelation of God; Christianity bore witness to that revelation, but being a religion, it was subject to all the foibles of any human construction. Paradoxically, it should be realized, as Christ was lifted up, Christianity was demoted and became, in effect, just another world religion, though the full implications of this would not be understood immediately.

The new opening to the religions gained impetus from the foundation and growth of the World Council of Churches (WCC) in 1948, after the horrors of World War II. For this opening, credit should go to the WCC units and committees for dialogue and mission, which in themselves and as forums for some of the finest Protestant theologians in the world, proposed for consideration ideas that have been at the forefront of Protestant efforts to come to grips with the postwar and postcolonial world. Several Indian theologians were included in this discussion (Visser 't Hooft 1963, 50-82). Nevertheless, in addition to the Barthian influence already noted, the major background of the WCC's views are movements begun by nineteenth-century theologians such F. D. E. Schleiermacher and early-twentieth-century historians and theologians such as Adolph von Harnack (Jongeneel 1988, 204).

Since most Protestant theologians of religions do not, strictly speaking, belong to the school of fulfillment theory, which is the center of discussion in this chapter, we shall give here a synopsis of the WCC theology of religions and mission articulated by Paul F. Knitter. He sees the mission theology of the WCC as following the replacement model. According to Knitter, this model means that, in principle, God wills to make all peoples Christians (i.e., to replace their former religions with Christianity). In that view, only one religion, Christianity, is intended and authorized by God, and Christianity is to be preached to the adherents of other religions (Knitter 2002, 19). This model is related to the fulfillment theory inasmuch as it sees the other religions as having only a provisional value, which Christianity is to take over. In Catholic thought, although other religions are preparation for receiving the gospel, many elements in their thought and practices can be taken into the church.

Churches belonging to the WCC embrace some 400 million Christians in 330 churches, denominations, and fellowships from 100 countries and territories throughout the world. Although the majority of those Christians would probably locate themselves in the so-called mainline Protestant churches, many of those mainline members closely adhere to views of Christian identity that are found among Evangelicals and Pentecostals. In addition, Orthodox Christians also have an important voice and participation in the meetings and projects of the WCC. A fact that causes some consternation among members of the WCC is that the variety and sometimes incompatibility of ideas among Protestant and Orthodox churches, as well as of Evangelicals who have remained members of WCC churches, make it difficult for the WCC to arrive at a totally consistent position in matters such as theology of religions and mission. As a result, even the replacement model, which has been considered the WCC's theology of religion, is not characteristic of all members.

As already noted, the classic Protestant theology of religion received its initial influence from the theology of Karl Barth, which was almost sanctioned as the position of the WCC at the World Missionary Conference in Tambaran, India, in 1938. There was also the influence of the Evangelical churches. The Tambaran conference advocated working with other faiths to overcome the dangers of fascism that were then looming large in Europe and other places. The Tambaran conference described the relationship between Christianity and other religions in terms of evangelization. Conversations between the gospel and other religious traditions seek to find points of similarity that will ultimately give way to the proclamation of the gospel. It was this perspective that defined the attitudes of the WCC toward other religions at its inception in 1948 and for the first three decades of its life (Knitter 2002, 43).

A new outlook, however, began to develop in Protestant circles, perhaps as a result of the growth of churches in Third World countries, developments that followed the collapse of colonialism and the teaching of Vatican II on the relationship of the church to the modern world and of Christians to other religions and cultures. In 1971, the WCC opened its Sub-Unit on Dialogue with People of Living Faiths and with that began to move beyond its classic theological appraisal of other religions. The new office was charged with the purpose of promoting greater respect for and dialogue with persons of other faiths. After the meeting of the subunit in Chiang Mai, Thailand, in April 1977, the WCC issued two years later its *Guidelines on Dialogue*. Admonishing Christians that they should not approach dialogue from a "position of superiority," the *Guidelines* also urged all followers of Jesus Christ not to consider dialogue only as a luxury or a pleasant pastime. Rather, dialogue with persons of other religions is a necessary "means of living out our faith in Christ in service of community with our neighbor" (WCC 1979, 11-12). At the World Assembly in Vancouver in 1983, the WCC reasserted that position.

Some have argued that the WCC position on the relation of Christianity to other religions suffers from a lack of sustained theological support. There are statements of stance or orientation toward persons of other faiths, but these do not articulate a *Christian* theological position. To resolve the tensions between dialogue and theology, however, the WCC subunit on dialogue and mission organized a meeting of specialists in Baar, Switzerland, in 1990. The study group sought to lay a more coherent theological framework for the WCC dialogue with other religions. All it managed to agree on, however, was a weak form of pneumatology that affirmed the presence of the Holy Spirit, who revealed God and saved persons in and through other religions. The next general assembly of the WCC (in Canberra in 1991) and subsequent general assemblies have ignored the Baar statement and its theological framework. Despite this, the WCC's appeals for an open, dialogic orientation to other traditions remain vigorous in spite of nervousness about engaging in deeper theological reflections and consultation on the issue. In the thinking of many in the WCC, Christianity, like all religions today, is challenged to reassess itself and to contribute to building a new culture that includes and sustains the salvation of all peoples as revealed in Jesus Christ (Raiser 1997, 23).

Conclusion

In this chapter, we have seen the positions of key authors whose ideas have continued to influence the theology of religions and mission. To be noted is the fact that the fulfillment model has paved the way for the so-called inclusive Christology and soteriology that mark the Catholic theology of religions and mission. Inclusive Christology appears to be favored by the majority of Catholic authors today and receives support in John Paul II's encyclical *Redemptoris Missio*, where he sees both Christ and the church as unique and constitutive means to salvation, though to a different degree and depth.

> While acknowledging that God loves all people and grants them the possibility of being saved (cf. 1 Tim 2:4), the Church believes that God

has established Christ as the one mediator and that she herself has been established as the universal sacrament of salvation. "To this catholic unity of the people of God, therefore, . . . all are called, and they belong to it or are ordered to it in various ways, whether they be Catholic faithful or others who believe in Christ or finally all people everywhere who by the grace of God are called to salvation." It is necessary to keep these two truths together, namely, the real possibility of salvation in Christ for all mankind and the necessity of the Church for salvation. Both these truths help us to understand the *one mystery of salvation*, so that we can come to know God's mercy and our own responsibility. Salvation, which always remains a gift of the Holy Spirit, requires man's cooperation, both to save himself and to save others. This is God's will, and this is why he established the Church and made her a part of his plan of salvation. (*RM* 9)

The authors we have discussed agree also that there can be other mediators, but they are so only in relationship with Christ and in the power of Christ (see *RM* 5). In this perspective, Rossano affirms that Christ is the origin, center, and destiny of the various religions, the one who brought them to birth, takes them up, purifies them, and fulfills them in order to take them to their eschatological goal, so that "God may be all in all" (1 Cor 15:28; see *LG* 17; *AG* 11; see Rossano in Anderson and Stransky 1981, 34).

With regard to the Protestant theology of religions, it suffices to say that in spite of the general nature of the WCC statements on the relationship of Christianity to other religions, the WCC's principled commitment to the necessity of interreligious dialogue invites people of all religions to sit down and talk with one another and to promote the reign of God in their communities. At another level, we have discussed the Protestant Independent movement. It is important to note that Evangelicals and Pentecostals tend to a strict interpretation of texts such as Acts 4:12 ("There is no salvation through anyone else, nor is there any other name under heaven given to the human race by which we are to be saved"). In taking this position, they agree with Catholics on the constitutive nature of the work of Jesus as the Christ, but they are nervous about Catholic tendencies toward what they call "universalism," by which they mean the teaching that salvation will be granted to all regardless of explicit faith in Christ. Clarification of these basic visions of the relationship of Christians to the religious "other" and of their salvific value is probably the most contentious issue to confront missiologists today.

7

MISSION AS *MISSIO DEI* AND SERVICE OF GOD'S REIGN

Overview

World War II, and its political and spiritual repercussions, prepared the ground for the emergence of the missionary theory of *missio Dei* and of mission as liberating service to God's reign. To this must be added that the end of the colonial era left the West with no justification for regarding itself as the center of the world. The churches in the former colonial territories started to emerge strengthened for independence from the "mother churches" in the West (Sundermeier in Müller et al. 1997, 432). At the same time the desperate situation of humans—a majority of whom are deprived of the most elementary goods and exploited ruthlessly by a privileged minority—created a sense of urgency in all churches. This general situation prepared the way for a new trend in mission theology.

When theologians and missiologists were confronted with the situation, they began by giving explicit attention to the theological backing or warrants concerning motivation for mission. First, they sought to understand the *basis of mission as coming from within Godself*. This was most notable in the Protestant world. The question of the goal of the Christian mission—whether framed as the conversion of nonbelievers, the *plantatio ecclesiae* or christianization (which has its influence also on the Catholic side)—was articulated in two ways: as God's activity in the world and as service to *shalom*. This path of mission theology began with a conference given by Karl Barth in 1932, entitled "Theology and Mission." Thus, Barth initiated modern Protestant reflection on the nature of mission. Barth develops the theory of mission as the *activity of God*. With this approach, Barth says that mission is, above all, a witness to the action of God in the world and for humankind. For Barth, the question of modalities of mission or of its authenticity does not arise. Mission as the activity of God is put totally in the realm of Christ and in his grace without any relationship to human good will. Some believe that this aspect of Barth runs the risk of becoming "Christomonism" (a position that eliminates the significance of any activity except that of Christ). The term that emerged later and is still popular today—*missio Dei*—was used for the first time at the Protestant missionary conference at Willingen in 1952. Here the influence of Barth's thesis reached its apogee, as the Barthian theologian Karl Hartenstein popularized the use of the term *missio Dei*. Hartenstein sees mission not as the responsibility of the missionary or the church but as the cause of the Trinitarian God. Perhaps as a reaction to a rigid, theocentric, even Christomonistic vision of mission, that understanding would find itself replaced by liberal Christians with an anthropocentric concept of mission. To grasp this struggle in context, David Bosch helpfully reminds us that German delegates at the Tambaran Conference of 1938, over against the shadow cast by the rise of National Socialism, articulated Barth's principles when they affirmed that "through a creative act of God, His Kingdom will be consummated in the final establishment of a New Heaven and a New Earth," and then, "We are convinced that only this eschatological attitude can prevent the church from becoming secularized" (Bosch 1991, 390). God's final reign and its effect will be, in the well-known Hebrew word for peace, a state of *shalom* in which God will be all in all, and universal reconciliation and peace will rule the universe.

In fact, after the Willingen Conference of 1952, mainline (or "historical") Protestant churches adopted *missio Dei* theology as a common vision of mission. Mission is not primarily an activity of the church but an attribute of God. The church is the movement of God toward the world. The church is an instrument of mission. The church exists because there is *missio Dei*, and not the contrary. To participate in mission is to take part in the movement of God's love for human beings, because God is the fountain of love (see Buono 2000, 74-76).

The thesis of Barth recognizes the value of mission as the mission of God. With right interpretation of the concept of *missio Dei*, this theory could help in articulating the conviction that the theological foundation of mission is based on the doctrine of the Trinity. Mission has its origin in God the Father, who sends his Son into the world and in the fact that the Father and the Son sent the Holy Spirit to the church to continue in time the salvific mission of the same God to the world. This is the reason for the existence and founding of the church by Jesus Christ himself. Therefore, the limit of Barth's thesis rests on his taking the foundation of mission as the fulfillment of Christian reconciliation. God has, rather, laid a unique foundation in grace in Christ and has willed that the fulfillment of the new creation cannot be realized without the existence and participation of that liberty which the same grace has shaped (see Colzani 1996, 50).

The problems created by Barth's thesis prepared the way for the birth of explicit reflection on the nature of mission as service to the universal reign of God's *shalom*. This too was influenced by the political and spiritual situation after World War II. Thus, beginning with Barth, missiologists began to give theological explanations for the motivation in mission. As in the thesis of Barth, some missiologists, in the first place, claim that God himself is the basis of mission and that the institution of *shalom* was its goal. From this background, missiologists began to ponder the theological significance of human agency in missionary activity. This, in turn, necessitated dealing seriously with the concept and theology of history. Missiologists also had to reflect on and articulate a responsible relation to the new political climate and the claim of so-called political theology that radical action for political change is an integral aspect of Christian mission. Thus, the relation between salvation as an eschatological gift and missionary activity within history came to the forefront (J. Aagaard 1973, 10-11). The first effort at tackling this problem was at the International Missionary Conference (IMC) at Whitby, Ontario, Canada, in 1948. The participants at the conference used the slogan "partnership in obedience." This concept sought to define the relationship between the "older" and "younger" churches in such a way that the common goal of one mission remained in sight. At the same time, with the slogan "expectant evangelism," the conference opened up a perspective toward new directions in the theology of mission in which eschatology and history are used to define the theology of mission itself. But which history was meant, and which understanding of history was to be used for the interpretation of missionary events? The differences of opinion on these questions resulted in two trends: the salvation-history model and the history-of-the-promise model. This tendency is found also in the works of some Catholic theologians such as the German authors Johann Baptist Metz and Ludwig Rütti. Their approach, particularly that of Metz, has been described as a historico-political reading of mission theology. The Latin American theologians of liberation (to be discussed in chap. 9) have been influenced to some extent by this trend.

We shall begin the discussion with the Protestant authors of the salvation-history model and the history-of-the-promise model.

The Salvation-History Model in Missiology

The salvation-history model is said to be the most widespread and, up to the present, the most influential of the models developed around the missionary theory of *missio Dei*. The theological span of its representatives is broad, among whom Walter Freytag and Georg Vicedom are counted as chief representatives. For the history-of-the-promise model, the chief spokespersons are the Dutch missiologist J. C. Hoekendijk (a Protestant) and Ludwig Rütti (a Catholic).

Walter Freytag (1899-1959)

Walter Freytag, regarded as one of Germany's most profound and influential missiologists, was born in Neudietendorf, a small town in Thuringia. He studied theology and philosophy at Tübingen, Marburg, and Halle, completing a doctorate in 1925. He was director of Deutsche Evangelische Missionshilfe, the central Protestant German agency for promoting mission work, and he taught missiology and history of religions at both Hamburg and Kiel universities. A man of many talents, Freytag devoted his gifts and strength to the cause of mission, with special emphasis on Christianity and non-Christian religions, the psychology of conversion, and what he called "the miracle of the church among the nations." Although he was equally unforgettable as a speaker, a teacher, and a writer, he left behind only one major book, *Spiritual Revolution in the East* (published in German in 1938 and two years later in English). In that book, Freytag set the stage for a new approach to the historiography of young churches. His lasting contribution to missiology has been preserved, in two volumes of collected essays and speeches, published after his untimely death at the age of sixty (see G. Anderson 1998, 228).

The starting point of Freytag's theory is that mission takes place "with a view to the end"; it prepares for it. This means that Freytag views history as a prologue, a preparation, a provisional stage during which we are waiting for the second coming of Christ. Freytag asserts that the end will break in when all peoples have heard the gospel. It is from this context that Freytag says that the overriding purpose of mission is the preparation of the people for the hereafter, ensuring for each a safe passage to heaven. According to Freytag, mission is God's reality in this world. He adds that the so-called realities of nature, world, and history should not be extolled more than the explicit testimonies of Scripture. For him, the world and history are important only because they make mission possible and because God's patience allows them (see Freytag 1961, 213ff.). Thus, Freytag affirms that the only real history is the history of missions; it is the hands on the clock of the world, telling us what time it is and when we may expect Christ's second coming (a view found also in Linz 1964, 132-36).

Besides this positive role, Freytag insists that history is the believer's enemy, an abiding threat, and a possible source of contagion, since the continuation of history only increases the "distance" between the dreary present and the glorious future. For Freytag, progress in world history consists, at most, in an increase of catastrophes. The New Testament knows no other progress in history than that the end is drawing near. Human history, meanwhile, stands under the sign of the advance of the demonic (Freytag 1961, 189-216). Our task is not to build up God's kingdom in this world, to christianize society, or to change structures. There are limits set to what we can and should do, and we should not anticipate now what will only become visible at the arrival of the new creation (Freytag 1961, 96, 200; Bosch 1991, 505). In Christological terms, Freytag sums up his idea as follows: "The life of Christ has to do with the day of his return. Gospel is never glad tidings of solved problems but a summons to a fight in which victory is certain" (quoted in Gensichen in Anderson et al. 1994, 440). Thus, in order to maintain the perspective of the *eschaton*, Freytag played down the salvation that had already been achieved in Christ's cross and resurrection. For him, the acts of God that constitute the *kerygma* contain as well the future acts of God. What matters most to him is, again, whether Christians in their whole life and existence are willing to become part of God's eschatological mission or whether they would stand in its way. This is the perspective with which, in Freytag's opinion, the church, too, would stand or fall, since it has "its life towards that end, the goal of God in the coming again of Christ" (Freytag 1958, 146). Freytag agrees that the gathering into a visible community of those who come to believe in Christ is an indispensable part of mission. Yet the church is more than mission. Its total being is not to be reduced to its missionary action. To do so is to let the church fall into the captivity of thinking that its significance is exhausted by its historical activity. Thus, Freytag concludes that it is not mission but the grace of God, manifested in baptism and Eucharist, on which the church has to rely. There might be times of emergency and pressure when the church would have to survive by relying on that ground only, even without any outgoing mission.

Freytag's idea, influenced by the traditional reluctance to open up toward the actual world—had to come to grips with some major theological problems that were to develop later in the 1960s: mission as participation in the *missio Dei*. Nor should it be forgotten that his speeches and essays were mostly composed in post-Nazi Germany, where Freytag had witnessed the subversion of German national and cultural values at the service of Hitler's ideology. More than that, the church had been largely silent when Hitler was gathering steam. According to Hans-Werner Gensichen, Freytag helps us grasp more profoundly the fact that Christian mission is rooted in the *missio Dei*, God's own self-giving. In the 1960s, then, the term *missio Dei* came to be used as a sort of technical term for mission. As pointed out above, Karl Hartenstein used it for the first time in his paper on the Willingen Conference in 1952. There he defined mission as "participation in the sending of the Son, the *missio Dei*, with the all-embracing aim of establishing the Lordship of Christ over the whole redeemed creation" (quoted in J. Aagaard 1973, 12).

Freytag described mission, with reference to Mark 13:10, as "part of God's own eschatological action, . . . as the sign of the coming end set up by Him" (1961, 189). To Freytag, this carried a dual emphasis. First, *missio Dei*, as the very term suggests, was meant to correct all undue emphasis on *missio hominum* ("the mission of human beings"). The signs of the times made it clear to everyone that the "loss of directness" in Western missions, their "endangered image," were more than a symptom of transitory weakness. Rather, they point to a more permanent defect, a habitual overestimation of human missionary action and its achievements, perhaps even to the "spectre of panmissionism," and thus to a new and peculiar kind of active disobedience in the disguise of restless activity (see Freytag 1961, 94; Gensichen in Anderson et al. 1994, 439).

Second, *missio Dei* made sense only in view of the end, the *eschaton*, which gave mission the proper perspective. It is believed that Freytag borrowed the eschatological emphasis from the Oscar Cullmann school of biblical exegesis. Cullmann interprets mission in radically salvation-historical terms. The new age has begun; the old has not yet ended. We live between the times, between Christ's first and second coming; this is the time of the Spirit, which means that it is the time for mission. As a matter of fact, mission is the most important characteristic of and activity during this interim period. It feels the present and keeps the walls of history apart; history is kept open by mission. According to Cullmann, until the missionary task is completed, it is "holding up" the end (see Cullmann 1965, 225-45). Freytag, for his part, deliberately restrained from giving the mission its place in a comprehensive scheme of *Heilsgeschichte* ("salvation history") whereby it might serve as an unfailing indicator of apocalyptic events to come, or even as a device of bringing those events nearer. Freytag, instead, found the dialectic of mission and eschatology fulfilled in the continuing call to mission, "to take part in the responsibility of God's outgoing into the whole world," to such an extent that those "who live in the obedience of faith are part of His action" (Freytag 1958, 146). Both Freytag and Cullmann wrote against the immediate background of the catastrophe of World War II. The perennial value of their views—chastened by their experience in the great debacle of war—lies in their unflagging insistence that there is no authentic mission without a fundamental eschatological disposition. For Freytag, in particular, this finds expression in his ever-recurring references to the *basileia*, the reign of God as the substance and goal of mission (see Bosch 1991, 506).

It is important to note, however, that the same problem that has been identified in Pietism is to be found also in Freytag's salvation-history model of mission. Freytag creates dualism between the present and the future, that is, if we are to follow his emphasis on *waiting* as counseling a kind of quietism and inactivity in the face of history's course. More true to a longer-term Christian theological view of history, human beings are called as Christians to claim this entire world for God, as part of God's reign. God's future reign impinges on the present, and in Christ the future has been brought drastically closer to the present. This means that Freytag's view of the world as, in effect, a reality totally forsaken by God denies that the world itself is of divine origin and reduces our conception of the historical firstfruits of redemption in Christ. Furthermore, we would become a victim of an insidious dualism if we were to follow Freytag's emphasis on being saved for the next life in ways that alienate and separate us from involvement in this world. A fixation on the parousia at the end of time means that we are evading our responsibilities in the here and now. Submitting to Christ as Savior is inseparable from submitting to him as Lord not only our personal lives but also political and economic systems in the corporate life of society. From the latter submission stems the mission of attempting to realize his lordship by our involvement in history.

Georg Friedrich Vicedom (1903-1974)

Georg F. Vicedom was born in northern Bavaria, Germany, and was trained in the seminary of Neuendettelsau. He pursued additional ethnological studies at Hamburg University and was a missionary in the highlands of central New Guinea. He later taught missiology at the mission seminary, at the faculty of Neuendettelsau, and at Erlangen University. His missiological studies and interest centered on anthropology, the biblical foundation of missions, the importance of mission for the church, and the dialogue of religions. Vicedom's bibliography contains more than four hundred titles, a dozen of them major books; the most significant for our present study is *The Mission of God* (1965) (see Anderson 1998, 701-2).

The term *"missio Dei"* and profound theological discussion associated with it in the salvation-history model have become widely known since 1958 through Vicedom's German book entitled *Missio Dei* (English translation, 1965). In this book, Vicedom takes God rather than humanity as his point of departure and, appealing to the Willingen declaration, quotes Karl Hartenstein: "Mission is not only obedience to the command of the Lord, it is not only the task of gathering the community, it is participation in the mission of the Son, the *missio Dei,* with the ultimate goal of establishing the reign of Christ over all his redeemed creation" (Vicedom 1958, 12). According to Vicedom, church and mission are not independent quantities but have their origin in the loving will of God, who is the ultimate acting subject of mission. Furthermore, since mission is "modeled on" the inner-Trinitarian missions, "its service, spirit and program of action are determined by the *missio Dei*" (Vicedom 1958, 14). Precisely because mission is founded on the doctrine of the Trinity, it is an expression of the unique reign of God and differs essentially from the "missionary" work of Islam, which denies the divinity of Christ and of the Holy Spirit. Again, since God always reveals Godself through actions, mission cannot be other than the continuation of the saving action of God through the communication of God's saving acts: "That is its authority and its obligation" (Vicedom 1958, 15). God does not abandon creation. Instead, God's action embraces the whole world and affects the here and now. God's love, says Vicedom, is particularly evident in Jesus Christ, sent to save humanity. Since God's love touches all, mission is directed universally and is fundamentally concerned with the reign (or kingdom) of God. The step from the kingship of God to Jesus Christ is easy, for he is the one who comes in the name of the Lord (Matt 21:9), worthy of all royal honor through glory in the highest heavens (Luke 19:38). He is the king who, in a true kingly fashion, cares for his own and pays back a hundredfold of what they have sacrificed for him (Luke 18:29-30). There is no power that is not subject to him and that will not be destroyed when his kingdom is established (Matt 28:18). Consequently, the reign of God and that of Jesus Christ are one and the same; whoever proclaims the name of Jesus also proclaims the lordship of God (Acts 8:12; 28:31). Jesus is God's response to the questions of humans and also the core of message about the kingdom (2 Tim 4:1) (Vicedom 1958, 24; see Müller 1987, 66-67).

Vicedom's view of mission harmonizes to some extent with Bengt Sundkler's theology of mission. Sundkler (1909-1995), Sweden-born missiologist and Lutheran pastor in South Africa and Tanzania, has put his stamp on a range of terms that have found wide acceptance in many circles. According to Sundkler, the history of mission begins with an event that is decisive for salvation history, the call of Abraham. It is God's answer to the lost state of humanity since Adam's fall and to their revolt in building the Tower of Babel. God works in a double fashion: God chooses people and treats them as examples, as "substitutionary" examples. In the course of the history of salvation, we have the election of a people, of a "faithful remnant," of the Son of Man, which finds its high point and turning point in the cross. From this point, the remnant continues: the election of the apostles and the founding of the church, which spreads throughout the world to announce the message of salvation in Christ to humanity. Agreeing with Cullmann, his colleague in biblical exegesis, Sundkler says that the length of time between the first and second coming of Christ is determined by the announcement of the lordship of Christ. Mission fills the period. It becomes the measure by which the end of history can be determined. As in Cullmann's ideas, according to Sundkler, mission is "crossing frontiers," and the office of a missionary alone serves this purpose (Matt 8:11-12). Mission's proper work is, according to Sundkler, the proclamation of the gospel to non-Christians. This is a spiritual service, and it is embedded in the idea of Christ's lordship: the royal rule of the love of Christ, which is understood as absolute and must be lived out absolutely (see Sundkler 1968, 121ff.; Sundermeier in Müller et al. 1997, 432-33).

Thus, in Vicedom's view of mission is found the synthesis of the discussions about the history-of-salvation model and mission. The *Heilsgeschichte* mission portrayed in the Old and New Testaments reaches its apex in the resurrection and exaltation of Jesus Christ, and the mission of the Christian is one of entering into and serving under the lordship of the same Lord and

Savior, Jesus Christ. The mission of the church portrayed in Matthew 28:18ff., in Vicedom's theology, is exactly this: the proclamation of the coming kingdom, the promulgation of the risen Lord's accession to the throne. *Missio* is, theologically speaking, the activity of the exalted Lord, the second person of the divine Trinity, from the time of his ascension to his second coming. Thus, the church has only one task, namely, carrying on the history of salvation by proclaiming the perfection of God's reign, announcing Christ's kingdom in the gathering of the community "until he comes again" (Vicedom 1958, 37).

There are many positive aspects of Vicedom's mission theology. One major weakness (and it is analogously applicable to other authors of the history-of-salvation model) is the scant attention given to the values of the present age, and especially to the merits of Christ's earthly ministry and the paschal mystery. In other words, the salvation-history model plays down the significance of the world and history, separating them dualistically into two realms. It is criticisms of this aspect of the salvation-history model that have given rise to the model we discuss next, the history-of-the-promise model.

The History-of-the-Promise Model

Objections to the salvation-history model have been advanced from various perspectives. One states that history fades out as a concern of the Christian community if universal history is divided into salvation and world history rather than seeing history-as-a-whole as the object of divine care. Ultimately, if one follows the salvation-history model to its logical conclusion, only Israel and the church matter, and even they have a purely instrumental value. In that case, mission no longer has the whole world in view. Furthermore, the salvation-history model, it is alleged, sees humanity largely as a mass of damnation (*massa perditionis* in the classic Latin phrase), and God is portrayed as concerned only with the rescue of the few who are chosen for salvation. Again, if apocalyptic thought gains the upper hand over eschatology, then the church stands alone in the center of all thought, plans, and actions. Mission as mission to the world falls out of sight. These criticisms, first advanced by J. C. Hoekendijk (at the Willingen Conference of 1952) against the history-of-salvation model gained worldwide attention and some acceptance through a study entitled "The Missionary Structure of the Congregation." This study, which was commissioned at the General Assembly of the World Council of Churches at New Delhi (1961), gave a central place to Hoekendijk's thesis.

In the history-of-the-promise model, just as in the salvation-history model, the concept of the *missio Dei* is a point of departure for articulating a theology of mission. The salvation-history model emphasizes the relationship of the mission of the Son and that of the church, initiated by the Holy Spirit, which are considered to be the mission of "God-as-such." In the history-of-the-promise model, however, mission is understood as the predicate of God. "God is a missionary God" (Hoekendijk). God makes Godself known. The goal of God's all-embracing work of salvation is the world. This model has representatives in both Catholic and Protestant circles, though with varying degrees of emphasis. On the Catholic side, the new model is identified with the political-theology background of Johann Baptist Metz and Ludwig Rütti, who was influenced by Jürgen Moltmann. In addition, there is influence from H. J. Margull, Walter J. Hollenweger, Manfred Linz, and others. For our purposes, we shall discuss two authors: Johannes C. Hoekendijk and Ludwig Rütti.

Johannes Christiaan Hoekendijk (1912-1975)

Johannes Christiaan Hoekendijk, a Dutch missiologist, was born and raised in western Java, Indonesia, where his parents were missionaries until 1925. He studied theology at the State University of Utrecht. Hoekendijk served as missionary consul in Indonesia for one year (1945-1946) and then had to return to the Netherlands because of health problems. He became secretary of the Netherlands Missionary Council (1947-1949) and of the Department of Evangelism of the World Council of Churches from 1949 to 1953. He taught practical theology and church history at Utrecht University from 1953 to 1965, and in 1965 he was appointed to the chair of World Christianity at Union Theological Seminary in New York, where he remained until his death. Hoekendijk participated in the ecumenical discussions on mission with views that have often been labeled radical (see Anderson 1998, 297).

Hoekendijk's major academic work is his dissertation *Kerk en Volk in de Duitse Zendingswetenschap* ("Church and People in German Missiology" [1948], which was translated into German with an added appendix in 1967). Some of his important earlier essays are collected in *The Church Inside Out* (1966), and some of his contributions to the WCC study project on the missionary structures can be found in *Planning for Mission*, edited by Thomas Wieser (1966). One can find even more in G. Coffele, *Johannes Christiaan Hoekendijk: Da una teologia della missione ad una teologia missionaria* (1976).

Hoekendijk begins his theology of mission by asserting that the *missio Dei* is history in a comprehensive sense. He views God as a being who makes himself (i.e., "Godself") known in promise to the world. There is no "resident" God, but only the God of the exodus, who enters into history and reconstitutes it through the word of promise and so brings about the divine purpose. The world apart from God does not exist. It is not static. It has no longer an inflexible framework but a malleable, transformable one. The world discovers itself in progressive movement. If in the salvation-history model history exists only for the sake of mission, in this case the situation is reversed. Mission, including the church, exists only for the sake of history. The church is at the service of history and is both challenged and put into question by it. The church must be converted to the all-embracing service of society. If the church is in any sense universal, then it can exist only for the sake of universal history.

Hoekendijk's theology of mission is based on the understanding of the phrase *missio Dei* as entailing God's self-revelation as the One who loves the world; God's involvement in and with the world; and the nature and activity of God, which embrace both the church and the world, and in which the church is privileged to participate. *Missio Dei* enunciates the good news that God is a God-for-people. In this context, *missions of the church* (the *missiones ecclesiae* or the missionary activities of the church) refer to particular forms of participation in the *missio Dei* in specific times and places, or responses to particular needs (Hoekendijk 1967, 346; Bosch 1991, 10).

Starting from a position that sees the church in purely instrumental categories, Hoekendijk feels free to launch attacks on the church as an institution, since, according to him, only God can make Godself "known." Mission is not a function of the church. Rather, the church is a function of mission. From this perspective, he says that the starting point for mission theology is the confrontation of the kingdom of God and the secular world. Influenced by the World War II experience and its aftermath and by the Protestant history of denominational and national churches, Hoekendijk insists that the church can be no more than a function of God's work for worldly *shalom*.

The term *shalom* was a central theme of the European team at the WCC Uppsala Assembly study project (1967) and at the Bangkok Conference on "Salvation Today" (1973). The goal of mission was identified as *shalom* and as *humanization* by Europeans and North Americans. Reports of both teams view conversion as something that happens primarily in the sociopolitical and economic sphere in the form of social change. Individual change as a result of personal faith, conversion, and knowledge of God is not a focus of these meetings. Part of the Uppsala Assembly report reads:

> We have lifted up humanization as the goal of mission because we believe that more than others it communicates in our period of history the meaning of the messianic goal. In another time . . . the fundamental question was that of the true God, and the church responded to that question by pointing to him. It was assuming that the purpose of mission was Christianization, bringing man to God through Christ and his church. Today the fundamental question is much more that of *true* man, and dominant concern of the missionary congregation must therefore be to point to the humanity in Christ as the goal of mission. (WCC 1967, 78)

Hoekendijk's stance, as represented in this report, had in effect become the standard public missiology of the WCC. Hoekendijk himself called *shalom* a secularized concept, a social happening, an event in interhuman relations, asking at one point, "What else can the churches do than recognize and proclaim what God is doing in the world? . . . it is the world that must be allowed to provide the agenda for the churches" (quoted in Bosch 1991, 383). Hoekendijk remains a major influence on the post-1970 paradigm of missiological thinking in the world of ecumenical (i.e., WCC-related) Protestantism, especially insofar as it is rooted in the idea of the world providing the agenda for the church and of the church having to identify completely with this agenda. This idea surfaced clearly at the Strasbourg Conference (1960), during which Hoekendijk, with his emphasis on the secular calling and role of Christianity, elicited more applause than other speakers from the participants (see Hoekendijk 1967, 309; Bassham 1979, 47ff.; Bosch 1991, 382).

There are noticeable weaknesses in Hoekendijk's history-of-the-promise theology of mission. First, this theology makes any consideration of the "religious" as a distinct sphere of human life a negligible factor. Social questions take precedence. The question can be fairly asked, What is the "religious element" in religion if the needs and self-understanding of the secular world set the agenda for the church? For Hoekendijk, religion signals conservatism, the status quo, the undervaluing of the world. His theology downplays missionary preaching and teaching, since all their function is reduced to revealing how God is at work above all in those secular movements where work for *shalom* is being carried on to bring the world to universal peace. This approach forbids missionary preaching from announcing salvation, but counsels the faithful to discover that salvation is involved with liberating this world (Sundermeier 1997, 436). In other words, the history-of-the-promise model ignores the question of eternal salvation, since according to it, creation is already saved; history as a whole is the implicit history of salvation.

Furthermore, in practical terms, missionary work is not a matter of going from the church into the world, but from within the world to the world. The missionary is not one with a special call, nor is the priest or minister. First and foremost, mission is for laypersons. People not already members of the church are not called to become members of the church (for this would be proselytism). According to Theo Sundermeier's summary of this missiological position, non-Christians should let themselves be brought into God's mission *in the world* but not by becoming Christians (1997).

Although one can appreciate the context in which the history-of-the-promise model was developed—a preoccupation with alleviating suffering in the world after World War II, the power of Dietrich Bonhoeffer's theology and example, and the optimistic spirit of the 1960s about what might be achieved soon by way of completely restructuring sociopolitical realities and attempts at identifying the "signs of the times"—this model has not fared well in recent missiological studies. As David Bosch affirms, there can be little doubt that this understanding of the scope of the *missio Dei* developed contrary to the meaning and intentions of Karl Hartenstein, who first used the term (see Bosch 1991, 392). By introducing the phrase, which he developed from a Barthian perspective, Hartenstein hoped to protect mission against secularization and horizontalization, and to reserve it exclusively for God. Exactly the opposite developed in Hoekendijk's version of the history-of-the-promise theology of mission. Moreover, for Barth, mission was to be understood in the context of the Trinitarian theology's classical doctrine of the *missio Dei* as God the Father sending the Son, and God the Father and the Son sending the Holy Spirit. Barth correctly expanded this to include the Father, Son, and Holy Spirit sending the church into the world. This linking with the doctrine of the Trinity, which constitutes the theological foundation of Christian mission, is totally absent from Hoekendijk's approach. In fact, the extreme positions of Hoekendijk have prompted L. A. Hoedemaker to challenge the utility of the concept of *missio Dei*. It can, he argues, be used by people who subscribe to mutually exclusive theological positions (see Hoedemaker 1988, 171-73). In addition, Hoekendijk's attacks on the institutional church represent a view that leads to absurdity. It is impossible to talk about the church's involvement in the world if its very right to exist is disputed a priori (see Gensichen 1971, 168).

The value of this model is its recognition that mission is God's mission. When interpreted rightly, especially with its concept of the *missio Dei*, the model has helped to articulate the conviction that the theological foundation for mission is based on the doctrine of the Trinity. Mission has its origin in the sending of the Son by the Father into the world, and in the sending of the Holy Spirit by the Father and the Son. The church is sent for the mission (by the Triune God) through the Son and in the power of the Holy Spirit. This is the deepest understanding and source of mission. It is also the foundation and the reason for the very existence of the church.

Ludwig Rütti (1936-)

Ludwig Rütti, a German Catholic theologian, discusses in his thesis, written under the mentorship of J. B. Metz, *Zur Theologie der Mission: Kritische Analysen und neue Orientierungen* ("Toward a Theology of Mission: Critical Analyses and New Directions," 1972), the theology of the Vatican II document *Ad Gentes*. Rütti's reading of *Ad Gentes* has in it aspects of the history-of-the-promise model along with the political-theological reading of the theology of mission that shows the influence from Metz (1969) and Moltmann (1967).

Of particular importance here is the mission theology of Metz, which has also had a tremendous influence not only on Rütti but also on Latin American liberation theology. Thus, to understand Rütti better, we may need to begin with a brief allusion to the mission theology of Metz. For Metz, the mission of the church is a political one, affirming the political character of the Christian message. For him, in an epoch of secularization, political language replaces metaphysics as the language of theology (Metz 1969). Confronted with the problem and the danger involved in defining mission from the point of view of political history and theological reflection, Metz says that the actual reality has made politics the proper arena for theological analysis and for mission studies. As one author puts it, the secularization of the world and of society has led to the radical thesis of the theology of God's death and to the politicization of the goal of the Christian mission (Buono 2002, 66). But for Metz, the mission of the church and the goal of mission are to make a critical proclamation of the future of humanity. With its service to the world, the church becomes a political principle of liberty. This is because, faced with the present reality of the growth of human dominion over the world, there is also a growth in human domination over humanity. In this case, therefore, the proclamation of the reign of God by the church should be made as a critical proclamation of God as the future of the human. In other words, Metz speaks of a mission theology in which the church's role is largely one of prophetically criticizing the unjust political order of the world.

This is the background out of which Rütti developed his mission theology. For him, the foundation of mission is not in the institution of the Twelve, nor in the missionary mandate, nor in the divine missions, since all these lead us to the past, which is fixed and cannot change the world. Rütti refuses any form of dualism between church and world, and thus he does not accept conversion to the faith or to the church as any part of the goal of mission. Thus he does not accept Vatican II's decree on mission (*Ad Gentes*) because, as he puts it, "Mission is the responsibility of Christians for the world in the hope of transformation." This function, he says, does not entail an activity that is exclusively the task of the church, but is based in the wider promise of God to "create a new world." Christ, in making a call to conversion, was really calling for the kingdom that begins to realize itself through human activity in history. This is the paschal gift. Hence, the last lines of his book read: "The duty of Christians, re-clothed by the promise for a new world, is not to maintain or defend a church, but consists in the efficacious responsibility for the hope present in the world; responsibility that looks for men and women to make participants of this hope and work" (Rütti 1972, 345).

In this missiological approach we have a very low vision of ecclesiology and no appreciation of the deeper sacramental aspect of the church as the body of Christ and an instrument of the Spirit. Participation here and now in communion with God, experiencing the forgiveness of sin and the regeneration of life by the power of the Spirit, is of little interest, presumably because this concerns individuals. Again, one asks, Has the *religious* been dropped out of religion as concepts of faith and mission or the mystery of the Holy are diffused? The theory conflates without distinction human history and the history of salvation, thus downplaying the supernatural dimension of salvation.

Conclusion

There is no doubt that these concerns expressed in the theories of *missio Dei* and mission as service to the reign have shaped the way mission is viewed by many today. However, Christian mission, *sui generis*, has its basic foundation in Scripture, and its meaning has been enriched in Christian tradition and its central dimensions clarified by the magisterium of the church. While some are uncomfortable with invoking tradition and magisterium, when they are understood correctly, they do not contradict Scripture. Rather they deepen our insight and understanding of the Scripture and provide us with the faith assurance needed in the mission. In the Vatican II document on divine revelation (*Dei Verbum* 6), it is clear that tradition and Scripture are "bound closely together, and communicate one with the other," and both flow "from the same wellspring" and move toward "the same goal" (*DV* 9) and make up a "single deposit of the Word of God, which is entrusted to the Church" (*DV* 10). We are, then, confronted with the question whether elements in missiologies we have been discussing represent a fruitful development of God's word concerning the mission of Christians or an unbalanced selection of elements that in themselves may be helpful but cannot be represented as an integral theology of mission.

In the teaching of Vatican II and of Pope John Paul II (recall chap. 1), mission is portrayed as having had and displaying today a multidimensional character that is credible and faithful to its origins. To say this is to acknowledge that one should guard against the temptation to reduce the Christian mission to social service or assign to it a mainly political agenda. Social and political factors, though important and thoroughly consonant with the church's own deeper understanding of the obligation to work in the realm of history, should not be presented as if they have precedence over the specifically religious dimension of the Christian mission. The essential content of the Christian proclamation cannot be modified or ignored even as we discuss social and political problems and are shocked by war, genocide, poverty, the spread of HIV/AIDS, and the domination of two-thirds of the world's peoples by one-third. Social and political issues must be faced, but responses to them depend on changing circumstances. At the center of the Christian mission is the proclamation of the message that salvation in Jesus Christ is both universal in its extension and offered to all peoples and all times, and is the final answer to the world's problems. Mission above all must be a clear proclamation that, in Jesus Christ who died and rose, salvation is offered to all men and women, as gift of God's love and mercy. This salvation does more than meet material or even spiritual needs; it reaches fulfillment in communion with the Father, beginning here in this life, reaching fullness in eternity (*EN* 9). A secularized world finds this message of transcendence hard to grasp, but the church's message is that our commitment to that transcendence is an aid, not an impediment, to concern for the world's immanent problems.

Human elements, as a matter of fact, are responsible for the world's sufferings, and contemporary sciences such as political economy and sociology help us identify better than in past ages how the political disequilibrium of the world and society has come about. Recognizing the growth of such sciences, however, should not give rise to theological models that diminish the credibility, nature, and goal of the church and of the Christian mission. From the dawn of Christianity, the church, with the chair of Peter the apostle, as the center of communion, has been the visible agent of the mission. Rodney Stark (1997) has shown convincingly that the early church grew precisely because it saw no contradiction between proclaiming its message about Jesus as the Christ and creating a community that witnessed God's love by caring for the sick and poor. The twentieth century has shown the human condition to be one in which humanity has endured more suffering than in any other period in history. That theologians would seek to accentuate the need of Christians to overcome the unjust structures that cause such suffering is both salutary and understandable. Thus, although the rise of the theological tendencies studied above cannot be denied or discounted, they should not be used to attack the church and the essence of its missionary vocation. Any theology of mission worthy of the name should bring into relief the indispensable role of the church and its leaders in missionary ventures precisely in their attempts to articulate a gospel in which the dignity of the human being as a child of God is central. A central criterion of any missiological position's adequacy must lie in how it attends to the primary place of the specifically religious character of Christian mission. We refer, of course, to the way in which Jesus the Christ leads humanity to know God, the Holy One, as our healer and savior. Any approach contrary to such principles, it must be said, works against the nature of mission itself. In fact, the present-day emphasis on ecumenical and religious dialogue, on inculturation and human development, will be self-defeating if a mission theology does not highlight the religious character of our mission and the crucial role of the church and religious leaders in that regard.

Part Three

NEW PERSPECTIVES

8

MISSION AS ECUMENICAL DIALOGUE

In the period following the Second Vatican Council, the church has borne deeper witness to the importance of ecumenical dialogue. She has shown an ever more profoundly missionary consciousness as well as a deeper sensitivity in the area of ecumenical activity. She is the church of both *euntes docete* ("Go and teach" [Matt 28:19]) and of the prayer *ut unum sint* ("That all may be one" [John 17:21]; *Ut Unum Sint* is also the title of John Paul II's 1995 encyclical letter on ecumenism). There is, therefore, a close bond between mission and ecumenism, which needs to be studied thoroughly (see *AG* 6). At the same time, as we hope to show, ecumenical dialogue should today be considered one of the church's new ways of evangelization. The present chapter is not a summary of the works of authors who write on ecumenical dialogue, but a study of the missionary dimension and challenges of ecumenism as they developed in the Catholic Church. The chapter will show the universal influence of this development and conclude with some trajectories for strengthening and deepening ecumenical collaboration among the churches.

The Origin and Development of the Terminology

The word *ecumenism* comes from the Greek word *oikoumenē,* which in turn comes from *oikeō* ("to inhabit") and therefore, in the final analysis, from *oikia* ("house"). In ancient Greek, *hē oikoumenē tēs gēs* indicates all the earth inhabited by humanity or the whole of humanity as opposed to the uninhabited regions of the earth. Here *oikoumenē* indicates the world inhabited by both the Greeks and the barbarians.

After the conquests of Alexander the Great in the fourth century B.C., the concept became limited to the Greek-speaking, Hellenized world—Alexander's empire as opposed to the territories where it was impossible to communicate with the inhabitants. In contrast to *polis,* which had a narrow spatial limitation, *oikoumenē* later indicated the entire world formed in the Hellenistic culture. In this usage the term assumed a clear political coloring. Later it was possible to transfer the concept to the Roman empire, which was only too willing to identify its growing empire as the civilized world. The *oikoumenē* was now the empire, and the emperor was its lord and defender. In this way, in Roman imperial worship, Nero, as well as Marcus Aurelius, was honored as the "good spirit of the *oikoumenē* [world]" as the "benefactor and savior of the entire world." Greek-speaking Judaism did not participate in this cult, although in the Septuagint *oikoumenē* translates various Hebrew concepts mostly relating to the world, to the earth, and above all to all the inhabited earth (see Neuner 2000, 8).

Oikoumenē *in the New Testament*

In the New Testament we find the preeminent meanings of *oikoumenē* in the Hellenistic era, namely, "world" and "empire." The word does not appear often in the New Testament, probably because of its political connotation. Despite this fact, there are some illustrative passages in the New Testament, and the term is found in the Septuagint. For example, at the time of the emperor Augustus the order went out that all the world (*oikoumenē*) should be enrolled (Luke 2:1). The first disciples were dragged before the courts and accused of inciting the whole *oikoumenē* to revolt. In these passages *oikoumenē* indicates the Roman empire and its structures, but this concept had a very negative connotation. This becomes clear particularly in the account of the temptation, where Satan shows Jesus all the kingdoms of the world (Luke 4:5), and in the book of Revelation where *oikoumenē* indicates Satan's dominion over the whole world (12:9; 16:14). When the New Testament says that God's kingdom will be preached throughout the whole *oikoumenē* (Matt 24:14) and that God has established the day "on which he will judge the world [*oikoumenē*] in righteousness" (Acts 17:31), it refers to the world or to all human beings, since they are the recipients of the good news and salvation. Therefore, in New Testament terminology *oikoumenē* is an ambivalent concept. This is why Hebrews 2:5 speaks of the *oikoumenē* or world to come in subjection to Jesus Christ and compares this with the *oikoumenē* that passes, that is, with this world.

In the Patristic Period

In the patristic period the two meanings already mentioned are preserved: the whole world and the empire with its structures. Unless otherwise specified, I follow the work of Josef Neuner (2000). The *Letter of Clement* in a prayer of thanksgiving says that God created the world (i.e., the *oikoumenē*). This includes reality in its totality, including the angelic and spiritual powers (*Clement* 60.1). In the *Martyrdom of Polycarp* the formula *katholikē ekklēsiē* ("catholic churches") is used several times, and this is explicated with another formula, "in the whole *oikoumenē*" (see *Martyrdom of Polycarp* 8.1). Thus universality (*katholika*) and ecumenicity (*oikoumenē*) are words that now explain each other. In this way the normal meaning of world was established, applying the concept of *oikoumenē* also to the ecclesiastical sphere. The church is "catholic" because it is spread all over the world. In Origen and Basil the church appears as the new *oikoumenē*, as the cosmos sanctified through the gospel. Her members are the inhabitants of the *oikoumenē* and do not merely belong to the *ethnē*, that is, to the nations, who live outside the *oikoumenē*.

This idea is found also in St. Augustine, according to whom there is a connection between orthodoxy and the worldwide spread of the church. While heretical groups are each limited to a precise region, the universal church guarantees the true faith. In Africa there are Donatists, but not Anomoeans. These, instead, are found in the East, where there are no Donatists. The Catholic Church, however, is found all over the world; she covers it like a vine, whereas heretics have only a regional diffusion. Only the universal church is true and legitimate, in contrast to the regional heresies. Therefore *oikoumenē* is synonymous with the entire Eastern and Western church, whose orthodox warrants are bolstered by her universal diffusion.

From the time of the emperor Constantine onwards, the concept of *oikoumenē* enters the church's official language with the beginning of the so-called ecumenical councils (Neuner 2000, 9). Constantine summoned the Council of Nicaea in 325, "so that it might be for the salvation of the whole world" (Eusebius, *Life of Constantine* 65). The one Catholic Church in the *oikoumenē* corresponds to the emperor's *one* lordship over the *oikoumenē*. This linguistic use is taken up again by the Council of Constantinople (381), when it describes the Council of Nicaea as an "ecumenical council." According to this terminology, "ecumenical" is what is recognized throughout the church as valid and universal and, therefore, binding from the point of view of imperial law. In this context, ecumenical means official, binding for all, and orthodox. Whatever an ecumenical council decided definitively was the expression of a binding Christian doctrine; anyone who opposed or did not accept its declarations placed themselves outside the faith, outside the church, and, as the church came to dominate society, outside the approved social order.

Toward the end of the fourth century *oikoumenē* indicates the orthodoxy of the whole empire. When three great theologians of the Eastern Church—Basil the Great, Gregory Nanzianzen, and John Chrysostom—are described as "ecumenical teachers," it means that their teaching is accepted as a norm and canon for the whole church. Until the early Middle Ages the rector of the University of Constantinople was given the title *didaskalos tēs oikoumenēs* ("teacher of the world"), which gave him competence and binding authority in theological and canonical matters.

In the sixth century a conflict arose between Rome and Constantinople around the concept of *oikoumenē*. In the meantime the adjective *oikoumenikos*, according to Neuner, had "become a kind of synonym to indicate Constantinople and the territories subject to the Byzantine influence." Here we remember the dispute on the *oikoumenikos–universalis* adventure between Gregory the Great and John the Faster (see Neuner 2000, 10). The imperial city represented the *oikoumenē*, the empire, and its culture. In 449 a witness attributes the title of "ecumenical patriarch" to Dioscorus of Alexandria, indicating first of all his role at the synod, over which he was to preside on the emperor's behalf.

The Council of Chalcedon (451) several times describes the bishop of Rome as "bishop and ecumenical patriarch," a title that the popes did not adopt or claim for themselves. Indeed, the pope who was given this title had not claimed it for himself. Instead "ecumenical" was understood in the sense of an imperial role, ascribing by implication to the pope the role of defender of the universal, orthodox faith. As such the title carried with it a claim of jurisdiction over the universal church. Pope Gregory the Great was described as the *universalis papa* ("universal pope"), but he refused the title and asked to be called instead the *servus servorum Dei* ("servant of the servants of God"), because he did not want to place himself above the other bishops. Despite this exhortation, after Gregory's death subsequent bishops and patriarchs of Constantinople were also called "ecumenical" or "universal" patriarchs and bishops, thus setting the stage for irreconcilable and competing claims to superiority between the Western and Eastern patriarchs. Such conflicts did arise and were among the reasons Rome gave for excommunicating the patriarch of Constantinople Michael Cerularius in 1054. Among the complaints they allege, "he even calls himself ecumenical patriarch."

In Medieval and Modern Times

Within the space of a millennium *oikoumenē* and "ecumenical" were used to describe the universal church and her claim that she alone possesses the truth (see Neuner 2000, 11). A new way of understanding *oikoumenē* that extended its meaning is found in seventeenth- and eighteenth-century Pietism. Pietism broke the confines of the Protestant regional churches and had a universal, worldwide way of reflection. The community of the Moravian Brethren considered themselves the *ecclesiola in ecclesia*: the invisible church is made visible in its members' union with one another. This concept of "ecumenical" indicates consciousness of a world communion of all Christians and their churches.

In the Protestant world, beginning in the middle of the nineteenth century, the concept of "ecumenical" was generally used to describe the missionary ideal and the universality of the Christian proclamation. In 1846 the Evangelical Alliance was founded, its objective being to establish "an ecumenical federation" of true believers beyond every confessional and national confine. In 1881 the Methodists organized their first Ecumenical Methodist Conference, where problems and interests of world Methodism were discussed, but not their relationship to other confessions and other churches. In 1900 an "ecumenical missionary conference" was held in New York. This title was used for the very first time in the history of missionary conferences, "because the plan it proposes touches the entire extension of the inhabited world." The purpose of this conference was to assign mission territories on a world level to individual churches and individual missionary societies. This attempt to divide the world for missionary purposes and to reserve a particular territory for each church and each missionary society, avoiding overlapping as much as possible, was defined as "ecumenical."

In the Contemporary Period

In the modern age it can be said that "ecumenical" conferences were summoned to discuss the rival behavior of different denominations, which strive to surpass one another in their ability to win new converts and establish new social services in mission territories. This kind of competitive behavior means that the people being wooed wonder about the real motive that drives missionaries to act. Furthermore, it confuses the local people about the choice of denomination to follow and becomes a situation of real scandal. In their zeal to surpass the rival party, the competition leads to useless duplications of social services. What is worse, this rivalry tends to increase already existing ethnic divisions between members of the local population. Therefore, in the modern age, ecumenical dialogue begins with the need to address such issues in the missionary situation. The objective of ecumenical dialogue (in the sense of "worldwide" and "missionary") is to bring churches into closer contact with one another for the sake of mission and its credibility. The biblical passage that classically calls for ecumenical commitment is Jesus' prayer of farewell according to John's Gospel: "That they may all be one" (John 17:21). Here prayer for Christian unity is one of Jesus' main requests, the center of his prayer for his community. Unity is an essential sign of the Christian community; it is a precious blessing in itself, a sign of its election and its nature as God's real community. This idea has its roots in the Old Testament; it is found in the Qumran community, which called itself *yaḥad*, "union" (Schnackenburg 1987, 220).

Furthermore, according to John's Gospel the community's unity is based on God's unity and makes it visible. Unity is given to the church, created together with her essence. It cannot be achieved by human hand, but it must be maintained in fidelity to the origin; it is not a goal to be achieved, but a gift given to the church. If she renounced her unity, she would defile her essence and would be unfaithful to her vocation. Therefore, ecumenism is fidelity to Jesus' prayer and to Jesus' will: that all those who believe in him should be one as he is one with the Father and the Father is one with him. Ecumenism is especially the possibility, the call, and the command to strive for the union of Christians and the union of all their churches, so that there will be one church, one faith, and one Lord. In fact, the exhortation of John's Gospel shows that the threat to unity is not something external alone, but it calls into question the very community in its existence and in its pretensions. In the early church this conviction was taken up in the creed and translated into the affirmation that declares that unity is an essential sign of the church.

Therefore, church unity is a gift that churches can accept and receive as the expression of a communion that is already present and finds its ultimate foundation in God. The exhortation of John's Gospel shows that believers' unity was already endangered at that time. And yet saying that does not tell us what the enemies of unity were seeking. Were different factions accusing one another of not believing orthodox doctrine concerning Christ? Was there something else at stake? For this and other reasons we can apply Jesus' prayer to today's ecumenical situation only on certain conditions (see Neuner 2000, 20 n. 35). Moreover, the New Testament, particularly the Pauline Letters, shows an attempt to overcome the parties and factions that arose in communities and to restore the unity that had been broken through a human error. The overall perspective is one in which God conferred unity and therefore Christians are commanded to preserve it or restore it where it has been broken through human fault.

This command of Jesus is the authentic driving force for ecumenical dialogue. With ecumenical dialogue the church continues her missionary mandate, because division in the church contradicts her essence and denies Jesus' command. In other words, the church needs union, not because it is useful, desirable, or pleasant but because union belongs to the essence of the life of the church (see Visser 't Hooft 1967, 211).

Vatican II and Ecumenical Dialogue

Vatican II (in the decree on ecumenism, *Unitatis Redintegratio*) stresses the importance of ecumenical dialogue when it declares that, because of the divisions among Christians, the Catholic Church "finds it more difficult to express in all actual life her full catholicity in all its aspects" (*UR* 4). The decree *Unitatis Redintegratio* describes the restoration of unity among all Christians as one of the principal concerns of the council and declares that the division among Christians not only openly contradicts the will of Christ but also scandalizes the world and damages the holy cause of preaching the gospel to every creature.

Ad Gentes (6) takes up the same theme and declares that church unity is closely connected to her mission. All baptized persons are called to come together in one flock so that they may bear unanimous witness to Christ their Lord before the nations. The decree continues: "And if they cannot yet fully bear witness to one faith, they should at least be imbued with mutual respect and love."

After the council, the Catholic Church made further progress on the path she had undertaken. *Evangelii Nuntiandi* (1975) insists on the necessity of "a collaboration marked by greater commitment with the Christian brethren with whom we are not yet united in perfect unity" (*EN* 77). Today plans for dialogue between the Catholic Church and various other confessional communities, including the Evangelicals, are an integral part of the ecclesial scene, and the great Protestant missiologist David Bosch traces both the extent and importance of this post–Vatican II effort (1991, 462-67).

From a non-Catholic perspective, Roman Catholic participation in official dialogues sometimes seems problematic. Non-Catholics point out, for example, that the Catholic Church is not a member of the World Council of Churches (WCC), because that framework, at a symbolic level, would require her to accept de jure equality among the world's churches, something she cannot do because since very early times, Rome has claimed that the Petrine ministry gives her primacy. Yet through the Pontifical Council for Promoting Christian Unity she does consult with the WCC and has long been a full participant in the WCC's Faith and Order Commission. The Faith and Order Lima agreement on baptism, Eucharist, and ministry (1982) initiated a series of fruitful meetings among churches around the world aimed at forging greater understandings of the sacraments and ministry in the life of the churches. By one count, there were 185 responses to the Lima document by the year 2001. In 1993 delegates to the Fifth World Assembly of the Commission on Faith and Order of the World Council of Churches, held in Santiago de Compostela, recommended that the commission commence a major study of "a universal ministry of Christian unity."

In several parts of the world regional conferences of Catholic bishops have joined regional groupings of WCC churches. Additionally, there has been a history of Roman Catholic dialogues with churches such as the Anglican and the Lutheran, as well as with families of churches such as Evangelicals, the Orthodox, and Pentecostals. In 1976 and 1981—to give just two examples from a long series of meetings that continue today—the Anglican-Roman Catholic International Commission (ARCIC) published two documents on the question of authority in the church; these discussed the episcopal ministry and its relationship with a primatial office of unity in the universal church (see *Declaration of Venice* [1976]; *Declaration of Windsor*). In May 1999 ARCIC published *The Gift of Authority*, which approaches the structure of faith as a dialogical event. In dialogues with Lutherans, the most important event in the ecumenical-theological dialogues that have continued over a thirty-year period was the signing in Augsburg on October 31, 1999, of the Joint Declaration on the Doctrine of Justification, between Catholics and Lutherans. But the Roman Catholic/Lutheran Joint Commission report, *The Ministry in the Church* (March 13, 1981), is just one among several other important marks of growing Catholic–Lutheran mutual understanding.

The quest to repair church unity belongs to the very essence of Christian life. The Christian church cannot become accustomed to division, which contradicts Jesus' fundamental intention and the church's essence, just as she cannot become accustomed to heresy or a break with her apostolic origin. As Peter Neuner says, even a secular history cannot legitimize the fact that churches mutually reject communion in preaching, in the sacrament, and in ministry (see Neuner 2000, 21). According to Joseph Ratzinger (now Pope Benedict XVI), unless irrefutable reasons of truth and Christian ethics oblige us to break ecclesial communion, the separation is unlawful because it is an offense against the church's essence and it is culpable attachment to this separation, for whatever reason it may have arisen. "It is not unity that requires a justification, but separation" (Ratzinger 1982, 211). Therefore ecumenical dialogue is an important aspect of the missionary commitment of the Roman Catholic Church, whose center of communion is the see of Rome, whose bishop she believes was given the ministry of bringing about unity in the church (*UR* 2). In 1964, Pope Paul VI said the following about the papacy's role in furthering unity:

> That We, who promote this reconciliation, should be regarded by many of Our separated brothers as an obstacle to it, is a matter of deep distress to Us. The obstacle would seem to be the primacy of honor and jurisdiction which Christ bestowed on the Apostle Peter, and which We have inherited as his Successor. (*ES* 110)

As recently as 1995, Pope John Paul II spoke realistically about the fact that for many the Petrine ministry's claim to universal primacy is itself an obstacle to unity in the minds of many:

> the Catholic Church's conviction that in the ministry of the Bishop of Rome she has preserved, in fidelity to the Apostolic Tradition and the faith of the Fathers, the visible sign and guarantor of unity, constitutes a difficulty for most other Christians, whose memory is marked by certain painful recollections. To the extent that we are responsible for these, I join my Predecessor Paul VI in asking forgiveness. (*UUS* 88)

These statements were greeted with some grumbling from within the Catholic Church. In fact, it reflects an awareness of both Popes Paul VI and John Paul II that, beginning with Vatican II, it had become impossible to speak of church without speaking at the same time of mission and about the *one* mission of the *one* church. This represents an enormous, even paradigmatic change, and it did not come about as a result of the accumulation of new intuitions, but it was the result of the church's new understanding of herself. This change of paradigm is part of the new quest for totality and unity and of the attempt to overcome dualism and division. It is not the result of a lazy tolerance, of indifference and relativism, but of a new understanding of what it means to be Christians in the world. For this reason the commitment to ecumenical dialogue between churches in recent years has a meaning only if it is at the service of mission. Ecumenism is not a passive and somewhat reluctant convergence, but an active and deliberate way of living the Christian mission and of fulfilling it together. It is not the mere replacement of hostility with a correct but independent courtesy (Bosch 1991, 464). Still, as the issuance of and reaction to *Dominus Iesus* (the Congregation for the Doctrine of the Faith's statement on the universality, uniqueness, and finality of Jesus Christ [2002]) shows, ecumenical sensitivities run close to the surface. Attempts to give clear guidelines for theologians within the church about such issues are quickly picked up and criticized by other churches. Such reactions also indicate that the Catholic Church and other churches have come far in mutual understanding and tolerance, so that when something appears to set the clock back, it is closely scrutinized.

Classical Theological Divergences in Catholic–Protestant Dialogue

We wish now to indicate briefly some of the theological and missiological problems in ecumenical dialogue with Protestants. From a classical Catholic point of view, the problems of theological controversy are related to the theological formation of founders of Protestant churches and also to the way in which Reformers denied the preeminent role of the see of St. Peter as the center of communion. Protestants, of course, see the Reformers as trying to recover the essential teaching of the gospel and to remove accretions of traditions that they believed were obscuring the meaning of the gospel. In addition, at the time of the Reformation, all sides were vying with one another to—in their own minds—protect the gospel, bring salvation to the masses, open the way to Christ, and make a claim to be the true church of Jesus Christ. The theological discipline of ecclesiology was born from such debates at the beginning of the modern age, when ecclesial parties each wanted to establish their claim and their right. Leading up to Vatican II, Catholic ecclesiology was dominated by a controversialist theological approach that sought to show that the Catholic Church alone was the true church and possessed the means of salvation given to her by Christ. On the Protestant side, while ecclesiology was implicit in what was taught, the central preoccupation was a demonstration that faith was the path to salvation and that no human being stood between God and the sinner seeking the faith that would "justify" himself or herself.

The problems of controversialist theology start above all in this ecclesiological space. Catholics, in essence, thought that Protestants were throwing away a tradition that had brought human beings to faith and salvation for centuries. Protestants, on the other hand, thought that the elaborateness of the Catholic Church and its manifold rites and structures obstructed the teaching of Scripture on how human beings were made right before God. For the most part, the central doctrinal themes concerning the Trinitarian God and the relation of Jesus the Christ, the Holy Spirit, and the Father had been given in the first Christian era and were not called into question either by the schism between East and West in the eleventh century or in the sixteenth-century Reformation. Instead, the question of mediation was in dispute; that is, principles of ecclesiology, related sacramental doctrine, and the power and role of the ordained were in dispute. Consequently ecumenical problems are found above all in the field of sacramental doctrine and ecclesiology (see Neuner 2000, 192). From a Catholic perspective, basic aspects of Protestant theology reveal the outlines of the problem. From a Protestant perspective, these same issues are areas in which biblical truth was being retrieved and brought into relief. To many these points may seem too simple, but it is good to remind ourselves of them.

Faith justifies. First, it is generally considered that the starting point of theology is the concept that faith alone justifies (*sola fide*). For Protestants of the Reformation there is an enormous distance between God and his creation. However, in God's sovereignty and through grace alone (*sola gratia*) God takes the initiative to forgive, justify, and save human beings. Therefore the doctrine of justification became the greatest truth on which all other doctrines are based. Human merit gains nothing. Instead, one surrenders oneself in faith to God's graciousness. Consequently the starting point of the Reformation was not how much people could do for their salvation, but what God had already accomplished in Christ.

The theology of the fall. Second, Protestants saw a close connection between *sola fide* and the centrality of the doctrine of justification and the need for the forgiveness of sin, both of which, they taught, need to be seen from the perspective of the fall. Seen correctly, the Reformers taught, members of the human race are born sinners and lost, incapable of putting anything to right by their own efforts and destined to persist in errant behavior. The world is evil, and individuals have to be snatched from this evil. Thus, people have to be made aware of their dissolute condition so that they might be led to repentance and be relieved of the great burden of sin. Protestants emphasized individual sin and the essential sinfulness of all humanity.

The subjective dimension of salvation. Third, Protestant theology underlines the subjective dimension of salvation. God should not be seen as God in Godself (*Gott an sich*) whose nature becomes the object of metaphysical speculation. Instead God is "God for me," "God for us," the God who, through love of Christ, justified us through grace. Martin Luther inspired this tendency, and it resonated for many reasons, including the fact that, as the late Middle Ages became the early modern era, the individual was beginning to emerge from the group. As Protestant writers "theologized" this development, the question of salvation became a personal matter for the individual, especially for the individual who came to see mediation by a corrupt church as problematic. In thousands of different forms believers would insist on a personal and subjective experience of rebirth through the Holy Spirit, and began to believe that everything rested on the individual's responsibility (i.e., "capacity to respond [to God's promise]") rather than being a member of the group belonging to the church.

The priesthood of every believer. In the fourth place, the strong accent Protestantism placed on the individual's personal role and responsibility led Protestants to emphasize the priesthood of every believer. The believer is in direct relationship with God, a relationship that exists independently of the *community*. Rooted in solid biblical teaching, the Protestant idea of the priesthood of all believers led their theologians to accentuate the individual's role in offering himself or herself to God. They therefore denied the mediatory efficacy of the ordained priests of the church in this action. Instead, the church's officers were primarily ministers whose office was to proclaim the word of God. From a missiological perspective, this led also to an effective denial, or at least neglect, of the notion that the "Great Commission" of Matthew 28:19 referred to a grant of power to a holder of a universal ecclesiastical office.

Scripture alone. Fifth, the Protestant idea finds its focal point in the expression *Scripture alone.* Therefore the role of the sacraments is drastically reduced and subordinated to preaching. In many Protestant churches the liturgical center has been rearranged, and the altar (or the communion table) has been replaced by the ambo, which enjoys the place of honor on the podium.

These five key aspects of Protestantism, to which many others could be added, have some very important consequences for an understanding and development of mission, in the positive or negative sense (see Bosch 1991, 242-43). The first aspect—emphasis laid on the fact that faith justifies—can, on the one hand, become an urgent motive for involving people in missionary work. It can also paralyze any missionary effort. After all, we could say that since the initiative remains in God's hands, and God is the one who chooses those who will be saved, understandings of mission as an attempt to save peoples becomes blasphemous.

Second, looking at humanity only from the perspective of the fall could, on the one hand, safeguard the idea of God's sovereignty and thus guarantee that mission is, in the first and final analysis, God's work. But anxiety over human depravity can lead to promoting such a pessimistic view of humanity that life is viewed in fatalistic terms—human beings are mere pawns on a chessboard and human agency in history is diminished. This could lead to acquiescence and noninvolvement, because there is nothing human beings can do to change reality. Indeed, precisely because the emphasis on predestination and its attendant fatalism is so out of synchrony with contemporary life, the pressure to compromise on such elements can spill over into a diminishment of aspects of Christian faith that are certainly the core of revelation—God's Trinitarian nature and loving-kindness, the invitation to share in God's nature while on earth, Christic life as partnership with God in alleviating human misery.

Third, the emphasis placed on the subjective dimension of salvation can lead to an inflated view of the individual and his or her autonomy, a vision that could eclipse a parallel truth—that we find our supreme happiness in community and therefore need to be ready to cede our desires when they are in conflict with the common good. Thus, an exaggerated emphasis on the individual runs the risk of estranging individuals from the group and of destroying awareness of the fact that the human being is fashioned in the image and likeness of a Trinitarian God and that we are, by definition, communal beings.

Fourth, the accent placed on the priesthood of all believers retrieves the concept that every Christian has a call and therefore a responsibility to serve God and to be involved actively in God's work in the world, not as immature or "lesser members" of the church but as full members of the church's ministry. At the same time, overemphasizing this field of discourse may conceal the seeds of schism, of a variety of believers liable to interpret God's word differently and, in the absence of an ecclesiastical magisterium, each tending to a different way. The splintering of the world Christian movement into separate, competing churches is to be seen as the fruit of this ideology. It is a fruit far removed from the desires of the Reformers, a careful study of whom shows that they hoped to catalyze and renew the one church, not split it into factions.

Finally, the accent placed on Scriptures should be recognized as the milestone of the Protestant Reformation and a genuine achievement. At the same time, *sola scriptura* taken to its logical extreme can be so rigorously applied that the scriptural principle sometimes works against itself. If the only things one can rely on are those that are taught unambiguously, features of the church's life that unfold over time, such as the sacraments, no matter how helpful they are in Christian life, can be discarded. Ironically, this entire dynamic can end up with placing God, the things of God, and the Bible on one side and humankind on the other. Luther would say, "God and the Bible are two different things" (Oberman 1983, 234-39). David Tracy has written masterfully on the tragedy of the "analogical" Catholic imagination and the "dialectical" Protestant imagination opposing one another, when in reality both are needed for a sound Christian identity (Tracy 1981).

Issues in Catholic–Evangelical Dialogue

"Independent" Evangelicalism and Pentecostalism

For perspective, it is important to take note of a notable lacuna in what we have discussed above. We have *not* delved into the thinking of the movement that is today referred to as "Independent" churches and missions. The term "Independent" is used increasingly today to differentiate Evangelical and Pentecostal churches from "Ecumenical" churches (those that belong to the World Council). When we use "Independent" and "Ecumenical" in this sense below, we capitalize the words to draw attention to the fact that we are dealing with two distinct wings of Protestantism. An entire chapter could profitably be devoted to the Independent churches, if only to help Catholics better understand church families that we often throw together without properly understanding their differences. Roughly speaking, Evangelical and Pentecostal Independent churches are congregational in nature, by which we mean that each congregation is independent from every other. Insofar as they link with other churches, they follow a voluntary "associational" model. Most Ecumenical Protestants, on the other hand, are "connectional," a term that indicates that they are organized into units such as "synods" (Lutherans), "conferences" (Methodists), and "sessions" (Presbyterian). (Such connectional entities differ greatly from one area of the world to another, but these three are fairly common.) Following the congregational principle, Independents establish flexible links with like-minded churches for the purpose of, for example, preparing Bible translations and editions, educational programs for youth and adults, campus ministry at colleges and universities, or sending and maintaining missioners overseas.

In the year 1900, Independents constituted about 1.4 percent of the world's Christians. In 2000, they were approximately 19 percent. Ecumenical Protestants in 1900 were approximately 45 percent of the world's Christians; they were about 31 percent in the year 2000. During that same period Catholics have held fairly steady at 47.5 percent of the total number of Christians in 1900 and 53 percent in 2000, according to the World Christian Database. Independents are projected to be about 23 percent of the world's 2.6 billion Christians in 2025, while Catholics will be an estimated 50 percent and Ecumenicals about 32 percent. It is important to keep these numbers and percentages in mind when one thinks about Christian relations and dialogue on collaboration in mission and in relations with followers of other religions. While Protestant Independents disagree with Catholics on ecclesiology, they are fiercely orthodox on questions like Trinitarian theology and tend to be traditionalists in areas such as sexual ethics. This they share with Roman Catholicism, especially Third World Catholics. On the other hand, many Independents view with alarm Catholicism's relatively optimistic view that non-Christians can be saved without coming to explicit faith in Christ. If one compares the Lausanne Covenant statement (1974)—the theology of which is broadly agreed to by many Independent Protestants—with Roman Catholic documents such as Pope Paul VI's *Evangelii Nuntiandi* (1975) or Pope John Paul II's *Redemptoris Missio* (1990), the convergences and divergences of Catholic and Evangelical theology are quite apparent. But since even the members of WCC churches in Asia, Africa, and Latin America tend to share orthodox Trinitarian theology and a high doctrine of biblical authority, they also tend to have opinions that converge with both Catholics and Independents in many of these areas. It is therefore clear that the most important and interesting dialogues on theological and missiological matters over the next twenty years will be between Catholics worldwide and Christians in the global South. That conversation has only just started, and we do not discuss it at length in this book. Nevertheless, the reader should not be misled. Dialogues, debates, and discussions between these families of followers of Christ will be a major part of both ecumenical and interfaith discussions over at least the next generation and probably longer. Their impact on the theory and practice of mission will be considerable.

The best sources for information on the theology and demographics of these rapidly growing movements include the following: A. Scott Moreau et al., *Evangelical Dictionary of World Mission* (2000); A. Scott Moreau et al. *Introducing World Missions: A Biblical, Historical, and Practical Survey* (2004); David B. Barrett et al., *World Christian Encyclopedia* (2001). (Full information on these books may be found in the bibliography below.) For a shorter and more general exposition of the essentials of this new evangelicalism, a short book by John R. W. Stott, one of the Evangelical movement's acknowledged elder statesmen, is *Evangelical Truth: A Personal Plea for Unity, Integrity and Faithfulness.* On the much discussed and vexing question of what "Fundamentalism" is and what role it plays in all this, see George Marsden's *Fundamentalism and American Culture* (1980). Although Marsden's book deals with this theme only in the United States, the preponderant role of American Evangelicals in world mission makes it a good one from which to gain insight into the movement as a whole. On the scale and growth of Pentecostalism, probably the fastest-growing segment of the world Christian movement, see Dempster et al., *The Globalization of Pentecostalism* (1999) and Allan Anderson's *An Introduction to Pentecostalism* (2004). In the summer of 2006 the American Society of Missiology, in recognition of the one-hundredth anniversary of Protestant Pentecostalism, devoted its program to the renewal of Pentecostalism. In some measure, that signals a growing recognition on the part of missiologists that this is a movement we shall be hearing more from, both as a movement of Independent Protestants and also in terms of the so-called Charismatic Renewal that has brought it into the Catholic Church.

In all the books referred to above, one finds on display what has been termed the Evangelical and Pentecostal movements' greatest appeal: concentration on the essential message of the New Testament and acceptance of the absolute authority of the New Testament. A Catholic who reads such works cannot but be impressed by this. On the other hand, a Catholic critic will insist that in the journey through history, faith and culture enter into a dialogue that enriches liturgical and spiritual traditions, and that the principle of episcopal governance of the church and interpretation of the Scriptures under the successors of Peter is divinely willed. Other Protestant groups have started out with strong Trinitarian orthodoxy and conviction of the authority of the Scriptures, but this has not stopped them for splitting when they encountered the challenges of modernity. Will contemporary Independent Protestants do better? Can Catholics and Independents learn from one another? There is, accordingly, much for Catholics and Independents to discuss. As we move into the twenty-first century, these two embodiments of the Christian ideal are both the largest and most vital ecclesial families in existence.

The Way Ahead for Independents and Catholics

The history and characteristics of the basic issues in the dialogue with the Independents are intimately related to the general features in Protestantism discussed above. However, since the 1940s in North America and the 1960s in Europe, a specific Evangelical mission theology has laid claim to the missiological heritage of mainstream Protestantism, at which such Evangelicals look critically. The Evangelical tradition interprets this heritage somewhat differently from the churches that began the modern Protestant missionary movement (Fiedler in Müller et al. 1997, 144). Moreover, among the Evangelicals themselves there exist pluriform expressions of the basic issues in ecumenism.

In spite of the pluriform expressions of the Evangelicals, their theology is distinguished by certain common features: (a) a close relationship to Scripture, which is regarded as inspired and all-sufficient for life and doctrine; (b) emphasis on the atoning and redemptive work of Christ; (c) emphasis on the necessity of a personal decision of faith for conversion; (d) in at least some of its factions, the prioritization of evangelization and the building up of congregations directed toward work such as the pursuit of social justice and interreligious dialogue; (e) the conviction that all who do not believe in Christ are lost eternally; and (f) the actual expectation of the imminent return of

Christ, before which event the gospel must be preached to all nations (see Fiedler in Müller et al. 1997, 144-45).

A major area where Evangelical theology differs from the other traditions of Protestantism is its historical origin. The roots of today's "Independent-Church" Evangelical theology lie in the revival movements of the second half of the nineteenth century. Though it extends back to the Reformation, Evangelical mission theology came into its own in nineteenth-century evangelical movements, and above all through the Evangelical Alliance (established in 1846). These nineteenth-century movements, in turn, stand on the shoulders of earlier post-Reformation evangelical movements such as Pietism, Moravianism, Methodism, the Free Church movements in Europe, and similar awakening movements of the eighteenth and nineteenth centuries.

The revivals of the second half of the nineteenth century were mainly inter-denominational, and as far as mission theology is concerned, they found their typical expression in what were called "faith missions" in the years following World War II. They also placed strong emphasis on soteriology and, in general, have given little attention to ecclesiology. Furthermore, the understanding of unity in the Evangelical theology of mission is personal; that is, individual faith is primary and structural unity secondary. Continuity is understood as continuity of the same faith and doctrine, not as continuity of the apostolic origin of the church, whose faith and doctrine are safeguarded through its teaching authority. Further, as the name "Independent" suggests and as we said above, a growing percentage of the Evangelicals come from local congregations that are not linked to any of the mainstream denominations. Thus, a majority of the Independents' authors and missionaries belong to churches that do not consider disagreement and lack of unity a matter of major concern. In this they differ from Fundamentalists. Indeed, Evangelicals commonly seek to distance themselves from Fundamentalist divisiveness and polemics and to avoid unnecessary breaches in fellowship. There is very wide diversity in the ways Evangelicals understand and appreciate the Catholic Church, a spectrum that ranges between openness and being relatively closed.

Generally speaking, Evangelicals value unity and fellowship among Christians for more effective witness of the gospel and to foster interpersonal relationships of common faith, trust, and prayer, rather than relying on organizational or hierarchical structures. Their ecclesiological vision, accordingly, is a form of de facto functionalism. Furthermore, the Evangelicals *reject* liberal Protestantism in embracing: (a) the kinds of biblical criticism that undermine the divinity of Christ and the authority of the Scripture; (b) evolutionary theory; (c) a social teaching separated from the life-changing power of the proclaimed gospel (see Scherer in Müller et al. 1997, 147).

Two organizations in particular that have defined the missiological agenda of Evangelicals are the World Evangelical Fellowship (WEF, founded in 1951) and the Lausanne Committee for World Evangelization (LCWE, founded in 1974), often simply referred to as the Lausanne movement. Both organizations, while primarily North American in background and support, are seeking to develop a worldwide following and a global program. The two bodies have maintained close and cooperative relationships with each other, and many Evangelicals identify with both. The LCWE, as its name suggests, is not a council of churches or religious organizations but rather a loose coalition of individual persons, mission and evangelism agencies, and institutions sharing a common theological position and with a common missionary and evangelistic purpose. It is governed by an international committee of seventy evangelical leaders. Identification with the LCWE is made by signing the Lausanne Covenant and thereby covenanting with others "to pray, plan, and work together for the evangelization of the whole world" (Scherer in Müller et al. 1997, 148).

Between 1974 and 1989, the LCWE carried on its agenda by means of working groups on theology, mission strategy, intercessions, and communication. The LCWE joined in the planning of the 1980 Pattaya (Thailand) Consultation on World Evangelization. The most vital LCWE document in recent years comes from the Second International Congress on World Evangelization (Manila, 1989, often referred to as Lausanne II) and is entitled the *Manila Manifesto: An Elaboration of the Lausanne Covenant Fifteen Years Later*. The *Manila Manifesto* is in some way an updating of the Lausanne Covenant, but without departing from the covenant's essential affirmations. While possessing no official authority, these two documents embody a broad consensus of Evangelical opinion and conviction about mission and evangelization. Two paragraphs from the *Manila Manifesto* make interesting reading in our context:

> "Cooperation" means finding unity in diversity. It involves people of different temperaments, gifts, calling and cultures, national churches and mission agencies, all ages and both sexes working together.
>
> We are determined to put behind us once and for all, as a hangover from the colonial past, the simplistic distinction between First World sending and Two-Thirds World receiving countries. For the great new fact of our era is the internationalization of missions. Not only are a large majority of all evangelical Christians now non-western, but the number of Two-Thirds World missionaries will soon exceed those from the West. We believe that mission teams, which are diverse in composition but united in heart and mind, constitute a dramatic witness to the grace of God.

The most recent development of Evangelical missiology is emerging from dialogues with the Catholic Church. From 1977 to 1984 (and to the present), the Vatican Pontifical Council for Promoting Christian Unity participated in series of consultation meetings called the "Evangelical–Roman Catholic Dialogue on Mission" (ERCDOM). Evangelical participants come from many denominations. The focal point of all discussion is Christian mission. The Evangelicals do not officially represent any international body, although all were associated with the LCWE. The most striking recent statements (though unofficial) come from the Evangelical–Roman Catholic consultation (1994 document): *Evangelicals and Catholics Together: The Christian Mission in the Third Millennium*. The document suggests, as did the consultations from 1977 to 1984, that the commonalities between Evangelicals and Catholics are substantial, particularly when viewed against the background of the present-day world situations. Both are the most evangelistically assertive and most rapidly growing Christian communities in the world today. Both are alarmed at the growth in secularism and materialism in Western society; both see dangers posed to Christians throughout the world by the rise of Islamic fundamentalism; and both are concerned about the increasing moral chaos in the contemporary world, at both the individual and social levels. The document notes that in spite of the common concerns that Evangelicals and Catholics share over these realities of today, the relationship between the two Christian communities also presents many ongoing conflicts and tensions. These tensions, however, necessitate asking the question: How will the missionary endeavor started within the greatest century of missionary expansion in Christian history proceed into the third millennium? The growing consensus that appears to be emerging among young Evangelicals is a pragmatic one. That pragmatism is on display in another paragraph from the 1989 *Manila Manifesto*:

> Our reference to "the whole church" [in an earlier section] is not a presumptuous claim that the universal church and the evangelical community are synonymous. For we recognize that there are many churches which are not part of the evangelical movement. Evangelical attitudes to the Roman Catholic and Orthodox Churches differ widely. Some evangelicals are praying, talking, studying Scripture and working with these churches. Others are strongly opposed to any form of dialogue or cooperation with them. All are aware that serious theological differences between us remain. Where appropriate, and so long as biblical truth is not compromised, cooperation may be possible in such areas as Bible translation, the study of contemporary theological and ethical issues, social work and political action. We wish to make it clear, however, that common evangelism demands a common commitment to the biblical gospel.

In essence they agree that collaboration with Catholics on a limited range of issues is possible, while acknowledging both that some Evangelicals will not want to do so and that differences between Catholics and Evangelicals remain real. Some suggest that Evangelicals and Catholics may grow closer in the years that lie ahead while still maintaining a degree of distance between them, especially in regard to certain basic doctrinal differences. However, while we wait for the day when Catholics and Evangelicals may unite, one thing is certain—that both communities have missionary potentials from which the initiated cooperation in mission remains to be worked out and tested in all levels of the church's life (see Scherer in Müller et al. 1997, 150).

Toward Ecumenical Collaboration

How should the gospel preacher behave toward other Christian confessions, present and working in the same area where the preacher proclaims the good news? What operative criteria should he or she follow in this interreligious and interconfessional context? We find the answer to these two extremely important questions in the conciliar and postconciliar documents (see Saraiva Martins 1994, 136ff.). The thought contained in them can be reduced to the following basic principles: a fraternal attitude and collaboration based on the things common to all Christians.

Cultivating Fraternal Attitudes

First, the herald of the gospel must have a fraternal attitude toward Christians of other ecclesial communities or confessions, orientations that are based on both truth and love. According to the teaching of Vatican II: "One cannot charge with the sin of separation those who at present are born into these communities and in them are brought up in the faith of Christ, and the Catholic Church accepts them with respect and affection as brothers" (*UR* 3).

Second, to develop a feeling of fraternity, missionaries should be familiar with the outlook of Christians from other communities. They should be familiar and know about their life and spirit, gaining a knowledge that is obtained only through experience and serious study pursued in fidelity to the truth, that is, without prejudices. This obviously presupposes a more adequate knowledge of their respective doctrines and history, their spiritual and liturgical life, their religious psychology and cultural background. *Unitatis Redintegratio* notes that through cooperation with members of other churches in efforts to "relieve the afflictions of our times . . . all believers in Christ are able to learn easily how they can understand each other better and esteem each other more, and how the road to the unity of Christians may be made smooth" (*UR* 12). Furthermore, the missionary must pay attention to the way in which he or she presents the gospel. It "should in no way become an obstacle to dialogue with members of other ecclesial communities" (*UR* 11). Therefore the missionary who works in an ecumenical context must observe the following criteria.

On the one hand, Catholics are exhorted to present the good news clearly in its entirety, since "[n]othing is so foreign to the spirit of ecumenism as a false irenicism that would harm the original purity of the Catholic doctrine and obscures its genuine meaning" (*UR* 11). On the other hand, in preaching and explaining the gospel, the missionary will explicate it in such a way that it can be understood also by Christians of other confessions. Therefore our language will be supremely respectful of the integrity of the message and at the same time open to others. Again, in ecumenical dialogue (although the text refers explicitly to theologians, the message applies to missionaries), *Unitatis Redintegratio* declares that missionaries should act always "with love for the truth, with charity, and with humility" (*UR* 11)—three virtues that must animate every search, above all in the area of faith. However, the decree on ecumenism added, with regard to the truth of Catholic doctrine, that it must not be forgotten that "in Catholic doctrine there exists an order or 'hierarchy' of truths, since they vary in their relation to the foundation of the Christian faith" (*UR* 11). Furthermore, with regard to authentic Christian values, the document adds that it is also necessary that the missionary should recognize authentically Christian values deriving from our common heritage that are to be found among other ecclesial communities (see *UR* 4). Finally it is extremely important that, in ecumenical dialogue, the accent should be placed on what unites us rather than on what separates us. This was John XXIII's principle, confirmed by his immediate successor. In his first encyclical, *Ecclesiam Suam,* Paul VI declares, "we readily accept the principle of stressing what we all have in common rather than what divides us. This provides a good and fruitful basis for our dialogue, and we are prepared to engage upon it with a will" (*ES* 109).

Collaboration

A fraternal spirit, one of understanding and respect expected of Christians of all confessions, is not enough. *Unitatis Redintegratio* calls Catholics to work together with Christians of other traditions, noting that in a world where "cooperation in social matters is so widespread today, all men without exception are called to work together; with much greater reason is this true of all who believe in God, but most of all, it is especially true of all Christians, since they bear the seal of Christ's name" (12). There must be real collaboration between them. The Vatican II missionary decree *Ad Gentes* says that missionaries "should be properly prepared for fraternal dialogue with non-Christians" (*AG* 16). Since cooperation on all levels of social life, both national and international, is becoming increasingly closer, it would truly be a scandal if Christians did not seek a sincere and loyal collaboration in those areas where this is possible (see Saraiva Martins 1994, 140).

Areas for Collaboration

There are at least four major areas for collaboration between Catholics, Orthodox, and Protestants, and where possible, that collaboration and dialogue should extend to working with persons of other faiths as well.

On the social level. Vatican II indicated various areas for collaboration on a social level between Catholics and Protestants in areas of the world where social and technological changes are under way.

> It [cooperation among Christians] should contribute to a just appreciation of the dignity of the human person, to the promotion of the blessings of peace, the application of Gospel principles to social life, and the advancement of the arts and sciences in a truly Christian spirit. It should use every possible means to relieve the afflictions of our times, such as famine and natural disasters, illiteracy and poverty, lack of housing, and the unequal distribution of wealth. (*UR* 12)

In other words, Catholics, Orthodox, and Protestants can and must act together in the name of Christ and in the name of the gospel they proclaim. They must be the interpreters, *defenders, and promoters of human dignity* and of fundamental human rights, against every kind of social, political, or economic oppression and against any tyranny that crushes human dignity or does not respect human rights sufficiently. In the name of the message of fellowship they proclaim, they must be defenders and promoters of the fundamental equality of all men and women, fighting together against every form of discrimination or marginalization for reasons of a political, cultural, or religious nature.

In working for peace and reconciliation—the application of the gospel in zones of conflict. Another area where Christians of different confessions can collaborate is that of *peace*. In a world threatened by war, all Christians must defend peace with all their might. Believing in Christ, the Prince of Peace, involves working and committing oneself fully in a constant and intense work of peace, as the expression of liberty, harmony, and fraternal love among all men and women. In dechristianized societies, that is, in areas where the fundamental values of the gospel are becoming less and less important—for example, where ethnic conflict is going on among Christians—it is essential that members of different Christian confessions work together to examine and solve the common burning problems that this situation in modern society places with increasingly greater urgency before them. They must work together to animate the human community and its structures with the gospel, to vivify them with its spirit and transform them with its life-giving virtues.

This is the meaning of the social application of the gospel, in which all members of the various churches and Christian communities must be involved.

In recent years, four American missiologists have proposed that "reconciliation" ought to be a central focus of mission efforts (see Bevans and Schroeder 2004; Burrows 1998; and Schreiter 1996). They recognize that, on one level, reconciliation (*katallagē*) is not an oft-used word in the New Testament in either its verbal or substantive forms. On another level, however, it captures major elements of the gospel (forgiveness of sin, for example) and is in profound harmony with what contemporary peace studies show is the most effective dynamic for ending conflict and creating not just an absence of war but peace, the biblical concepts of *shalom* and *eirēnē*. The logic of the case, in the view of Burrows, is that continuing to think of mission in terms of expanding the church falls into the trap of the church presenting itself as a marketer selling a product. Reconciliation, on the other hand, involves conversion at the deepest level and entering deeply into the mystery of the death of Christ as the instrument of divine-human reconciliation, and taking hints on what our mission is from the self-giving of Jesus as portrayed in 2 Cor 5:18-19. Only the kind of spirituality that has led the missioner to gospel-inspired death to self will enable him or her to be an agent promoting the reconciliation of peoples in conflict.

Collaboration in the arts and sciences and in human promotion. There should also be this same collaboration in the arts and sciences. As indicated in both *Gaudium et Spes* (40-44) and Pope Paul VI's *Ecclesiam Suam* (98, 108), the church seeks to engender a Christian presence in culture in a spirit of dialogue, so that the many cultures of the world develop with a truly Christian spirit. In the same context, Christians of all churches must collaborate in using every kind of remedy to meet the many forms of deprivation of our time (hunger, illiteracy, poverty, lack of housing, the unjust distribution of wealth). A separate discourse on this topic is not necessary. This effort includes the defense and promotion of human rights. Defending and promoting human rights and the human being's legitimate aspirations involve struggling against these forms of poverty, which unfortunately still afflict large groups of modern society. Recently, these forms of poverty, which are largely human-made, have been described as a threat to peace if not well addressed, since they are signs of injustice in the society.

Furthermore, by working together on a social level in all the different areas indicated, heralds of the gospel carry out a real act of evangelization. In fact Christian social activity is part of evangelization. Indeed working for human beings, defending human beings, and promoting human liberation are already forms of evangelization. Christian mission includes the duties of proclamation, witness, and service (see Saraiva Martins 1994, 144).

Collaboration at religious and pastoral levels. Collaboration is also possible on religious and pastoral levels, above all in the field of research. Interconfessional collaboration in this field should begin within missiology and the other sciences more closely related to it, for example, religious sociology, ethnology, and so forth. Research or study in common should then extend to an examination of all those more important problems whose solutions could help the cause of evangelization: secularism, relativism, the present expansion of Islam, the dialogue with great religions, the traditional religions and cultures, and the alarming phenomena of sects. To a great extent this is already the case in societies devoted to missiological studies. Groups such as the South African Missiological Society, the British-Irish Association for Mission Studies, the International Association for Mission Studies, the International Association for Catholic Missiology, and the American Society of Missiology actively seek the collaboration of members of the various Christian families. Most missiologists indeed find it hard to imagine a research or writing project in which they do not collaborate with and seek advice from colleagues from other Christian traditions. That spirit needs to be extended.

As far as possible, then, collaboration should be encouraged also on a level of pastoral activity. Conscious of the necessity of this collaboration and animated by the spirit of unity, the minister of one confession will try to get to know the viewpoint of ministers of other Christian communities. They will avoid taking actions that are competitive and engender rivalry. Thus, a fraternal attitude is necessary among members of different confessions (pastors, missionaries, and so on). This collaboration is already a reality in many places. The reason why an ever-greater spirit of collaboration is needed between the churches is, in the teaching of Vatican II, that "through such cooperation, all believers in Christ are able to learn easily how they can understand each other better and esteem each other more, and how the road to the unity of Christians may be made smooth" (*UR* 12). Working together creates a sense of unity; one understands better the absurdity of division; there is a greater desire to reestablish unity as soon as possible among the various followers of Christ. While full communion at an institutional level may be a distant hope, collaboration in practical matters can demonstrate a unity of heart and mind inspired by the gospel at a much more basic human and spiritual level.

All ideals and hopes notwithstanding, John Paul II noted in his apostolic exhortation *Catechesi Tradendae* that

> the communion of faith between Catholics and other Christians is not complete and perfect; in certain cases there are even profound divergences. Consequently, this ecumenical collaboration is by its very nature limited: it must never mean a "reduction" to a common minimum. (*CT* 33)

Other churches and missionary bodies (recall our citation of the *Manila Manifesto* of the Lausanne Movement above) are similarly realistic. Full communion of faith between Catholics and other Christians is not foreseeable; there are real divergences. Nor should we underestimate the profound divergences that exist among the various tendencies of churches that go under the name Protestant. Increasingly it seems to be the case that a conservative Anglican may find herself feeling theologically and spiritually closer to a moderate Catholic than to a liberal Anglican. And a conservative Catholic may find himself feeling more at home with a member of the Russian Orthodox or a Pentecostal church than with a liberal Catholic. Cultivating an ecumenical heart and mind that seeks grounds for dialogue and communion with people who may not be of the same church as oneself, accordingly, has become complex not just in mission but in general ecclesial life.

All the more, therefore, it is necessary that in collaboration with other Christians, there is a clear awareness of divergences and avoidance of misunderstanding about them. Clarity is needed in this regard. Collaborating does not mean renouncing one's own or one's church's principles and beliefs. Rather it means coming together, despite divergences, in order to carry out together, as far as possible, the mission of illuminating all humanity with the light of the gospel by both our words and our deeds. True ecumenism, according to John Paul II, must respect doctrinal and theological convictions (see *CT* 32). That said, there are elements common to all Christians that could be called the theological foundation of ecumenical collaboration, particularly in the field of missionary activity. These elements are baptism and faith (see *UR* 3). The Lima statement of the World Council of Churches on baptism, Eucharist, and ministry has the following words in its preface. They are noteworthy for our discussion of collaboration and mutual understanding:

> In leaving behind the hostilities of the past, the churches have begun to discover many promising convergences in their shared convictions and perspectives. These convergences give assurance that despite much diversity in theological expression the churches have much in common in their understanding of the faith. The resultant text aims to become part of a faithful and sufficient reflection of the common Christian Tradition on essential elements of Christian communion. In the process of growing together in mutual trust, the churches must develop these doctrinal convergences step by step, until they are finally able to declare together that they are living in communion with one another in continuity with the apostles and with the teachings of the universal Church.

The first element common to members of different churches and Christian communities is baptism, which unites them to Christ. In other words, baptism celebrated in a Catholic, Protestant, or Orthodox Church is *valid,* and therefore it is recognized by the Catholic Church (see *LG* 15; *UR* 3). Agreement on such principles in the texts of both Vatican II and of the Faith and Order Commission's Lima process means that most Christians recognize baptism celebrated in another church to be, simply, *Christian* baptism, a rite that justifies and unites the baptized person to Christ. Therefore, those baptized in these faiths are Christians in the true sense (our brothers and sisters). This does not, however, mean that all differences are erased. Some Protestants, for instance, believe that only "believer's baptism" is valid, by which they mean baptism sought by an adult or a person who has reached a level of maturity at which he or she can maturely choose to be baptized.

The consequence of Vatican II and the Lima process is that for a wide spectrum of Christians baptism is recognized as the first sacramental bond of communion and, therefore, also the first basis for collaboration between members of the various Christian churches and communities. For this reason, united in baptism, they must act together in everything that is permitted by their baptismal communion. In order to avoid any possible doubts for Catholics, however, the *Directory on Ecumenism* (Flannery 1996, 483-501, 515-32) gives precise and concrete instructions on this matter. These instructions should be read carefully and taken into account, above all by pastors/missionaries when they have to deal with non-Catholics and Christians who wish to enter the church. For Lausanne movement Protestants, however, the theology of baptism has never been defined, because Lausanne Evangelicals and Pentecostals have a variety of ideas about what constitutes valid baptism and whether collaboration with Roman Catholics, Orthodox, and Ecumenical Protestants is to be pursued (Lausanne 1989, no. 9).

The second common element and the basis of ecumenical collaboration is faith in God the Father, in Christ the Son of God and the Savior, and the Holy Spirit—that is, faith in the Blessed Trinity (*LG* 15). This faith cannot but be a strong incentive for members of the various Christian churches to act together, to oppose more effectively the flood of religious indifference or atheism that is spreading more and more in the various levels of modern society. Indeed, active collaboration among all those who have faith, against its powerful enemies, is proof of the authenticity and validity of this faith (see Saraiva Martins 1994, 148).

Finally, Sacred Scripture and acceptance of its preeminent authority in the life of the church is an important common element that unites all Christians. All Christian confessions hold the Bible in a position of honor as a rule of faith and of life. They read it and in it seek contact and union with God as well as enlightenment for their behavior. The degree to which the Bible is understood as the Word of God and how the Bible's authority is explained, however, is a question on which consensus breaks down. Nevertheless, there is clear consensus that diligent reading and constant meditation on this Word, which is the Word of love and unity, should lead Christians to collaborate in making it known to all humanity—and indeed, through it to free all men and women from every form of slavery, beginning from the radical slavery of sin.

Formation in Ecumenism

What we have been discussing means that heralds of the gospel—in particular, pastors and missionaries—must have a sound ecumenical formation on a spiritual and doctrinal level. To a brief unfolding of how seriously the Catholic Church wants this taken we now turn.

Spiritual formation. The Second Vatican Council declares that a sound spiritual formation is needed based on renewal or interior conversion. In regard to relations with other Christians, the council points out that the renewal of the church and of each of her members has an extraordinary ecumenical importance (*UR* 6), since "[i]t is from newness of attitudes of mind, from self-denial and unstinted love, that desires of unity take their rise and develop in a mature way" (*UR* 7). Furthermore, the reason for the movement toward unity is for the renewal of the church, understood as an increase of fidelity to her own calling (see *UR* 6). Therefore, the *Directory on Ecumenism* declares that in ecumenical formation priority should be given to conversion of heart, to spiritual life and its renewal (see Flannery 1996, 70). The *Directory* goes on to say that,

> the ecumenical spiritual life of Catholics should also be nourished from the treasures of the many traditions, past and present, which are alive in other Churches and ecclesial communities; such are the treasures found in the liturgy, monasticism, and mystical tradition of the Christian East; in Anglican worship and piety; in the evangelical prayer and spirituality of Protestants. (Ibid.)

This means that if ecumenical renewal is to be authentic, it must first of all be deeply rooted in the life of the church, in liturgy, and in sacraments. In this way there can be a greater guarantee of her authenticity and depth. Renewal also includes prayer for Christian unity. Furthermore, this renewal will be finalized to fulfill the church's mission in the world.

Doctrinal formation. The ecumenical formation of pastors and missionaries also includes the doctrinal dimension of theological education. First of all, according to *Unitatis Redintegratio* (10), theology must be studied and taught with due regard for the ecumenical point of view. Theology is at the service of the church and her activity and therefore also at the service of her ecumenical activity. For example, they must speak about the church and study her original unity and the fact that they belong to the people of God.

Concretely, the ecumenical approach to theology means understanding it, developing it, teaching it, and studying it not in a controversial manner but with a healthy openness to problems regarding church unity. It also means explaining the truths of the faith "more profoundly and precisely, in such a way and in such terms that our separated brethren can also really understand it." That is, they must show the bond that exists between the various parts of the creed and church unity (*UR* 11; *Directory on Ecumenism*, Flannery 1996, 71-75).

An ecumenical approach to theology brings with it requirements for acquiring a healthy ecumenical mentality in the theological field. First of all, we must take into account the conciliar declaration which states that ecumenical activity "cannot be other than fully and sincerely Catholic, that is, loyal to the truth we have received from the Apostles and the Fathers, and in harmony with the faith which the Catholic Church has always professed" (*UR* 24). Furthermore, the organic order must be respected, that is, the hierarchy in the truths of Catholic doctrine. There must be a clear distinction between the truths of faith and theological doctrines and, consequently, between "the same deposit of faith or truth contained in the doctrine and the way in which they are presented" (*UR* 17). Finally, it is necessary to admit legitimate diversity regarding the way of expressing the truth, legitimacy based on the different methods and ways theologians use to study it (see 17; Saraiva Martins 1994, 153).

Conclusion

Our discourse leads us to conclude that in a program of studies for the prospective missionary, a specific course should be introduced on ecumenism. This sort of study, according to the *Directory on Ecumenism*, should articulate:

- the historical origins, the progressive development, and the present state of the ecumenical movement;

- the doctrinal foundations of ecumenism, with special attention to bonds existing between the various Christian churches or communities;

- the purpose and method of ecumenical activity;

- the relationship between ecumenism and evangelization;

- the various forms of union and collaboration between Catholics and Christians of other confessions;

- knowledge of the life of different Christian communities, theological and doctrinal trends within them, their spirituality, their liturgy, and so forth;

- in-depth study of the various problems related to ecumenism, including specific questions arising from the ecumenical movement on hermeneutics, ministry, divine worship, "inter-communion," tradition, false irenicism (Flannery 1998, 75).

In the same way, in this kind of course, it is important that there be an in-depth discourse on spiritual ecumenism and its many forms; on the relations that exist at present between the Catholic Church and other churches and ecclesial communities and their federations, as well as between the various non-Catholic Christian communities, and finally, on the special importance of the World Council of Churches (WCC) in the ecumenical movement and the present state of relations between the Catholic Church and the above body. Therefore, the tendencies that are at the foundations of the division among churches should not continue to be viewed mainly as controversial issues or obstacles for Christian unity. Rather, they provide the material for deeper dialogue and mutually enriching, in-depth theological reflection and study. A dialogue on the historical background of the basic theological thoughts that were at the base of the division among Christian churches must be encouraged. Past tendencies to look for a way to suppress the historical memory of an aggrieved party or to defend past mistakes and pretend that they do not matter anymore must be abandoned. If there is no sincere effort to arrive at mutual understanding of neuralgic points, experience shows, such mistakes or misdeeds pop up unexpectedly at the least provocation at critical moments, much to the detriment of amicable relations.

All this points to the importance of dialogue and continued theological study of those important trends of thought that marked and have continued to influence the relationship among churches. Dialogue and study of the historical background of the division among Christians will help in identifying commonalities and divergences, where they exist, between those churches, and work for greater understanding and collaboration among them.

9

MISSION AND THE CONTEXTUAL THEOLOGIES

Emergent theological thought in the Third World continues to exert great influence and emotion both within the Third World itself and in the nations of the Northern Hemisphere with their ancient roots in Christian theology. The Christian world today is awash with claims that Latin American (liberation) theology, Asian theology, and African theology represent the future of the church and call into question classical theologies. A first question is, What are we to make of such claims and such theologies? These emergent theological tendencies in the young churches could be described as the missiological reflections of the newly evangelized, but in the case of Latin America, many of the churches producing these theologies are now as many as five hundred years old. Certainly, they represent efforts by the Christians of those regions to interpret the Christian message and to provide models for thought and reflection that have grown from their own context, cultural heritage, and experience as a people with certain ways of living and reflecting on the mystery of the Christian faith. The reflections are also efforts of theologians to relate the Christian message to the sociocultural, political, and economic reality of their regions. Rooted in the common faith in Jesus Christ, his gospel message, and in communion with all the local churches of the universal church-family, with the chair of Peter as the center of communion (in the case of Catholics), they are attempts by theologians to make their own contributions to the development of the common Christian heritage.

There are two main tendencies common in emergent Third World theologies. The first is the emphasis on Christology—the attempt to interpret the mystery of Christ from the perspective of the concrete religiocultural experience of a people. This effort falls within the context of inculturation. The second is the issue of human promotion or liberation—attempts by theologians to relate the gospel message to the sociocultural, political, and economic context of a given people.

This chapter will discuss the trends in Third World theologies from a

Catholic perspective and attempt to explicate their historical significance for mission on a continent-by-continent basis. The aim is to show the significance of dialogue with contextual theologies for the promotion of Christian mission and to present it as a new trend in mission studies.

Historical Background

In 1976 the Ecumenical Association of Third World Theologians (EATWOT) was born in Dar-es-Salaam, Tanzania. It met to promote the sharing of theological reflection among Third World Christian theologians. Dates and themes for the first several conferences are as follows:

- 1976, Dar-es-Salaam, Tanzania—the emergent gospel

- 1977, Accra, Ghana—African theology

- 1979, Colombo, Sri Lanka—Asian theology

- 1980, São Paulo, Brazil—basic Christian communities

- 1981, New Delhi, India—synthesis to review the work done and to begin a cycle of general assemblies, to be celebrated every five years.

After seven years, Third World theologians felt that the time had come to start a dialogue with the "progressive" theologians in Europe and North America. Thus, some forty theologians from the Third World and roughly the same number from Europe and North America gathered in Geneva in 1983 to examine the nature of the differences that separated them and to find a common ground for doing theology in a world divided by cultures, religions, racism, gender, market economy, and the class concept of politics, as well as the new forms of media orientation.

Other EATWOT assemblies followed:

- 1986, Oaxtepec, Mexico—convergences, divergences, and fruitful exchange between Third World theologies

- 1991, Nairobi, Kenya—Third World spirituality: a cry for life

- 1996, Manila, the Philippines—the search for a new just world order: challenges for theology.

Other meetings of groups that took their origins in the EATWOT process occurred after 1996. For instance, from August 24 to August 30, 1997, a meeting devoted to theological reflection for the Indios peoples of Latin America was held in Cochabamba, Bolivia. Its theme was indigenous wisdom as a source of hope. More than two hundred delegates gathered together to continue reflection on this new form of theology, which can be subdivided into two main currents: (1) the more radical *Indio-Indian* theology, which seeks to return to the myths and traditions of the preconquest past, excluding elements introduced in evangelization, which are seen as the ideology of the conquistadors; (2) the more moderate *Indio-Christian* theology, which tries to reformulate the relationship of past and present indigenous elements within the Christian milieu and seeks a synthesis between two seemingly irreconcilable "loves"—that of the indigenous peoples with their original way of life, on the one hand, and the church with its plan of salvation, on the other hand. In the final document of Cochabamba we read: "We must study our own cultures more and more, return without respite to the sources of our wisdom and discover in the lives of our peoples the manifestations of God, Father and Mother, also revealed in Christ."

At the same time, theologians in Asia, above all in India, say they cannot give a decisive answer to the question of adapting basic theological concepts from the Western tradition because the concepts are missing in Asian culture. Thus, according to Dalston Forbes (president of the Sri Lankan Association of Theologians):

> We are immersed in these problems, like in the first Christian centuries, when Christians came up against Greek thought; an understandable expression of the Christian message had to be found according to that culture and those philosophical categories. Gradually, also through debates and errors, orthodox ways of expression emerged. But it took centuries [in the West].

Forbes adds,

> We are the first generation of Indian theologians who have looked at this unknown world of Buddhism and Hinduism. We feel like Christopher Columbus when he discovered America: he thought he had understood everything and he had not understood anything. We are suspected of betraying Jesus and instead we are looking for new ways of conveying the message we have inherited, based on the questions Buddhists ask us. (Cited in Oborji 2001a, 67)

Samuel Rayan, another Indian theologian, declares,

> When we people of the Third World gather together to study theology and to share risky commitments, we are not an exclusive club of professionals and academicians, but brothers and sisters struggling for the liberation of peasants, laborers, the poor, the illiterate, young people without a voice. We try to see that they are with us, that they have an opportunity to express themselves in their own way, and that what

divides become essential ingredients in the theological production. Our method and our conviction require that the gospel should be addressed to the poor and that the oppressed, having been awakened, should be the subject of theology. (Ibid.)

The starting point for African theologians is found in their final message to the Pan-African Conference of Third World Theologians in Accra, Ghana (December 17-23, 1977). The theologians declared:

We believe that African theology must be understood in the context of African life and culture and the creative attempt of African people to shape a new future for themselves . . . from the African situation . . . defining itself according to the struggles of the people in their resistance against the structures of domination. Our task as theologians is to create a theology that arises from and is accountable to African people.

It is on the basis of this that Kofi Appiah-Kubi, one of the organizers of this conference, said:

That the Gospel has come to remain in Africa can not be denied, but now our theological reflections must be addressed to the real contextual African situations. . . . How can we sing the Lord's song in a strange land, in a strange language, in a strange thought, in a strange ideology? (see Psalm 137, 4). For more than a decade now, the cry of the Psalmist has been the cry of many African Christians. We demand to serve the Lord in our own terms. . . . The struggle of African theologians, scholars, and other Christians in ventures such as this consultation is to find a theology that speaks to our people where we are, to enable us to answer the critical question of our Lord Jesus Christ: "Who do you (African Christians) say that I am?" (Appiah-Kubi and Torres 1979, viii)

The tone employed by Appiah-Kubi to describe the main concern that accompanies the theological commitment is common among Third World theologians, as we shall see. It is important to rise above reactions to the tone, which can be hard for many to do, and to see that the concern of the theological endeavor of Third World theologians falls under what is today known as contextual theology. Contextual theology is a form of Christian theology that is necessary today in view of the increasing awareness of the reality of the plurality of religions, cultures, philosophies, different opinions, and sociopolitical systems. In its missiological task of incarnating the Christian faith on every continent, missiology must tackle the discussion of the *Sitz im Leben* ("situation in life," i.e., in "ordinary" experience) of the various places in the light of the religious, sociocultural, political, and economic realities. As a comprehensive book on contextual theology, Stephen Bevans's

Models of Contextual Theology gives a good overview of the phenomenon in general and then gives introductions to six models of these theologies, including an example from both First World and Third World theologians. We cannot go into depth here but will endeavor to present a reliable overview.

Contextual theology deals with two main topics: (1) the role of culture in evangelization (theology of inculturation), catechesis, liturgical development, and dialogue with religions; and (2) the relationship between the gospel and human promotion (and liberation theology, human development, and trans-formational development). In the first case, inculturation and interreligious dialogue, theology must assert the compatibility of a contextual theology with the gospel as expounded and understood in communion with the universal church (see *RM* 52, 54). With regard to the second, discussion of the sociopo-litical and economic reality, the task of an appropriate contextual theology is to identify ways to proclaim the gospel through which the church offers it as a force for liberation that leads to conversion of heart and to culturally appro-priate ways of thinking and acting that are capable of fostering human dignity, development, and a healthy solidarity among peoples (*RM* 59).

In our context (which has its origin in the political and economic language of recent years), the term "Third World" refers to those countries or conti-nents in the Southern Hemisphere and elsewhere (sometimes called the nations of the global South) that do not enjoy the same economic develop-ment and self-determination as do the peoples and nations of Western Europe, North America, Japan, Australia, and New Zealand (a body of nations sometimes referred to as the global North). Thus, the term "Third World" belongs basically to the field of sociopolitical and economic analysis (see Müller 1987, 175). In theological discussions, some prefer the term "Two-Thirds World," which refers to the fact that two-thirds of the world's people live in the global South; but we use the original terminology, because it relates explicitly to the original philosophical insight that the peoples of the Third World are not equal participants in the decision-making and world-shaping functions of the world's geopolitical system, whereas the countries of the North tend to dominate those of the South and to keep them under con-trol not only with colonialism but also with postcolonial forms of exploita-tion. The kind of domination implied in the term indicates that the countries of the South are granted, as it were, a façade of political pseudo-indepen-dence, but in actual fact they are dominated by economic and military pow-ers. The term Third World has supplanted the expression "underdeveloped countries" in the media and specialized writings. To compare and provide shorthand ways of identifying the Third World over against the First and Second Worlds (the former world of Soviet communism and today's Chinese and Korean communist worlds), theologians try to interpret the levels of eco-nomic development between countries in the various zones. The EATWOT group of Third World theologians themselves accepted and popularized the use of this term when they adopted its name for their international association, the Ecumenical Association of Third World Theologians. As it stands today, although it is not a perfect term and its competitors each have certain aspects that commend them, it has no derogatory overtones and is employed here to assist in discussing the concerns of theologians in three large areas of the Christian world to address the challenges presented by the situations in their contexts.

Continental Perspectives

The present chapter does not pretend to treat in detail all the major currents and crosscurrents in the Third World theologies as we know them today. It will also be difficult to cover all the efforts in various countries. Therefore, I shall outline here only the basic tenets of these theologies in Latin America, Asia, and Africa, fully aware that developments in each area deserve a multi-volume treatment. Asian theologians have undertaken the most comprehensive study I am aware of in the attempt to provide a guide to the principal writings in that region. When they did so, their labors were collected in three large volumes (respectively, 726, 734, and 816 pages in length; see England et al., 2002-2004). Yet this entire collection consists only of basic introductions to the various countries, short introductions to the principal authors, and a list of their works. The attempt to do the same for Latin America and Africa would yield a similarly large work.

Latin America

Latin American theology developed from the sociocultural situation of a region in which native cultures and peoples were dealt heavy blows by the Spanish and Portuguese colonial eras and in which the resultant *mestizo* ("hybrid") cultures and nations have not achieved their full economic potential. It is not easy to say anything that is systematically true for the whole of Latin America, because the historical sources are scattered over a large, diverse continent. Moreover, one is dealing with the simultaneous presence of Africans, as well as with the local religious traditions of the aborigines and Iberian Catholics. What has captured center stage in the theological and ecclesial worlds, however, is a developing theology very much concerned with the continent's long experience of foreign economic, political, and cultural domination. The structures of injustice in Latin American society have influenced greatly the pastoral practice and theology of the church in that region. Thus, we shall consider here the Latin American theology of liberation, which is the most outstanding and best-known theological effort there. It is important to realize, however, that in recent years, the rapid increase of

Protestant Evangelicalism and Pentecostalism, on the one hand, and attention to traditional Indian religious elements within Catholicism, on the other, have led to other strains of theology that are of equal interest to missiology. It is no longer possible to say that Latin America is characterized only by a traditional Roman Catholic theological outlook.

Three social factors have been decisive for the development of liberation theology in Latin America (which has gone on to influence socially conscious theology in virtually ever other country in the Third World):

- a situation of domination and oppression

- the emergence of a consciousness of the possibility of liberation

- and the lack of effective political channels to harness collective effort toward a constructive implementation of that consciousness.

The situation of oppression has a long history. The current form is rooted primarily in the structure of European colonialism, which included both the widespread death of millions in epidemics brought by the invaders, and then the evils of slavery, in which black Africans were imported to replace the dead Indians. These structures became operative in Latin America from the beginning of the Spanish-Portuguese colonization and produced a dominant class of whites who controlled huge tracts of land and all mineral resources. The wars of independence and the political situation resulting from them were not capable of breaking with this structure. Then followed the emergence of today's neocapitalist hegemony, which is dominated by British and American imperial institutions and their evolving contemporary forms of exploitation.

Latin American liberation theology emerged out of this context and more particularly from disenchantment with the failed development programs of the 1950s and 1960s, when a vague hope prevailed that the mass poverty of Latin America could be solved by technological solutions and development projects. When these attempts failed, many Latin Americans became convinced that such schemes had only consolidated traditional social structures without coming to grips with the causes of underdevelopment. This in turn led many Christians at the grass roots to seek a radical break with the prevailing system. Moreover, the teaching of Vatican II, Paul VI's encyclical *Populorum Progressio* (1967), and the deliberations of CELAM (Consejo Episcopal Latinomericano, the Conference of Latin American Bishops) at Medellín in 1968 made many Christians wake up to the stark reality of injustice. Many theologians began contrasting the conciliar statements with the unbearable reality of the continent.

From this situation came the birth of Latin American liberation theology. The theology takes the concrete situation in Latin America as its starting point. It sought to do this, however, not in a theoretical way but rather by starting from an analysis of the concrete experience of Christians in their daily lives and in the liberation process. Theology of liberation saw itself articulating their problems, faith experiences, and insights in the light of the reality of the Christian mystery. This reflection takes place not only on a purely academic level but also among the common people in basic, face-to-face communities. The theology produced was concerned with reflection on the praxis of liberation, that is, it saw itself as a reflection on concrete action by the oppressed, both individuals and entire peoples, starting with the specific and practical option for the poor and oppressed. The whole of reality is judged and the Word of God interpreted from this perspective. The reflection attempted to analyze how liberative action had succeeded or not, and then to return both to the Word of God and to experience to correct mistakes and move forward in a continuous circle of experience and action, reflection, prayer, and then another return to action.

For the authors of liberation, theology is a reflection on the activity of the church in an arena larger than its sacramental system and the work of priests and bishops. Its goal is to discern the presence of the Holy Spirit leading the people to the kind of liberation spoken of in Luke 4:18-19:

> The Spirit of the Lord is upon me,
>   because he has anointed me
>   to bring good news to the poor.
> He has sent me to proclaim release to the captives
>   and recovery of sight to the blind,
>   to let the oppressed go free,
>   to proclaim the year of the Lord's favor.

Theology, according to those espousing liberation thought, should be concerned not only with the life of the church but also should seek to draw inspiration from the problems of the world and history. The memory of Pope John XXIII and the Vatican II document on the relationship of the church with the modern world, *Gaudium et Spes,* as applied to the Latin American context by CELAM at Medellín, were its inspiration. Only in so doing, they taught, could theology really express God's word in a new way for our own time. In other words, liberation is the core concept of a theology that understood human history as a process of liberating humanity in a biblical sense and refused any dualistic hermeneutics that walled off the spiritual and sociopolitical dimensions of life in hermetically sealed worlds. Through this process a new society with a new humanity gradually would develop. Liberation theology attempted to induce a principle of permanent cultural revolution into history, the goal of which is a world "where every person, no matter what race, religion or nationality, can live a fully human life, freed from servitude imposed by others or by natural forces over which humanity has not sufficient control" (*PP* 47). As the missiologist Heribert Bettscheider puts it, three levels of meaning are to be distinguished in the concept of liberation:

- Liberation refers to the aspirations of oppressed social classes and peoples. Their oppression is the result of conflicts that cannot be solved by a process of development. This is possible only through radical liberation.

- On a deeper level, liberation means a process in which humanity takes its fate into its own hands. It is a dynamic process in which men and women gradually develop all their dimensions to find themselves in the end new persons in a qualitatively different society.

- Finally, the process of liberation has a theological aspect. The Bible describes Christ as Savior and liberator. He frees humanity from sin, the ultimate cause of any rupture of friendship, of injustice, and of oppression. Christ truly liberates—that is, he makes possible a life of community with him which is the foundation of true community (1997, 273).

The three processes, Bettscheider notes, do not run along parallel lines. Instead, they are mutually inclusive and find their full foundation in the gospel message of a liberation that pertains to realizing the relationship between progress within the temporal sphere and the eschatological reign of God. The liberation of humanity and the growth of the reign of God are both oriented to the perfect community of human beings with God and with one another.

Leading authors of the Latin American liberation theology include Helder Camara, Leonardo Boff, Clodovis Boff, Juan Luis Segundo, Elsa Tamez, Juan Sobrino, José Miguez Bonino, Segundo Galilea, and Gustavo Gutiérrez. Gutiérrez's book *Theology of Liberation* (published in Spanish in 1971) is the fundamental text for liberation theology. He has as his context the poor of Lima, Peru, his native city. Gutiérrez always insisted that theology was the "second step," reflection arising out of pastoral activity. Theology becomes a critical reflection on Christian praxis. The aim of praxis must be to emancipate and to create a new humanity (Gutiérrez 1988, 11-13). Gutiérrez, like many other liberation theologians, advanced a teaching that emphasized the social dimension of sin, which, according to him, is more than the sum of individual wrongful acts. Thus the redemption from sin won by Christ must be more than the redemption of individual souls. It must also redeem, that is to say "transform," the social realities of human life. In concert with other theologians, Gutiérrez speaks of the full measure of redemption that must await the second coming of Christ, but quickly adds that redemption, as Paul teaches, is in some sense already present. It is the responsibility of Christians to work to extend that redemption in space and time, and thus the effort to undo social sin is a constitutive part of what it means to be a Christian (ibid., 74). It is from this perspective that Gutiérrez concludes that the church with its theology should be part of this effort of liberation. In this way, according to him, the church will be able to make its specific contribution of integral liberation (sociopolitical, anthropological, and soteriological-theological), having as its lasting criteria the judgment of the Word of God and the living tradition of the faith—hence, the concrete realization of her mission in anticipation of the values of the eschatological reign of God (ibid., 160ff.).

Gutiérrez and other liberation theologians have given the church and the world new perspectives on the Christian understanding of liberation, especially by insisting that sociopolitical, anthropological, and soteriological readings of the term "liberation" belong together because they offer diverse epistemological sources and a corresponding hermeneutical analysis, which results in epistemological autonomy at each level. Moreover, they show the faith character of such interpretation and how it all leads to salvation in Christ. Still, liberation theology has been criticized for attempting to develop a unique hermeneutical analysis of the process of salvation-liberation, through a kind of philosophy and ideology that systematize both the method and the criteria of the research. In their understanding of orthopraxis (i.e., correct action), liberation theologians are said by critics to put too much emphasis on social action for this-worldly human liberation, thereby marginalizing the specifically eschatological dimension of the Christian mission. Liberation theologians have not succeeded in convincing their critics that they have shown how to achieve the proper balance between orthodoxy and orthopraxis, and here lies the heart of the criticism against the theology of liberation.

The Congregation for the Doctrine of the Faith issued two documents on the theology of liberation. The first document, entitled *Libertatis Nuntius* (Instruction on Certain Aspects of the Theology of Liberation), was issued on August 6, 1984. On March 22, 1986, the congregation issued another document, entitled *Instruction on Christian Freedom and Liberation*. This second document augmented some conclusions not deeply touched upon in the first one. In it, the theme of liberation is situated in the context of the history of freedom since the beginning of modern times and gives a description of the situation of freedom in the world. Progress in the realization of freedom is described, but the ambiguities of modern liberation processes are also pointed out. The document also notes that the liberating mission of the church aims at the comprehensive salvation of humanity and the world. The power of the gospel penetrates into human history; it purifies and vivifies it. At this point the document emphasizes in a special way the love that creates an option for the poor. It also emphasizes that structural changes in society are absolutely necessary. In general, however, it insists that, in the distinction between doctrine and action, doctrine must come first, because it is right teaching that is the Christian criterion for determining which actions are right or wrong. Thus, priority should be given to the faith as the source and as that which inspires the right action of the Christian.

Asia

To speak of "Asian theology" is probably even more difficult than to speak of Latin American theology, since we are dealing with an enormous continent. Asia is the birthplace of the great world religions—Hinduism, Buddhism, Confucianism, Islam, and, although it is often forgotten, Judaism and Christianity. Christians constitute only a small minority of Asians, except in the Philippines, the only country in Asia with a Christian majority. The characteristic feature of Asian Christian theology is the emphasis on interreligious dialogue. Thus, a significant theological effort in Asia is centered on formulating Christological doctrines. Indeed, most of the significant nontraditional Christological experiments being worked out today are emerging in South Asia, that is, in India and Sri Lanka, and in the Philippines. We shall make a brief presentation of Indian theology, Korean theology, and Japanese theology.

Indian theology. The aspect of Indian theology we shall consider here is *cosmic (Logos) Christology*, which has found its chief exponent in Raimon Panikkar. Faced with the universal orientation of religions (especially explicit in both Hinduism, where all religions are seen as fundamentally equal, and in Christianity, where Christ is the mystery of God for the whole world), Panikkar inquires about the possibility of a Hindu-Christian dialogue. Since only God and not the individual understanding of God can be the meeting place in God, who is present in the concrete history of humanity under different names, the basic assumption for Panikkar is that Logos—the nameless, the absolute, the transcendent—is infinite. The infinite can manifest itself in infinite ways. Creation, the cosmos, is a manifestation of the Logos. Humans are manifestations of the infinite Logos. According to Panikkar, wherever *humanitas* reaches its perfection, we have a perfect manifestation of the Logos. Jesus of Nazareth is a perfect manifestation of the Logos, for in him *humanitas* has reached its perfection (see Panikkar 1968, 122; Parappally 1995, 137-60).

The foundation of Panikkar's Christology is his concept of *cosmotheandric experience* and the new religious consciousness that emerges from such experience. Cosmotheandric experience is based on Panikkar's conviction that ultimate reality is both one and many. The many are one and the one is many because there is a real interpenetration of the cosmic, the divine, and the human as distinct but real dimensions of the whole (see Panikkar 1993, 65ff.). For Panikkar, God (*theos*) and humanity (*anthrōpos*) and cosmos (*cos-*

mos) are constitutive dimensions of the one reality. The world is really part of the "Whole." Such a concept enables God, the Logos, to manifest itself in all things and in every person. Panikkar is fond of quoting the Vulgate translation of Wisdom 1:7: "For the Spirit of the Lord fills the world, and is all embracing, and knows what man says." Every human being, then, has the potential to become both a Christophany (a manifestation of the Christ-principle) and a theophany (a manifestation of the divine; see Panikkar 1968, 138).

The more sociopolitical perspective of Stanley Samartha and M. M. Thomas is different from this approach. The context of Christology is not Hinduism, as a religious experience of the mysterious divine, but the concrete Indian situation at the present time confronted as a religious, social, and political task for both Christianity and Hinduism. Theologians such as D. S. Amalorpavadass, G. M. Soares-Prabhu, and Michael Amaladoss, among others, see the changing Indian society and Hinduism, mainly in its Advaita-Vedanta form, as promising contexts for articulating a more adequate Christology. Drawing on the liberation theology of Latin America in recent years, theologians such as M. M. Thomas, Samuel Rayan, J. Desrochers, and S. Kappen have increasingly elaborated a Christological basis for a holistic liberation of the poor and marginalized (against the caste Hinduism) of Indian society. In this connection, a "Jesuan theology" that emphasizes the solidarity and sympathy of Jesus with the oppressed stands in the foreground. Similar approaches to a cosmic Christology can be found in Sri Lanka in the context of Buddhism (see Klaes 1997, 61-63).

Korean theology. Korean theology (often called "Minjung" theology after its best-known strand) arose in the 1970s in the context of the political oppression of the Korean people and the struggle for survival of Korean church groups. Through it, an attempt is made—especially by participating in the suffering of the people—to discover the essential identity of the Korean people and culture (including, e.g., the importance of shamanism and the strong influence of Confucianism) and to make the suffering of the Korean people theologically fruitful. There has not yet appeared a comprehensive Korean Christology, but several theologians have developed some historical sketches. For instance, Byung-Mu Ahn discusses how the enslaved and deprived people (as subjects of their own destiny) could realize their theological importance and achieve their Christic identity through a collective-corporative interpretation of the passion of Jesus. Jesus' unconditional acceptance of the people (*ochlos*, not *laos*) is fundamental. The death of Jesus is not *for* the people but is *participation* in the destiny of the people. And the way Jesus endured his suffering and death is recognized as an act of God overcoming hatred and violence. Because of Jesus' resurrection, his disciples are urged to go "outside the camp" (Heb 13:13ff.) to encounter oppressed people and to set forth on an exodus from every form of domination and oppression. In the course of history, the church of Christ must fight, hope, and suffer for liberation until the fulfillment of the messianic reign (see Ahn 1985, 49-58).

The fact that Korea is the site of a rapidly increasing Christian population means that it will have both the well-trained personnel and the critical mass for theological and missiological production that could make it the scene of important Asian Christian reflection. Not to be ignored either is the fact that Korea is now, after the United States, the source of the largest cadre of missionaries (chiefly Protestant) serving outside their own homeland.

Japanese theology. In Japan, Christological studies form part of the effort toward the indigenization of the Christian churches. Theologians make use of the underlying Shinto, Confucian, and Buddhist concepts and consciousness to open up, for Japan and the whole world, a new approach to the message of Christ. Ultimately, this message is always one about the experience of the *im*-mediateness of God to people and among people. This attempt is found in K. Kitamori's work, which draws on Buddhist ideas and the attitudes of the samurai. It reveals itself as "the pain of God," in which the love of God overcomes divine anger because of human opposition. Christ's cross reveals that the all-determining love of God is always suffering love and pain, stemming from the hopeless pain of the world (see Kitamori 1965). Shushaku Endo (born 1927), in his work *Silence,* is concerned with the immeasurability of the compassionate love of Jesus. Endo emphasizes the motherly love of God, the compassionate Christ (not the Christ who liberates from suffering), and a Christ-experience that can be fully understood only by drawing on Zen Buddhist experience and the teaching of *satori.*

Japanese Christologies are influenced to a large extent by Buddhist ideas. The key issue is the experience of the self-emptying of the redeeming God in Christ so that men and women really become fully human. Kosuke Koyama speaks of the risen Christ who died on the cross with "no handle" and who "did not handle us." K. Takizawa emphasizes the enlightening experience of Immanuel, the God who from eternity is a fundamental fact of existence, a "God for humanity" who is intimately *with* each creature of this creation and whose call Jesus has answered in a perfect way by losing his life, thus becoming the standard for all human answers. Naturally, the Christological impulses in economically successful Japan have not arisen out of the experience of the social and economic oppression of the people. Rather, the question of poverty and suffering has been dealt with within the context of self-emptying (see Klaes 1997, 63).

Africa

An overview. African Christian theology reflects on the gospel, Christian tradition, and the total African reality in an African manner and from the perspectives of the African worldview. The African reality in question includes the changing African society. Some prefer to speak of theologies, because they see much diversity in African culture and religion. Others stress a fundamental similarity in religious experience and in the nature of the emergent issues. Discussion of African theology is first and foremost reflection on the scene in sub-Saharan Africa, leaving aside the ages-old Coptic traditions in Egypt and Ethiopia. The principal trends of African theology include both inculturation and liberation (each with its own currents and crosscurrents). The theology of inculturation in this context refers to the discussion on the encounter of the gospel with the African cultures. The theology focuses on the role of cultures in evangelization and reflects on ways of deepening Christian faith in Africa. The theology of liberation in Africa is distinguished by three main currents:

- African liberation theology as developed in the independent part of Africa

- African women's liberation theology, developed along the path of injustices that women undergo both in traditional and modern African society

- South African liberation theology, developed in protest against racist ideology and white privilege; it focuses on poverty, social challenges, and structures for political and economic stability, and on the self-reliance of African churches and society. African liberation theology reflects also on oppressive cultural elements of both traditional and modern Africa, and on issues of discrimination, race, and color.

African theologians spontaneously seek a more universal Christian theology that will connect them and their people with the whole of humanity and the history of salvation. Thus, in the writings of African Christian theologians, one sees the effort to link the African ancestral worldview with the self-revelation of God in Jesus Christ. This is done by reflecting on Christian faith and exploring the universal dimensions of the African ancestral heritage, including its origins in the one supreme God. Africans in the diaspora, who for circumstances of history were uprooted from their ancestral heritage, also seek a world that is founded in the universal dimension of the kingdom of God. In whichever case, African theologians began to realize the strength that Africans could draw from their ancestral history and wanted to construct a theology that would bridge the gap between their colonial past and their new-found faith in Christianity.

This, in a nutshell, is the background for our understanding of the kind of language that has characterized the development of theological reflection in contemporary Africa. The origin of this theological effort on the continent has been traced back to the publication in 1956 of *Des Prêtres noirs s'interrogent* ("black priests question themselves"), in which a group of young African theologians raised questions about how theology was being done in Africa and whether or not things could be different in ways that would theologize in a more genuinely African way and by dealing with topics important to Africans. Since the time that first call was made to develop a genuinely African Christian theology to our own day, many volumes have been written and conferences and symposia held on a regular basis. Today we have the Pan-African Conference of Third World Theologians, and a number of research centers and universities have been founded with the specific aim of promoting studies and research on African theology. In addition, there are regional, national, and local associations of African theologians. But, in general, African authors operate within the broad scope of the nature of the meeting of the gospel message with African culture and reality.

A close look at the works of African authors reveals a theological language that puts a heavy accent on culture and the common origin of the human family. This accent and consciousness that emphasize the positive value of African culture and context as well as the universal brotherhood of the human family were first noticed in the early attempts by some authors to articulate African philosophy. Hence, in speaking of African theology, we are also dealing with the intrinsic connection between philosophy and theology in the development of that theology itself. In other words, a philosophical approach dominated the early attempts of African authors to articulate in writing the cultural and religious heritage of Africans in the light of the Christian faith and their experience as a people. In this regard, the leading voices came first from Francophone African countries (and later from the Anglophone and Portuguese-speaking countries of the continent as well as from Africans in the diaspora). The primary focus of these investigations in African Traditional Religion, culture, and customs was to articulate the latent African ontology, that is, its conception of "ultimate reality," and its relation to everyday human life and history. This springs from the question, How do we bring the African world view and traditional religion into contact with the liberty and historicity of the self-communication of God in Jesus? In these studies, African authors discovered that the Africans' preoccupation with life and security provides the ingredients for our understanding of African ontology, including the existence of divine beings, in particular of God as the supreme being who is the ultimate reality above all history and the root of the African religious formulation of the basis of life. The value that Africans attach to life, its prolongation and security, is the basis for our understanding of African ontology. In fact, all efforts in African Traditional Religion are geared toward the protection and guarantee of life and its maintenance. Thus, from this standpoint, authors began to study concepts of life among various people and to demonstrate the intuition that *life* stands out for Africans as the value around which all other values find their meaning.

The search and project for life that is meaningful, its continuity and dynamic progress toward fullness and realization (ancestral status, divinization), are fundamental for understanding an African person's perception of ontology and ultimate meaning (Uzukwu 1983, 9).

Therefore, while African theology acknowledges the challenge posed to missiology today by the radical relativism of some strands in the theology of religions—the predominant concern of Asian theologians, the dialogue with postmodernity, and West and East dialogue—for African authors, the basic issue is dialogue with cultures. African theologians insist that dialogue with cultures is linked to the question of creating a new cultural identity for Africans. This task is essential to deepening the faith of African Christians and promoting the work of evangelization on the continent. Africa today is under tension between a past scorned by many and a present that seems to have few prospects for a fully human future. In fact, it has not been easy for many African theologians to distinguish the present African reality from the historical uneasiness that has over the years characterized the relationship between the people of Africa and others. Theologians want to show the strength Africans can draw from knowledge of their ancestral history as a resource for creating a new cultural identity; and so the challenge, as seen by African authors, is to explore how African cultures, having come into contact with Christian and Western patterns of thought, can emphasize those things that unite the peoples of various races, cultures, and religions. How will this contact and facts of our common origin in God and faith in Jesus Christ encourage and enable people from every tradition to learn from the other and by so doing foster a more humane understanding of how to see ourselves, one another, and the world at large (Brown 2004: 3)? This is the spirit that has continued to permeate the development of theological reflection in contemporary Africa.

This approach has given African theology a language of evangelization interpreted in terms of inculturation and human promotion (or liberation). The two trends are not contradictory but rather complement each other. In fact, they represent two sides of the same process of making Christianity a truly African religion. So, nowadays, African theologians present a more unitary perception of inculturation and human promotion. This perception has produced a new term or language in African theology, namely, the theology of reconstruction. For all this, developing strands of African theology have a great catechetical value. The two areas where this is most evident are in the Christological and ecclesiological perspectives of African authors, to which we now turn.

African Christology. It is a credit to the fertility of contemporary African theologians that Christology is perhaps the aspect of theology that has received their greatest attention. For the decisive factor in every Christian life is the response to the question of Christ: "Who do you (African Christians) say that I am (Matt 16:15)?" (Appiah-Kubi 1979, viii). It is a well-known fact that Christology is the most fundamental aspect of Christian theology. Therefore, it behooves every church to make explicit its response to this question in a true and contextual manner. Without a proper understanding of Christ, his nature, his meaning, and his message, Christianity itself becomes inauthentic (Oguejiofor 1996, 18-19). Thus, many Christological models have recently sprung up from the pens of African theologians. Christ has been designated as the liberator, the ancestor, the first-born son, the master of initiation, the healer, the African king, the African chief, mediator, savior, redeemer with power, and so forth (see Schreiter 1991). All these are concepts and images very familiar to most African people, and they serve to illustrate the figure of Jesus Christ. African Christologies based on such specifically African concepts may be called "illustrative Christologies" (Karotemprel 2001, 19); some have called it "narrative theology" (Healey and Sybertz 1996). Such Christologies have the merit of being sufficiently inculturated in African culture. They also serve a catechetical purpose because people can readily relate to the images of Jesus Christ proposed by African Christologies.

Of these, the model of Christ as ancestor has received a lot of attention, especially in East and Central Africa. For some, it is, among other designations, the most distinctively African and the most profound. So much so, that the "notion of the ancestor is so deeply embedded in African religious consciousness that the idea of Christ as ancestor seems to have arisen independently in the minds of different theologians in different parts of the continent" (Moloney 1987, 509).

Championed by such theologians as Bénézet Bujo (from Congo), and Charles Nyamiti (from Tanzania), it is a motif that fits easily in most of Africa. Nyamiti's work, *Christ as Our Ancestor*, is perhaps the most elaborate presentation of the new Christology. Nyamiti examines the African's ancestral belief and concludes that there are basic similarities and differences between it and Christ's ancestorship. According to him, the five characteristics valid for both are natural relationship, supernatural status, mediation, being a model of behavior, and having title to regular, sacred communion (1984, 15-17). But the essential differences are not fewer in number. Nyamiti recognizes that Christ's relationship to humanity transcends family, clan, or racial boundaries; Christ is God-man and Son of God; he is a perfect model of behavior, and has, being God, a supernatural model of communication. Still there is a basic sameness in structure but with a difference in level and mode. Nyamiti thus defines "brother-ancestor" as a relative of a person with whom he has a common parent and of whom he is mediator to God and archetype of behavior; and with the brother-ancestor, thanks to his supernatural status acquired through death, a person is entitled to have regular, sacred communion. Because of Christ's relationship in the Trinity and his relationship with humanity, his ancestorship is divine-immanent, and, at the same time, he exercises the roles of mediator, prophet, king, and priest. Hence, for Nyamiti, the traditional titles of Christ are incorporated in his ancestorship.

With a slightly different nuance and in what looks like a more acceptable approach, Bénézet Bujo attributes to Christ the title of "Ancestor par excellence," that is, "Proto-Ancestor," in whom the whole life of the African Christian can be rooted (Bujo 1992, 77). To arrive at this title Bujo does not place Christ the ancestor at the level of biological lineage (as Nyamiti did), as if Christ is an ordinary human ancestor, that is, at the level of consanguinity. Rather, Christ the ancestor is of the transcendental level. Christ is the "Ancestor par excellence"; the "Proto-Ancestor"; that is, he is the "Unique Ancestor," who is the source of life and the highest model of all ancestorship. Bujo proposes a Christological-eucharistic ecclesiology, oriented toward the African concept of life. He examines the significance of Jesus as life giver, a central theme in the New Testament, especially in Pauline theology. Paul draws a parallel between the first and second Adam (see 1 Cor 15:45ff.; Rom 5:12ff.) and speaks of Christ as the first-born from the death, as the head of the body, the church (Col 15:20). In him resides the fullness of God, who has chosen to use him to reconcile all things (Col 1:19-20; Bujo 1992, 93). In the Gospel of John, Jesus is presented as one who has come so that his followers may have life and have it in abundance (John 10:10). He gives his life for the sheep (John 10:11-15). Jesus is the true vine, and we can only bear fruit when we remain attached to him (John 15:1-6). Even more, Jesus is the resurrection, and the one who lives in him and believes in him will never die (John 11:25-26). The exalted Jesus is the means through which God imparts his divine life to the world; he is, as it were, the bread of life, the source of eternal life (John 6:32-58), and therefore, the proto-life source.

In such examples of African theology, Christ is the life-giving ancestor who presides over the new family of God, the new extended universal family. The same Jesus Christ can be considered as the Great Healer, the Liberator, and the Great Master of Initiation. Throughout Africa there are processes of initiation that are viewed as rites of passage for every stage of human existence, but especially at the passage from adolescence to adulthood. Christ was initiated in the customs of his Jewish people. He was also initiated into God's plan, which was the route to his perfection through obedience in his death and resurrection. Christ's initiation into a new existence is the raison d'être of our being initiated into a new existence, and he himself leads us into the fullness of life. Thus, he comes to be the master of initiation, the elder brother in his father's foyer, initiating others into the same household (Sanon 1991, 85-102). Christ is also designated as the African king, who like traditional African potentates is very much concerned with the spiritual and physical well-being of the people. The African kings fulfilled significant sacramental roles for their communities, and through their annual festivals maintained harmony between their societies and their Ultimate Reality. Through an equally detailed examination of Christ's designation as king in the Scriptures, the visions and the conceptions of African kingship cultures can enrich the same concept in the New Testament, at least for the African mind (Manus 1993).

In the view of these theologians, it is meaningful for the African to speak of Jesus as Ancestor par excellence, because in him are fulfilled all the qualities and virtues that the Africans ascribe to their ancestors. In other words, the historical Jesus fulfills the highest ideals ascribed to the ancestors in African thought—he heals, he cures, he raises the dead, and so on. In short, he imparts the life force in all its fullness. This love and power he bequeaths, after death, to his disciples. It is precisely in his death and resurrection, with its soteriological meaning, that Jesus transcends the ancestors. This is Christology from below and provides a point of departure for a Christology in the African context (Bujo 1992, 80). Consequently, African theologians describe the church as the focal point from which the life of the proto-ancestor flows and spreads to all humanity. Thus, they see the Eucharist as the "ancestral meal" instituted by the proto-ancestor and as that which should stand at the heart of African ecclesiology. The Eucharist is not simply an object of contemplation. Rather, it is the very life of the church and the source of its growth, life that is not merely biological but mystical and spiritual. The purpose of the Eucharist (as with some African death-life rituals) is to impart life in all its fullness for the welfare of the whole community. This life is the Spirit. For African theologians, the ancestral model is Trinitarian, in that the Father, Son, and Spirit are the source, imparter, and substance, respectively, of the divine life in the community (Bujo 1992, 95; Nyamiti 1984, 64-65). An ecclesiology based on such an ancestral model presents a number of challenges to the life of the church. For in traditional African society, each member is expected to make his or her contribution to the vital force of the whole community. The meeting point of Christianity and ATR can be found in this concept of communitarian life, sharing, and relationality (Oborji 1998, 106).

Critics raise basic questions about the relevance of ancestral Christology theologically and socioculturally. Theologically, can the ancestor Christological paradigm really serve to reveal the whole person of Jesus Christ? How do we exploit this concept to capture all the richness of traditional Christology within the context of the theology of the Trinity? How about non-African Christian believers in Jesus Christ? It is not clear how the life of Christ is imparted to these biological ancestors, whether it is on the basis of common grace (as Nyamiti seems to say) or by a kind of universalism derived from the efficacy of the resurrection, as Bujo argues. If Christ is the mystical and spiritual brother-ancestor, how can he be related to biological ancestors who are not strictly within the community bound together by faith? Socioculturally, if this ancestor model is to be valid today, how long will it have relevance in Africa, given the momentum of the process of modernization, urbanization, and universal education? As a result, the ancestor paradigm may have to be reexamined and evaluated by future African theologians.

With ancestor Christology, African theologians want to demonstrate the meeting point for Christianity and ATR. Though their works are still tentative and have not been devoid of some criticisms, they offer us suggestions on how to relate ATR to the Christian mystery. For instance, Charles Nyamiti, as we noted, already applies the human ancestral relationship analogically to the inner life of God (Trinity) to show that there is a kind of ancestral kinship among the divine persons. He affirms that from an African perspective, Christ could be called our brother-ancestor because through him and in the divine Spirit, we have been reconciled with God and made partakers of the Trinitarian life. This has consequences for Christians who are now invited to live a life of sharing and communion in the pattern of the Trinitarian life (Nyamiti 1984, 61).

Thus, despite some flaws, one may find that in the ancestor Christology the concept of proto-ancestor is a promising attempt to interpret Jesus Christ, his salvific functions, and his relationship to the church and humanity in an African context (Karotemprel 2001, 19). Again, in spite of the theological problem inherent in using such a model to present a Christian mystery, one cannot deny the usefulness and relevance of inculturating Christology in the cultures of Africa. Nor should it be forgotten that *all* theological language is metaphorical and that no single image or metaphor can encapsulate the entire mystery of Christ. Taken together, a number of metaphors, images, and symbols create a total semantic field. It is in the totality of such devices that humans begin to grasp the mystery by which they are being saved. In addition, there is immense catechetical value in the whole attempt at presenting Jesus Christ in terms perceptible to Africans. As Christopher Mwoleka argues, the relationality in community life emphasized in African culture and traditional religion is already a providential, well-prepared ground for an African inculturation of the mystery of the Holy Trinity and church communion (Mwoleka 1976, 151). This is why dialogue with African culture and traditional religion is very important for the inculturation of Christianity in Africa.

African ecclesiology. At the 1994 synod of bishops, Special Assembly for Africa, the language of African theology contributed a formulation for consideration as a possible African image of the church: the church as family of God. This image of the church as family of God found great favor among African bishops at that synod for Africa. In evaluating the model of the church as family, the bishops appreciated the important role of African theologians in promoting the work of evangelization on the continent and addressed them as follows:

> African theologians: Your mission is a great and noble one in the service of inculturation. You have already begun to propose an African

reading of the mystery of Christ. The concepts of Church-as-Family, Church-as-Brotherhood, are fruits of your work in contact with the Christian experience of the People of God in Africa. The Synod knows that without the conscientious and devoted exercise of your function something essential will be lacking. (Synod of Bishops, Special Assembly for Africa, *Message 56*)

And in evaluating this image of the church as family, the bishops viewed it as a new model for evangelization and church formation. In the final message of the synod we read:

Churches of Africa, People of God in assembly throughout the world, it is primarily to you that we proclaim Jesus Christ (see I Corinthians 1:23). . . . The Synod has highlighted that you are the family of God. It is for the Church-as-Family that the Father has taken the initiative in the creation of Adam. It is the Church-as-Family which Christ, the New Adam and Heir to the nations, founded by the gift of his body and blood. It is the Church-as-Family which manifests to the world the Spirit which the Son sent from the Father so that there should be communion among all. (Synod of Bishops, Special Assembly for Africa, *Message* 24)

The bishops adopted this model for use in the work of evangelization on the continent today because of its anthropological basis in the African context. Highlighting the universal dimension of African ancestral heritage in relation to the history of salvation, the synod message says:

Jesus Christ, the only-begotten and beloved Son, has come to save every people and every individual human being. He has come to meet each person in the cultural path inherited from the ancestors. He travels with each person to throw light on his traditions and customs and to reveal to him that these are a pre-figuration, distant but certain, of Him, the New Adam, the Elder of a multitude of brothers and sisters which we are. (Ibid.)

In the postsynodal exhortation *Ecclesia in Africa*, John Paul II once again highlighted this path of African theology. He exhorts African Christians in the following words: "Today I urge you to look inside yourselves. Look to the riches of your own traditions, look to the faith which we are celebrating in this assembly. Here you will find genuine freedom—here you will find Christ, who will lead you to the truth" (*Ecclesia in Africa* 1995, 48).

These documents emphasize one thing in common, namely, the common origin that all humanity shares and the role of African traditional religion and culture in leading Africans to the self-revelation of God in Jesus Christ. African traditional religion, which has now found its fulfillment in Christianity, becomes, then, a kind of Old Testament for the African Christian. This is the fact that African authors have been trying to demonstrate in their writings since the emergence of theological reflection in contemporary Africa.

It should be noted that the core message of the African image of the church as family of God is not for the glorification of the African cultural and religious elements. As in every other human culture, there are many elements in African cultures that may not be compatible with the gospel message. So, they need purification and redemption (*RM* 54). Nor do we need to imagine that the church-as-family model simply adds an African nuance to the pastoral method of small Christian communities, as Fuellenbach seems very close to arguing (2002, 188). Rather, African ecclesiology developed in the context of proclamation and evangelization, with its inspiration generally from St. Paul, the great missionary. The inspiration is specifically from Paul's Letter to the Ephesians on reconciliation of Jews and pagans with each other and with God (Eph 2:11-22). Church as family received a very positive reception among Africans, doubtless because of its anthropological basis and the value Africans put on the extended family, bound together by ancestral blood and community life. But it is also possible to interpret church as family as an African accentuation of the communitarian dimension of family as an authentically African reading of the Vatican II concept of the church as communion or as the people of God (*LG* 4). This element from the cultural heritage of Africans, which has been uplifted and given a new meaning, is best seen as a way to promote genuine ecclesial communion in the universal church-family and an authentic brotherhood among nations.

In the first place, the African image of the church as family wants to point out the devastating effect on the human family of new forms of racism, ethnic exclusivism, and hidden violence of all forms of oppression, which, according to the African bishops, are caused by "envy, jealousy and the deceit of the devil." These, they say, continue to burden the human family:

> They have led to war, to the division of the human race into first, second, third and fourth worlds, to placing more value on wealth than on the life of a brother, to the provocation of interminable conflicts and wars for the purpose of gaining and maintaining power and for self-enrichment through the death of a brother. (Synod of Bishops, Special Assembly for Africa, *Message* 25)

This is not the end of the road, however. While attention has been drawn to the complexity of these problems, the reality is that there is a new offer of hope in Jesus Christ. So, the *Message* adds:

> But Christ has come to restore the world to unity, a single human family in the image of the Trinitarian Family. We are the Family of God: this is the Good News! The same blood flows in our veins, and it is the

blood of Jesus Christ. The same Spirit gives us life, and it is the Holy Spirit, the infinite fruitfulness of divine love. (Ibid.)

In other words, the church-family model intends to promote a healthy relationship between Africans themselves and people of other races, just as it presented some trajectories for strengthening and deepening the relationships among Africans of different ethnic or religious groups living in the same community and nation (Oborji 2003c, 158).

African theology seeks ways of achieving harmony, peace, and understanding among people of different ethnic groups in African societies and between the Africans themselves and peoples of other races. It also highlights the importance of helping us all to embrace the fact that we are all children of one God and therefore should accept one another as brother or sister. Furthermore, as an ecclesiology, it touches on the issues of the recognition of signs of growth or development into maturity found in the African churches and society. Consequently, considering all the factors, the African bishops and theologians, following the orientation given by Vatican II, wish that communion in the church should be interpreted dynamically as unity in diversity, so that their churches can inculturate the gospel in their cultures and develop new forms of Christian living, worship, and thought that are relevant to their people and at the same time in communion with the long tradition and theological expressions of the universal church-family. In so doing, the African local churches will be enabled not only to remain faithful to the common faith in the work of inculturation but also to communicate to the churches outside Africa—indeed, to the whole church—their experiences of God's grace operating in their particular sociocultural contexts.

Therefore, African theology in its ecclesiological formulation is saying that, just as Christianity has become the religion of so many millions of Africans, African cultural values must be respected and taken seriously. And it is wrong to continue to regard Africa as an appendage or as a junior member of the human race. There is no portion of humanity that is not part of the world and full participant and beneficiary of God's offer of salvation in Jesus Christ.

Conclusion

In nearly all theological works emanating in the Third World, traditional Western theologies are attacked, at least indirectly. The basis of such an attack is the realization that local socioeconomic forms of exploitation are inseparably linked to Western hegemony and economic power. This tendency is also seen in the way Western theology has falsely universalized its Christology. In the last two decades, however, Western theology has become increasingly conscious that its theology, too, is contextual, not universal, and has produced a number of important Christological studies in line with this realization. Thus, as is evident in the work of Robert J. Schreiter, First and Third World theologians are now engaged in a fruitful and mutually critical dialogue (see Schreiter 1989, 13ff.).

Therefore, the emergence of theological reflection in the Third World today should not create anxiety. In an age of globalization and interculturation, it is necessary to encourage an exchange of opinions and information among local churches, on theological and pastoral levels. This is why the theological works of Third World authors should not be ignored. If we want to follow the principle of listening, which is proposed by many contemporary authors, we must expose tendencies to despise and devalue what is produced by the people of the Third World countries. In a similar vein, the principle of dialogue should encourage Third World theologians to avoid concentrating only on their own regions and ignoring every theological category that does not originate in their own sociocultural situation. Any prejudice is counterproductive. Does the fact that the divine plan showed that the Christian message would pass through European culture to travel its long journey through history, just as it crossed Asia and North Africa at the beginning of its history, perhaps alter its value? The good qualities with which the Christian faith has been enriched in its contacts with many particular cultures (e.g., Semitic, Greek, Latin, African, and Asian) must be accepted insofar as they do not harm but, indeed, help build up the body of Christ in any given local context. This means that just as the Third World transfers and adapts technology to its own socioeconomic environment so, too, theologians can accept European theology and try to build upon it, completing it with original elements from their own culture. All this will open the road to real, intercultural theology.

Along the same line, Third World theologians should avoid the tendency to attack the past missionary efforts in their regions. It is true that this tendency is important for a critical moment in the development of Third World theology; nevertheless, we should not forget the many good things that occurred during this period. The work of Kwame Bediako, Lamin Sanneh, and Andrew Walls, indeed, reminds us how a balanced theological dialogue in this regard could proceed. Serious historical studies of the missionary period invite theologians to pass from critical attitudes to informed, constructive attitudes that see the shortcomings of the missionary era in context. While we recognize that there were real deficiencies on the part of missionaries, it is more productive to concentrate on the challenges to the church's mission today in every region. Saying this, however, is not intended to encourage the voices of those who defend the mistakes of the past and accuse Third World theologians who have entered into critical dialogue with historical memory of being unreasonably "touchy." Indeed, the widespread preoccupation with the past on the part of some Third World theologians—

matched by the equally widespread sense of historical mistakes on the part of writers whose origins are among nations formerly dominant in mission—underscores the relevance of engaging in serious dialogue with the emergent contextual theologies. A desire to suppress studies that research the past can be motivated not only by the desire to avoid pain or to achieve reconciliation among the different peoples but also by a desire to avoid responsibility. Defending mistakes is not a reliable strategy, because, in the long run, a failure to attend to these issues in the present may store up problems for the future. The most reliable strategy is sincere dialogue with a view to healing and reconciliation.

10

DRAWING THREADS TOGETHER

As we reach the end of this study of concepts and paradigms of mission that guided the evolution of missiology as a theological discipline and that articulated the way in which the church understands its missionary activity, we are left with several basic questions:

- What remained basic to all concepts and paradigms of mission?

- How much has changed since the first effort to define mission in theological terms was made?

- What represents the surest path and the most challenging elements for mission studies today?

- How *theological* is missiology?

Let us reduce all these questions to this: What is the subject matter of missiology today and how is that related to the preceding paradigms?

As I draw together the threads of our discussion in this general conclusion, I emphasize *proclamation, evangelization,* and *contextual theologies* as the most important among the many proposals that are offered as new directions for further development and research on mission studies.

In the first place, proclamation could be called the unifying term of all previous and contemporary missionary paradigms and theories studied in this book. This also seems to be the view of Pope John Paul II when he says:

Proclamation is the permanent priority of mission. The Church cannot elude Christ's explicit mandate, nor deprive men and women of the "Good News" about their being loved and saved by God. "Evangelization will always contain—as the foundation, center and at the same time the summit of its dynamism—a clear proclamation that, in Jesus Christ . . . salvation is offered to all people, as a gift of God's grace and mercy" (*EN* 27). All forms of missionary activity are directed to this proclamation, which reveals and gives access to the mystery hidden for ages and made known in Christ (cf. Eph 3:3-9; Col 1:25-29), the mystery which lies at the heart of the Church's mission and life, as the hinge on which all evangelization turns.

In the complex reality of mission, initial proclamation has a central and irreplaceable role, since it introduces man "into the mystery of the love of God, who invites him to enter into a personal relationship with himself in Christ" (*AG* 13) and opens the way to conversion. Faith is born of preaching, and every ecclesial community draws its origin and life from the personal response of each believer to that preaching (*EN* 15; *AG* 13-14). Just as the whole economy of salvation has its center in Christ, so too all missionary activity is directed to the proclamation of his mystery (*DeV* 42, 64). (*RM* 44)

Be it the early models of conversion, church formation, and the concept of mission as service of the reign of God, or the prevalent models of mission as adaptation-inculturation, dialogue with the religions and cultures, ecumenism, and human promotion, the central issue is always the Christian proclamation of salvation in Jesus Christ. The concern of theologians in all these paradigms studied in the present book is always how to promote the Christian mission and how the proclamation of the gospel could take flesh in the hearts of men and women who accept the offer of salvation in Jesus Christ. In other words, proclamation and incarnation of the gospel go together. The aim of proclamation is for the faith to take root and bear fruit, fruit in abundance, among those who accept it. Hence, proclamation can be called a process or, rather, the first stage of evangelization.

Contemporary missionary documents have underlined the central place of proclamation in missionary activity. This can be seen from the titles of most of these documents. Proclamation is at the base of the title given to the Vatican II missionary decree, *Ad Gentes*. In the 1974 synod of bishops on evangelization, delegates from each zone had wanted the postsynodal exhortation to carry the title of their own theme as expressed during the working sessions of the synod. Delegates from Latin America wanted the pope to emphasize the theme of poverty and to entitle the exhortation so. Those from Asia wanted the issue of religious dialogue to be the theme of the exhortation, while African delegates, who emphasized the theme of the incarnation of the gospel in local cultures, wished that the postsynodal exhortation be on the theme of inculturation. Delegates from the North Atlantic, for their part, looked forward to an exhortation on the issues of secularism and ecumenism. But in the end, Paul VI chose the theme of proclamation and entitled the exhortation *Evangelii Nuntiandi*. John Paul II gave a proclamation-based title to his missionary encyclical *Redemptoris Missio*, from which we quoted above. The pope also made the theme of proclamation the subtheme of his apostolic exhortations at the continental synods celebrated in preparation for the Jubilee Year 2000.

Most of the mission paradigms and theories studied in this book, in one way or another, help us to understand the aim and concept of Christian mission. They bring to the fore the scope of the Christian mission, especially the various activities and means through which the church executes it. Even the authors of those theories that emphasize the social dimensions of missionary activity do not negate, as such, the necessity of Christian proclamation. This does not mean, however, that the partial and incomplete missiology of authors who speak of political critique and social service as the only goal of mission should be overlooked. As we noted, the works of most of these authors lack a balanced presentation of the essential aspects of the church and mission. Some of these authors appear to have forgotten the Christological, eschatological, ecclesiological, and the specifically religious dimensions of the church and its mission. But the conciliar and postconciliar documents of Vatican II have helped to save contemporary missiology from the dangers inherent in those new tendencies and have clarified the ecclesiological concepts of the church as missionary and of the place and role of particular churches. This can be seen in the vision of the church as communion and in discovering in the particular churches all the characteristics and responsibilities of the universal mission of the church (*EN* 15; *RM* 62, 64, 85).

Furthermore, contemporary church documents affirm the uniqueness of Christ in salvation and in the missionary mandate of the church. The documents underline the "sent" character of the church, which is rooted in the mandate of Christ and the church's own universal character to preach to all (*AG* 1). The missionary mandate of the church, which is her nature (*AG* 2), has its origin in the plan of the Father and develops out of the mission of the Son and the Holy Spirit. Proclamation is therefore basic. Proclamation and preaching, however, are to serve the aim of implanting the church through which people enter into the new household of God and, through the word and sacraments, receive continual nourishment in their faith and for their participation in building up the reign of God on earth. Thus, in proclamation we have the call to conversion, anticipation of the forgiveness of sins and regeneration in the Spirit, the beginning of the evangelization process, church formation, and service to the reign of God. But, for the word proclaimed to take root in the hearts, minds, and cultures of the people, inculturation, dialogue with the religions and cultures as well as commitment to human promotion and liberation must become part and parcel of the evangelization process. Moreover, in an age where the grey noise of advertising blankets every continent, the most effective vehicle for proclamation may well be the witness of selfless dedication to help free the oppressed from domination and misery.

Love is to animate the work of proclamation and the witness to the gospel involved in preaching. In other words, emphasis is placed also on service in love and the witness of a Christian life. To lead a profound Christian life is, for all Christians, the primary and most important contribution they can make to the spread of the faith. Such love for the faith and others has been described as an evangelization that is new in fervor, new in expressions, and new in methods. Therefore, in the missionary paradigms and theories studied in this book, there is a clear recognition of evangelization as fundamental to the Christian mission. This fact is evident in the debate between mission and evangelization sparked by Paul VI's apostolic letter *Evangelii Nuntiandi*. The two words are not contradictory, and neither replaces the other.

Finally, missiology today should not ignore the emerging theological reflections in the global South. In fact, it should make them a major object of its studies. Mission is said to be the mother of theology. That means that theology was born out of mission. With the recent rapid growth of Christianity in the Southern Hemisphere, it may not be an overstatement to say that the most significant theological reflections today are coming from the pens of Christians from that part of the globe. Theology is at its liveliest and truest where the life of the church is most vital. This does not mean that the theology of North Atlantic Christians is no longer valuable. Rather, what we are increasingly seeing is that North Atlantic theology is liveliest today where it is fertilized by the writings and developments from the global South. Again, the contextual theologies of the Third World do not speak only to the people of the global South but also to Christians of the North Atlantic. We are a world church in the midst of a world Christian movement. In their work, Third World theologians do not depend only on their local context; the source of their writing is the Bible, Christian tradition, and the theology handed down from the universal church by missionaries to the South. So, too, Third World theologians believe that their message is both for their own people and for all Christians.

In spite of the flaws and difficulties that can be found in the writings of some Third World theologians, it is evident that their reflections are already enriching Christian theology. Some of their chief concerns—religion, culture, human development, liberation, poverty, oppression, globalization, healing, and reconciliation—are now recognized as viable theological categories that enrich the traditional themes of systematic theology and give light to the practical goals that mission should pursue. Many of the so-called new forms of evangelization that are recommended as possible ways to reevangelize Europe were influenced by the contributions from Third World theologians. For instance, the history of the modern theology of religions and salvation will be incomplete without the recognition of the contributions of Asian theologians. In the same manner, the current theology of inculturation and the meaning of religions have been enlarged greatly by the reflections of African theologians, just as the theology of liberation and human promotion owe their resurgence in contemporary theology to the efforts of Latin American authors.

In addition, contemporary European and North American theologians, while defining the theological themes mentioned above, enlighten the universal church on the meaning of ecumenism and secularism and remind us all of the dangers of relativism and religious fundamentalism. Some North Atlantic theologians have started to enter into dialogue with their counterparts from the global South. This new trend needs to be encouraged and pursued in the spirit of mutual love, respect, and equality. There should be no display of superiority if we are to arrive at a positive result that promotes the pursuit of Christian mission. Again, dialogue with contexts includes dialogue with the concrete reality or situations of the contemporary world, which is characterized by religious fundamentalism, new religious movements, ethnicity, poverty, discrimination, and globalization. It includes also dialogue with various groups or persons who are marginalized by the status quo, for example, women, minority groups, and peoples of different color. The aim of dialogue with the context is not to compromise the faith or to align oneself with any group or ideology but to engage in studies and theological reflection that can assist the church in developing a missionary language that meets the challenges of the modern world to liberate all our brothers and sisters and enables them to reach their full potential and freedom in God's kingdom.

Nevertheless, the emphasis on dialogue should not lead to the hasty conclusion wherein it becomes the goal of mission. The traditional aim and concepts of mission studied in this book are still valid. Dialogue is in the service of them. The aim of mission remains evangelization and church formation. It is carried out through the missionary activities *ad et inter gentes*, in pastoral care, in the new evangelization, as well as in the Christian witness of our faith in Christ. Whichever way one approaches the matter, the various categories of missionary activity and the emerging forms of understanding the aim of mission all have their place in the classical meaning of mission. It is important that the classical meaning of mission be retained, because the church today is confronted as never before with new forms of modern humanity's indifference to religion and the clear reality that the vast majority of people have not yet heard the gospel. Moreover, the work of evangelization is just in its infancy stage in many countries of the global South, while secularism and religious indifference have brought about an entirely new missionary frontier in many nations of the North Atlantic.

There is also a growing consciousness of the deteriorating state of relations among diverse peoples and nations in the contemporary world. This has led to wars, to unnecessary stereotyping, to the fermenting of religious fundamentalism and dangerous ideologies, and to reliance on the media as the guide to modern life. All this poses a great obstacle to the pursuit of mission today. This scenario must not be viewed as a crisis but rather as a moment of transformation, and an opportunity for a new springtime for mission. It is a reality that offers a new drive as a sign of missionary vitality (*RM* 2). The urgency of the church's mission today is a fact that has been expressed with great force at the recent continental synods of bishops

(Europe 1991/1999, Africa 1994, Americas 1997, Asia 1998, Oceania 1999).

Consequently, the actual missionary situation with its diverse challenges and call for commitment offers us also promising signs of an increase in missionary vitality, particularly in the young churches, and an opportunity for collaboration among the various Christian families. It is for this reason that we have emphasized in this study the importance of dialogue with emergent contextual theologies in promoting mission studies and the missionary activity of the church.

BIBLIOGRAPHY

Aagaard, Anne Marie
    1974. "Missio Dei in Katholischer Sicht." *Evangelische Theologie* 34:420-33.
Aagaard, Johannes
    1973. "Trends in Missiological Thinking during the Sixties." *International Review of Mission* 62:8-25.
Ahn, B. M.
    1985. "The Korean Church's Understanding of Jesus." In *Voices from the Third World* (EATWOT) 8:49-58.
Allen, John L., and P. Schaeffer
    2001. "Reports of Abuse." *National Catholic Reporter.* March 16, 2001.
Allen, Roland
    1956. *Missionary Methods: St Paul's or Ours?* London: World Dominion Press; Grand Rapids: Eerdmans, 1962.
Almario, C. R., ed.
    1993. *Evangelization in Asia.* Quezon City, Philippines: Claretian Publications.
Anderson, Allan
    2004. *An Introduction to Pentecostalism: Global Charismatic Christianity.* Cambridge: Cambridge University Press.
Anderson, Gerald H., ed.
    1998. *Biographical Dictionary of Christian Missions.* New York: Macmillan.
Anderson, Gerald H., Robert T. Coote, Norman A. Horner, and James M. Phillips, eds.
    1994. *Mission Legacies: Biographical Studies of Leaders of the Modern Missionary Movement.* Maryknoll, N.Y.: Orbis Books.
Anderson, Gerald H., and Thomas F. Stransky, eds.
    1974-81. *Mission Trends.* 5 vols. New York: Paulist Press; Grand Rapids: Eerdmans.
Appiah-Kubi, Kofi, and Sergio Torres, eds.
    1979. *African Theology en Route.* Maryknoll, N.Y.: Orbis Books.
Arrupe, Pedro
    1978. "Catechesis and Inculturation." *AFER* 20:97-134.
Barreda, J. A.
    2003. *Missionologia: Studio introduttivo.* Cinisello Balsamo, Milan: San Paolo.
Barrett, David B., Todd M. Johnson, and Peter Crossing, eds.
    2006. "Missiometrics 2006: Goals, Resources, Doctrines of the 350 World Christian Communities." *International Bulletin of Missionary Research* 30:27-30.
Barrett, David B., Todd M. Johnson, Christopher Guidry, and Peter Crossing, eds.
    2003. *World Christian Trends, AD 30-AD 2200: Interpreting the Annual Christian Megacensus.* Pasadena, Calif.: William Carey Library.

Barrett, David B., Todd M. Johnson, and Thomas Kurian, eds.
  2001. *World Christian Encyclopedia.* 2 vols. New York: Oxford University Press.
Barth, Karl
  1957. "Die Theologie und die Mission in der Gegenwart." In *Theologische Fragen und Antworten,* 3:100-126. Zollikon-Zurich: Evangelischer Verlag.
  1978. *Church Dogmatics* 1/2. Edinburgh: T & T Clark.
Bassham, Rodger C.
  1979. *Mission Theology 1948-1975: Years of Worldwide Creative Tension—Ecumenical, Evangelical, and Roman Catholic.* Pasadena: William Carey Library.
Bediako, Kwame
  1995. *Christianity in Africa: The Renewal of a Non-Western Religion.* Maryknoll, N.Y.: Orbis Books.
Beinert, W.
  1983. "Jesus Christus, der Erlöser von Sünder und Tod: Überblick über die abendländische Soteriologie." In *Schuld, Sühne und Erlösung,* ed. K. Rivinius, 196-221. Sankt Augustin: Steyler Verlag.
Bellagamba, Anthony
  1992. *Mission and Ministry in the Global Church.* Maryknoll, N.Y.: Orbis Books.
  1993. *The Mission of the Church: A Commentary and Reflection on the Encyclical Redemptoris Missio.* Nairobi: St Paul.
Benedict XV (Pope)
  1919. *Maximum Illud,* apostolic letter.
Berkhof, Henrikus
  1979. *Christian Faith.* Grand Rapids: Eerdmans.
Bettscheider, Heribert.
  1997. "Liberation." In *Dictionary of Mission: Theology, History, Perspective,* ed. Karl Müller et al., 269-75. Maryknoll, N.Y.: Orbis Books.
Bevans, Stephen B.
  2002. *Models of Contextual Theology.* Rev. ed. Maryknoll, N.Y.: Orbis Books.
Bevans, Stephen B., and Roger P. Schroeder
  2004. *Constants in Context: A Theology of Mission for Today.* Maryknoll, N.Y.: Orbis Books.
Bhakiaraj, Paul Josuah, and Roger E. Hedlund, eds.
  2004. *Missiology for the 21st Century: South Asian Perspectives.* Delhi: ISPCK/Mylapore Institute for Indigenous Studies.
Blauw, Johannes
  1962. *The Missionary Nature of the Church: A Survey of the Biblical Theology of Mission.* Grand Rapids: Eerdmans; London: Lutterworth Press.
Bosch, David J.
  1980. *Witness to the World: The Christian Mission in Theological Perspective.* Atlanta: John Knox.
  1983. "The Structure of Mission: An Exposition of Matthew 28:16-20." In *Exploring Church Growth,* ed. Wilbert R. Shenk, 218-48. Grand Rapids: Eerdmans.
  1991. *Transforming Mission: Paradigm Shifts in Theology of Mission.* Maryknoll, N.Y.: Orbis Books.
Brennan, J. P.
  1990. *Christian Mission in a Pluralistic World.* Middlegreen, Slough: St Paul Publications.

Bria, I.
  1976. "The Renewal of the Tradition through Pastoral Witness." *International Review of Mission* 65:182-85.
  1978. "The Liturgy after Liturgy." *International Review of Mission* 67:86-90.
  1986. *The Witness of the Orthodox Churches Today.* Geneva: WCC.
  1987. "Unity and Mission from the Perspective of the Local Church: An Orthodox View." *Ecumenical Review* 39:265-70.
Brown, Lee M., ed.
  2004. *African Philosophy: New and Traditional Perspectives.* Oxford: Oxford University Press.
Bsteh, Andreas
  1966. "Zur Frage nach der Universalität der Erlösung." *Wiener Beiträge zur Theologie* 14:185.
Bühlmann, Walbert
  1978. *The Missions on Trial.* Slough: St Paul Publications.
  1983. *God's Chosen Peoples.* Maryknoll, N.Y.: Orbis Books.
Bujo, Bénézet
  1992. *African Theology in Its Social Context.* Maryknoll, N.Y.: Orbis Books.
Buono, Giuseppe
  2000. *Missiologia: Teologia e prassi.* Milan: Paoline.
  2002. *Missiology: Theology and Praxis.* Nairobi: Paulines Africa.
Burchard, Chr.
  1980. "Jesus für die Welt: Über das Verhältnis von Reich Gottes und Mission." In *Fides pro mundi vita*, 13-27. Gütersloh: Gerd Mohn.
Burrows, William R.
  1998. "Reconciling All in Christ: An Old New Paradigm for Mission." *Mission Studies* 15, no. 29:79-98.
Camps, Arnulf
  1983. *Partners in Dialogue: Christianity and Other World Religions.* Maryknoll, N.Y.: Orbis Books.
Camps, Arnulf, et al., eds.
  1988. *Oecumenische inleiding in de Missiologie.* Kampen: Kok. English translation, 1995. *Missiology: An Ecumenical Introduction.* Grand Rapids Eerdmans.
Caprile, Giovanni
  1974. "Il sinodo dei Vescovi" (3rd General Assembly, 27 September-26 October 1974). Rome, *La Civiltà Cattolica.*
Castro, Emilio.
  1978. "Liberation, Development, and Evangelism: Must We Choose in Mission?" *Occasional Bulletin of Missionary Research* 2:87-90.
Cavallotto, G.
  1996. *Catecumenato antico: Diventare cristiani secondo i Padri* and *Iniziazione cristiana e catecumenato: Divenire cristiani per essere battezzati.* Bologna: EDB.
CELAM (Latin American Episcopal Conference)
  1979. *Documents of the Third General Conference of Latin American Bishops, Puebla (1979).* Puebla: National Secretariat for Latin American Bishops' Conference.
Charles, E. Tamba
  1996. *Inculturating the Gospel in Africa: From Adaptation to Incarnation.* Rome: Pontificia Università Gregoriana.

Charles, Pierre
   1932. *Principes et méthodes de l'activité missionnaire en dehors du Catholicisme.* Louvain: Editions de l'Aucam.
   1938. *Les Dossiers de l'action missionnaire,* vol. 1 (2nd ed.). Aucam/Brusselles, Louvain: Universelle.
   1939. *Missiologie* (an anthology), Vol. 1. Louvain.
   1947. *La prière missionnaire.* Louvain: Editions de l'Aucam.
   1954/56. *Études missiologiques.* Paris: Desclée de Brouwer.
Chenu, B.
   1987. *Théologies chrétiennes du tiers monde.* Paris: Centurion.
Chupungco, Anscar J.
   1994. *Worship: Beyond Inculturation.* Washington, D.C.: Pastoral Press.
Coffele, G.
   1976a. *Johannes Christiaan Hoekendijk.* Rome: PUG.
   1976b. *Johannes Christiaan Hoekendijk: Da una teologia della missione ad una teologia missionaria.* Rome: Città Nuova.
Collet, Giancarlo
   1984. *Das Missionsverständnis in der gegenwartigen Diskussion.* Mainz: Matthias-Grunewald-Verlag.
   2004. ". . . *Fino agli Estremi Confini della Terra": Questioni fondamentali di teologia della missione.* Brescia: Queriniana.
Colzani, Gianni
   1996. *Teologia della missione.* Padua: Edizioni Messaggero.
Comblin, Joseph
   1977. *The Meaning of Mission: Jesus, Christians, and the Wayfaring Church.* Maryknoll, N.Y.: Orbis Books.
   1991. *La Forza della Parola: La Missione.* Bologna: EMI.
Congar, Yves M. J.
   1961. *The Wide World My Parish.* Baltimore: Helicon Press.
   1965. *The Mystery of the Church.* London: Chapman.
   1968. *The Revelation of God.* London: Longman & Todd.
Congregation for the Doctrine of the Faith (CDF)
   1984. *Instruction on Certain Aspects of the Theology of Liberation* (Libertatis Nuntius).
   1986. *Instruction on Christian Freedom and Liberation.*
   1992. *Letter to the Bishops of the Catholic Church on Some Aspects of the Church Understood as Communion.*
   1998. *The Primacy of the Successor of Peter in the Mystery of the Church.*
   2000. *Declaration* Dominus Jesus: *On the Unicity and Salvific Universality of Jesus Christ and the Church.*
   2004. *"Notification . . . on the Book* Jesus Symbol of God.*"*
Cracknell, Kenneth, and C. Lamb, eds.
   1986. *Theology on Full Alert.* London: British Council of Churches.
Crossan, John Dominic
   1991. *The Historical Jesus: The Life of a Mediterranean Jewish Peasant.* San Francisco: HarperSanFrancisco.
Cullmann, Oscar
   1965. *Heil als Geschichte: Heilsgeschichtliche Existenz im Neuen Testament.* Tübingen: Mohr.

1967. *Salvation in History*. London: SCM Press.
1986: *The Christology of the New Testament*. London: SCM Press.
Daniélou, Jean
1950. *The Salvation of the Nations*. New York: Sheed & Ward.
1957. *Holy Pagans of the Old Testament*. London: Longmans.
1962. *The Scandal of the Truth*. London: Burns & Oates.
1972. *Foundations of Mission Theology*. Maryknoll, N.Y.: Orbis Books.
Davies, J. G.
1966. *Worship and Mission*. London: SCM Press.
Dempster, Murray W., Byron D. Klaus, and Douglas Peterson, eds.
1999. *The Globalization of Pentecostalism: A Religion Made to Travel*. Oxford: Regnum Books International.
Dianich, S.
1985. *Chiesa in missione*. Turin: Paoline.
Dinh Duc Dao, J.
1993. "Missiography: Present Situations and the Emerging Tendencies of Mission." In *Mission for the Third Millennium: Course of Missiology*, ed. Paolo Giglioni, 27-46. Rome: Pontifical Missionary Union.
1994. *Inculturazione Testi di Lavoro su Fede e Culture*, XV. Rome: Editrice Università Gregoriana.
Dulles, Avery
1970a. "Current Trends in Mission Theology." *Theology Digest* 20:26-34.
1970b. "Mission Theology for Our Time" (SEDOS Symposium on *World Mission*), pp. 6-23.
1974. *Models of the Church*. Garden City: Doubleday.
1983. *Models of Revelation*. Dublin: Gill & Macmillan.
Dupuis, Jacques.
1991. *Jesus Christ at the Encounter of World Religions*. Maryknoll, N.Y.: Orbis Books.
1994. "Evangelization and Mission." In *Dictionary of Fundamental Theology*, ed. René Latourelle and Rino Fisichella, 175-82. New York: Crossroad.
1998. *Toward a Christian Theology of Religious Pluralism*. Maryknoll, N.Y.: Orbis Books.
Echegaray, Hugo.
1984. *The Practice of Jesus*. Maryknoll, N.Y.: Orbis Books.
England, John C., Jose Kuttianimattathil, John Mansford Prior, Lily A. Quintos, David Suh Kwang-Sun, and Janice Wicekeri, eds.
2002. *Asian Christian Theologies: A Research Guide to Authors, Movements, Sources*. Vol. 1, *Asia Region, South Asia, Austral Asia*. Delhi: ISPCK; Manila: Claretian; Maryknoll, N.Y.: Orbis Books.
2003. *Asian Christian Theologies: A Research Guide to Authors, Movements, Sources*. Vol. 2, *Southeast Asia*. Delhi: ISPCK; Manila: Claretian; Maryknoll, N.Y.: Orbis Books.
2004. *Asian Christian Theologies: A Research Guide to Authors, Movements, Sources*. Vol. 3, *Northeast Asia*. Delhi: ISPCK; Manila: Claretian; Maryknoll, N.Y.: Orbis Books.
England, John C., and A. C. C. Lee, eds.
1993. *Doing Theology with Asian Resources*. Auckland, New Zealand: Pace Publishing.

Esquerda Bifet, J.
  1991. *Pastoral for a Missionary Church*. Rome: Urbaniana University Press.
  1995. *Teologia de la Evangelición*. Madrid: BAC.
Exeler, A.
  1978. "Vergleichende Theologie Statt Missionswissenschaft? Provozierende
    Anfrage eines Nichtfachmanns." In *". . . denn Ich bin bei Euch" (Mt 28, 20):
    Perspektiven im christlichen Missionsbewusstsein heute*, ed. Hans Waldenfels,
    199-211. Einsiedeln: Benziger.
Fabella, Virginia, and Sergio Torres, eds.
  1983. *The Irruption of the Third World*. Maryknoll, N.Y.: Orbis Books.
Farley, Edward
  1983. *Theologia: The Fragmentation and Unity of Theological Education*.
    Philadelphia: Fortress Press.
Flannery, Austin
  1996. *Vatican Council II*. Vol. 1, *The Conciliar and Post-Conciliar Documents*.
    Rev. ed. Northport N.Y.: Costello Publishing.
  1998. *Vatican Council II*. Vol. 2, *More Post-Conciliar Documents*. Rev. ed. North-
    port: N.Y.: Costello Publishing.
Fornberg, Todd
  1995. *The Problem of Christianity in Multi-Religious Societies of Today*. Lewis-
    ton, N.Y.: Edwin Mellen Press.
Forte, Bruno
  1975. *La chiesa nell'Eucaristia*. Napoli.
  1995. *La Chiesa della Trinità: Saggio sul mistero della Chiesa, comunione e mis-
    sione*. Cinisello Balsamo: San Paolo.
Freytag, Walter
  1938. *Die Junge Christenheit im Umbruch des Ostens*. Berlin: Furche-Verlag.
  1940. *Spiritual Revolution in the East*. London: Lutterworth.
  1958. "Changes in the Patterns of Western Missions." In *The Ghana Assembly of
    the International Missionary Council*, ed. R. K. Orchard, 138-47. London:
    Edinburgh House.
  1961. *Reden und Aufsätze*. Vol. 2. Munich: Chr. Kaiser Verlag.
Fuellenbach, John
  2002. *Church: Community for the Kingdom*. Maryknoll, N.Y.: Orbis Books.
Gatti, E.
  1980. *Temi biblici sulla missione*. Bologna: EMI.
Geffré, Claude
  1987. *The Risk of Interpretation*. Mahwah, N.J.: Paulist Press.
Gensichen, Hans-Werner
  1960. "Were the Reformers Indifferent to Missions." In *History's Lessons for
    Tomorrow's Mission*, 119-27. Geneva: World Students Christian Federation.
  1961. *Missionsgeschichte der neueren Zeit*. Göttingen: Vandenhoeck & Ruprecht.
  1971. *Glaube für die Welt: Theologische Aspekte der Mission*. Gütersloh: Gerd
    Mohn.
  1994. "Walter Freytag, 1899-1959." In *Dictionary of Mission: Theology, History,
    Perspective*, ed. Karl Müller et al., 435-44. Maryknoll, N.Y.: Orbis Books.
Gibellini, Rosino, ed.
  1975. *La nuova frontiera della teologia in americalatina*. Brescia: Editrice Querini-
    ana.

1978. *Teologia nera.* Brescia: Editrice Queriniana.

1986. *Il dibattito sulla teologia della liberazione.* Brescia: Editrice Queriniana.

1994. *Paths of African Theology.* Maryknoll, N.Y.: Orbis Books.

Giglioni, Paolo

1990a. *Ministeri e servizi per la missione.* Bologna: EDB.

1990b. "Perché una 'Nuova' Evangelizzazione?" *Euntes Docete* 43:5-36.

1993. "The Church's Missionary Activity." In *Mission for the Third Millennium: Course of Missiology,* 169-212. Rome: Pontifical Missionary Union.

1996. *Teologia pastorale missionaria.* Città del Vaticano: Libreria Editrice.

1999. *Inculturazione: Teoria e prassi.* Città del Vaticano: Libreria Editrice.

2000. "Nuova Evangelizzazione o Evangelizzazione Nuova." *Euntes Docete* 53:15-27.

Gilkey, Langdon

1987. "Plurality and Its Theological Implications." In *The Myth of Christian Uniqueness: Towards a Pluralistic Theology of Religions,* ed. John Hick and Paul F. Knitter, 37-51. Maryknoll, N.Y.: Orbis Books.

Glasser, Arthur F., and Donald A. McGavran

1983. *Contemporary Theologies of Mission.* Grand Rapids: Baker Book House.

Gort, Jerald

1980a. *World Missionary Conference: Melbourne, May 1980: An Historical and Missiological Interpretation.* Amsterdam: Free University.

1980b. "The Contours of the Reformed Understanding of Christian Mission." *Calvin Theological Journal* 15:47-60.

Grentrup, T.

1913. "Die Definition des Missionsgriffes." *Zeitschrift für Missionswissenschaft* 3:265-74.

Gutiérrez, Gustavo

1983. *The Power of the Poor in History.* Maryknoll, N.Y.: Orbis Books. Spanish orig., 1979.

1988. *A Theology of Liberation.* Maryknoll, N.Y.: Orbis Books. Spanish orig., 1971.

Hahn, Ferdinand

1965. *Mission in the New Testament.* London: SCM Press.

Haight, Roger

1999. *Jesus Symbol of God.* Maryknoll, N.Y.: Orbis Books.

Healey, Joseph, and Donald Sybertz

1996. *Towards an African Narrative Theology.* Nairobi: Paulines; Maryknoll, N.Y.: Orbis Books.

Hengel, Martin

1983. *Between Jesus and Paul: Studies in the Earliest History of Christianity.* London: SCM Press.

1986. *Earliest Christianity.* London: SCM Press.

Hennelly, Alfred T., ed.

1993. *Santo Domingo and Beyond.* Maryknoll, N.Y.: Orbis Books.

Hernández, Angel Santos

1958. *Adaptación Misionera.* Bilbao: El Siglo de la Misione.

1965. *Bibliografía Misional.* Vol. 1, *Doctrinal.* Vol. 2, *Histórica.* Santander: Sal Terrae.

1991. *Teología Sistemática de la Misión.* Estella (Navarra): Editorial Verbo Divino.

Heschel, Abraham J.
  1969. *Dio alla ricerca dell'uomo.* Turin: Borla. English translation, *God in Search of Man.* New York: Farrar Straus Giroux, 1976.
Hick, John
  1973. *God and Universe of Faiths: Essays in the Philosophy of Religion.* London: Macmillan.
  1977a. *The Centre of Christianity.* London: SCM Press.
  1977b. *The Myth of God Incarnate.* London: SCM Press.
  1980. *God Has Many Names: Britain's New Religious Pluralism.* London: Macmillan.
Hick, John, and Paul F. Knitter, eds.
  1987. *The Myth of Christian Uniqueness. Towards a Pluralistic Theology of Religions.* Maryknoll, N.Y.: Orbis Books.
Hickey, Raymond, ed.
  1982. *Modern Missionary Documents and Africa.* Dublin: Dominican Publications.
Hoedemaker, Libertus A.
  1977. "Hoekendijk's American Years." *Occasional Bulletin of Missionary Research* 1:70.
  1988. "Het volk Gods en de einden der aarde." In *Oecumenische inleiding in de Missiologie,* ed. Arnulf Camps et al., 167-80. Kampen: Kok.
  1994. "Hendrik Kraemer (1888-1965)." In *Mission Legacies: Biographical Studies of Leaders of the Modern Missionary Movement.* Edited by Gerald H. Anderson, Robert T. Coote, Norman A. Horner, and James M. Phillips, 508-15. Maryknoll, N.Y.: Orbis Books.
Hoekendijk, Johannes Christiaan
  1966. *The Church Inside Out.* Philadelphia: Westminster.
  1967. *Kirche und Volk in der deutschen Missionswissenschaft.* Munich: Chr. Kaiser Verlag.
Hwa, Yung
  1997. *Mangoes or Bananas? The Quest for an Authentic Asian Christian Theology.* Oxford: Regnum International.
Irvin, Dale
  1998. *Christian Histories, Christian Traditioning: Rendering Accounts.* Maryknoll, N.Y.: Orbis Books.
Irvin, Dale, and Scott W. Sunquist
  2001. *The History of the World Christian Movement.* Maryknoll, N.Y.: Orbis Books.
Jenkins, Philip
  2002. *The Next Christendom: The Coming of Global Christianity.* New York: Oxford University Press.
John XXIII (Pope)
  1959. *Princeps Pastorum,* encyclical letter.
  1961. *Mater et Magistra,* encyclical letter.
John Paul II (Pope)
  1979. *Redemptor Hominis,* encyclical letter on Jesus the redeemer of humankind.
  1979. *Catechesi Tradendae,* apostolic exhortation.
  1979. *L'insegnamenti di Giovanni Paolo II,* 2:192. Vatican City: Libreria Editrice.

1986. *Dominum et Vivificantem,* encyclical letter on the Holy Spirit.

1988. *Sollicitudo Rei Socialis,* encyclical letter on social justice.

1988. *Christifidelis Laici,* apostolic exhortation.

1990. *Redemptoris Missio,* encyclical letter on the permanent validity of the missionary mandate.

1995. *Tertio Millennio Adveniente,* apostolic letter.

1995. *Ecclesia in Africa,* apostolic exhortation.

1995. *Ut Unum Sint,* encyclical letter on ecumenism.

1996. *Vita Consecrata,* apostolic exhortation.

Jongeneel, Jan A. B.

1988. "Kraemer und Samartha, zwei 'feindliche' Brüder." *Zeitschrift für Mission* 14:197-205.

1989. "Voetius' zendingstheologie, de eerste comprehensieve protestantse zendingstheologie." In *De onbekende Voetius,* ed. J. van Oort, 117-47. Kampen: Kok.

1995. *Philosophy, Science and Theology of Mission in the 19th & 20th Centuries.* 2 vols. Frankfurt: Peter Lang.

Kähler, Martin

1971. *Schriften zur Christologie und Mission.* Munich: Chr. Kaiser Verlag.

Kalilombe, Patrick A.

1984. *From Outstation to Small Christian Communities.* Eldoret, Kenya: Gaba Publications.

Karotemprel, Sebastian, ed.

1995. *Following Christ in Mission: A Foundational Course in Missiology.* Nairobi: Paulines Publications-Africa.

2001. "Introduction: Christology and Mission Today," in *Christologia e Missione Oggi,* ed. G. Colzani et al., 15-31. Rome: Urbaniana University Press.

Kasper, Walter

1976. *Jesus the Christ.* New York: Paulist Press.

Kitamori, K.

1965. *Theology of the Pain of God.* London: SCM Press.

Klaes, N.

1997. "Christology." In *Dictionary of Mission: Theology, History, Perspective,* ed. Karl Müller, 60-65. Maryknoll, N.Y.: Orbis Books.

Knitter, Paul F.

1985. *No Other Name? A Critical Survey of Christian Attitudes Toward the World Religions.* Maryknoll, N.Y.: Orbis Books.

2002. *Introducing Theologies of Religion.* Maryknoll, N.Y.: Orbis Books.

Kraemer, Hendrik

1947. *The Christian Message in a Non-Christian World.* London: Edinburgh House Press.

1961. *Religion and the Christian Faith.* London: Lutterworth.

Kraft, Charles H.

1991. *Communication Theory for Christian Witness.* Rev. ed. Maryknoll, N.Y.: Orbis Books.

1996. *Anthropology for Christian Witness.* Maryknoll, N.Y.: Orbis Books.

2005. *Christianity in Culture: A Study in Biblical Theologizing in Cross-Cultural Perspective.* Maryknoll, N.Y.: Orbis Books.

Kramm, T.
    1979. *Analyse und Bewährung theologischer Modelle zur Begründung der Mission.* Aachen: Missio Aktuell Verlag.
Lange, René
    1924. *Le Problème Théologique des Missions.* Collectanea Xaveriana 3. Louvain.
Lausanne Committee for World Evangelization
    1974. *Lausanne Covenant.* http://www.lausanne.org/Brix?pageID=12891.
    1989. *Manila Manifesto.* http://www.lausanne.org/Brix?pageID=12894.
Legrand, Lucien
    1992. *Mission in the Bible: Unity and Plurality.* Maryknoll, N.Y.: Orbis Books.
    2000. *The Bible on Culture.* Maryknoll, N.Y.: Orbis Books.
Linz, Manfred
    1964. *Anwalt der Welt: Zur Theologie der Mission.* Stuttgart: Kreuz Verlag.
López-Gay, Jesús
    1988. *Missiologia Contemporanea.* 2nd ed. Rome: Urbaniana University Press.
    1993. "Contemporary Missiology." In *Mission for the Third Millennium: Course of Missiology,* 9-31. Rome: Pontifical Missionary Union.
López-Gay, Jesús, ed.
    1994. *La missione della Chiesa nel Mondo di oggi.* Rome: Pontificia Università Gregoriana.
Lubac, Henri de
    1946. *Le fondement théologique des missions.* Paris: Éditions du Seuil.
    1958. *Catholicism: A Study of Dogma in Relation to the Corporate Destiny of Mankind.* New York: Sheed & Ward.
Luzbetak, Louis J.
    1963. *The Church and Cultures: An Applied Anthropology for the Religious Worker.* Techny, Ill.: Divine Word Publications.
    1967. "Missionary Adaptation." In *The New Catholic Encyclopedia,* 1:120-22. New York: McGraw-Hall.
    1988. *The Church and Cultures: New Perspectives in Missiological Anthropology.* Maryknoll, N.Y.: Orbis Books.
Manus, Chris U.
    1993. *Christ, the African King.* Frankfurt: Peter Lang.
Marsden, George F.
    1980. *Fundamentalism and American Culture: The Shaping of Twentieth Century Evangelicalism, 1870-1925.* New York: Oxford University Press.
Masson, Joseph
    1962. "L'église ouverte sur le monde." *Nouvelle Revue Théologique* 84:1032-43.
    1966a. *Vers l'église indigené: Catholicisme ou Nationalisme?* Brussels: Editions Universitaires Les Presse de Belgique.
    1966b. *L'attività missionaria della Chiesa (testo e commento dell' Ad gentes).* Rome: Editrice Università Gregoriana.
    1975. *La missione continua: Inizia un'epoca nuova nell'evangelizzazione del mondo.* Bologna: EMI.
Maurier, Henri
    1993. *Les Missions.* Paris: Cerf.
McGavran, Donald A.
    1973. "Salvation Today." In *The Evangelical Response to Bangkok,* ed. Ralph Winter, 27-32. Pasadena, Calif.: William Carey Library.
    1980. *Understanding Church Growth.* Grand Rapids: Eerdmans.

McGavran, Donald A., and Arthur F. Glasser
  1983. *Contemporary Theologies of Mission*. Grand Rapids: Baker.
McKenzie, John L.
  1968. "The God of Israel." In *The Jerome Biblical Commentary*, ed. Raymond E. Brown et al., 2:737-46. Englewood Cliffs, N.J.: Prentice Hall; London: Geoffrey Chapman.
  1985. *Dictionary of the Bible*. New York: Macmillan/London: Geoffrey Chapman.
Menasce, J. P.
  1951. "Traditions Juives sur Abraham." *Abraham Pére des Croyants*, 191-94. Paris: Cahiers Sioniens.
Metz, Johann-Baptist
  1969. *Theology of the World*. New York: Herder & Herder.
Mitterhöfer, J.
  1974. *Thema Mission*. Vienna: Herder.
Moloney, R.
  1987. "African Christology." *Theological Studies* 48:509.
Moltmann, Jürgen
  1967. *Theology of Hope*. New York: Harper & Row.
  1975. *The Experiment Hope*. London: SCM Press.
  1993. *The Church in the Power of the Spirit: A Contribution to Messianic Ecclesiology*. Minneapolis: Fortress.
Mondin, G. B.
  1973. *Le Christologie Moderne*. Rome: Urbaniana University Press.
Moreau, A. Scott, Gary B. McGee, and Gary R. Corwin
  2004. *Introducing World Missions: A Biblical, Historical, and Practical Survey*. Grand Rapids: Baker.
Moreau, A. Scott, Harold A. Netland, and Charles E. Van Engen, eds.
  2000. *Evangelical Dictionary of World Mission*. Grand Rapids: Baker.
Motte, Mary, and Joseph Lang, eds.
  1982. *Mission in Dialogue*. Maryknoll, N.Y.: Orbis Books.
Müller, Karl
  1978. "'Holistic Mission' oder das 'umfassende Heil.'" In *". . . denn Ich bin bei Euch" (Mt 28, 20): Perspektiven im christlichen Missionsbewusstsein heute*, ed. Hans Waldenfels, 75-84. Einsiedeln: Benziger.
  1987. *Mission Theology: An Introduction*. St. Augustin: Steyler Verlag.
  1989. *Josef Schmidlin (1876-1944): Papsthistoriker und Begründer der Katholischen Missionswissenschaft*. Nettetal: Steyler Verlag.
Müller, Karl, Theo Sundermeier, Stephen Bevans, and Richard Blies, eds.
  1997. *Dictionary of Mission: Theology, History, Perspective*. Maryknoll, N.Y.: Orbis Books.
Mushete, A. Ngindu
  1991. "Modernity in Africa." In *Trends in Mission*, ed. Willi Jenkinson and Hellene O'Sullivan, 143-54. Maryknoll, N.Y.: Orbis Books.
  1994. "An Overview of African Theology." In *Paths of African Theology*, ed. Rosino Gibellini, 9-26. Maryknoll, N.Y.: Orbis Books.
Mveng, Engelbert
  1990. *Identità Africana e Cristianesimo*. Turin: SEI.
  1994. "Impoverishment and Liberation: A Theological Approach for Africa and

the Third World." In *Paths of African Theology*, ed. Rosino Gibellini, 154-65. Maryknoll, N.Y.: Orbis Books.

Mwoleka, C.
1976. "Trinity and Community." In *Mission Trends*, ed. Gerald H. Anderson and Thomas F. Stransky, 151-55. New York: Paulist Press/Grand Rapids: Eerdmans.

Myklebust, Olav G.
1955/57. *The Study of Missions in Theological Education*. Oslo: Egede Institute.
1961. "Integration or Independence? Some Reflections on the Study of Missions in the Theological Curriculum." In *Basileia*, 330-40. Evangelische Missionsverlag.
1989. "Missiology in Contemporary Theological Education." *Mission Studies* 6:87-107.

Neuner, Josef
2000. *Teologia ecumenica: La ricerca dell'unità tra le chiese cristiane*. Brescia: Queriniana.

Newman, John Henry
1989. *An Essay on the Development of Christian Doctrine*. Notre Dame: University Press.

Nida, Eugene A.
1960. *Message and Mission: The Communication of the Christian Faith*. New York: Harper & Row.
1968. *Across Cultures*. New York: Harper & Row.

Nida, Eugene A., and William D. Reyburn.
1981. *Meaning Across Cultures*. Maryknoll, N.Y.: Orbis Books.

Niebuhr, H. Richard
1951. *Christ and Culture*. New York: Harper Brothers.

Nunnenmacher, Eugen
1993. "The Missionary Nature of the Church." In *Mission for the Third Millennium: Course of Missiology*, ed. Paolo Giglioni, 105-68. Rome: Pontifical Missionary Union.

Nyamiti, Charles
1984. *Christ as Our Ancestor: Christology from an African Perspective*. Gweru, Zimbabwe: Mambo Press.

Oberman, Heiko
1983. *Luther: Mensch zwischen Gott und Teufel*. Berlin: Severin & Siedler. English translation, *Luther: Man Between God and the Devil*. Garden City, N.Y.: Doubleday, 1992.
1986. *The Dawn of the Reformation: Essays in Late Medieval and Early Reformation Thought*. Edinburgh: T. & T. Clark; Grand Rapids: Eerdmans, 1992.

Oborji, Francis Anekwe
1998. *Trends in African Theology Since Vatican II: A Missiological Orientation*. Rome: Leberit.
1998/99. "Tendencies in the Third World Theologies." *Encounter* 4:26-35.
1999. *La teologia africana e l'evangelizzazione*. Rome: Leberit.
2000. "In Dialogue with African Traditional Religion." *Studies in Interreligious Dialogue* 10:57-76.

2001a. "Trends in Third World Theologies: Missiological Perspectives." *Omnis Terra* 35:66-75.

2001b. "Towards African Model and New Language of Mission." *AFER* 43:109-33.

2001c. "Missiologia contemporanea: Storia e nuove sfide." *Euntes Docete* 54:143-57.

2001/2002. "Towards a New Language for Missiology in Africa." *Encounter* 5:44-65.

2002a. "Poverty and the Mission-Charity Trend: A Perspective from Matthew." *International Review of Mission* 91:87-101.

2002b. "The Missionary Dimension of Ecumenical Dialogue." *Omnis Terra* 36:20-32.

2002c. "Revelation in African Traditional Religion: The Theological Debate since Vatican II." *Studies in Interreligious Dialogue* 12:5-22.

2002d. *Teologia della missione: Storia e nuove sfide.* Rome: Leberit.

2003a. "Missiology in an African Context: Toward a New Language." *Missiology* 31:321-38.

2003b. "The Mission ad gentes of the African Churches." *Omnis Terra* 37:55-164.

2003c. "Building Relationships in Pluralistic Communities: An African Perspective." *Studies in Interreligious Dialogue* 13:158-74.

2004a. "Africa: Rethinking the Mission-Charity Paradigm." *SEDOS Bulletin* 37:182-89.

2004b. "African Traditional Religion Between Pluralism and Ultimate Reality." *Studies in Interreligious Dialogue* 14:129-59.

2005. *Towards a Christian Theology of African Religion: Issues of Interpretation and Mission.* Eldoret, Kenya: Gaba Publications.

Odasso, Giovanni
1998. *Bibbia e Religioni: Prospettive bibliche per la teologia delle religioni.* Bologna: EMI.

Oguejiofor, O. J.
1996. *Philosophy in the Evolution of Contemporary African Christian Theology.* Nsukka, Nigeria: Fulladu.

Ohm, Thomas
1959. *Asia Looks at Western Christianity.* New York: Herder & Herder.
1962. *Machet zu Jüngern alle Völker: Theorie der Mission.* Freiburg: Erich Wevel Verlag.

Okolo, Barnabas C.
1994. "African Liberation Theology: Concept and Necessity." *SEDOS Bulletin* 26:102-3.

Orchard, R. K.
1958. *The Ghana Assembly of the International Missionary Council.* London: Edinburgh House Press.

Panikkar, Raimon
1968. *The Unknown Christ of Hinduism.* London: Darton, Longman and Todd.
1981. *The Unknown Christ of Hinduism: Toward an Ecumenical Christophany.* Rev. ed. Maryknoll, N.Y.: Orbis Books.

1993. *The Cosmotheandric Experience: Emerging Religious Consciousness.* Maryknoll, N.Y.: Orbis Books.

2004. *Christophany: The Fullness of Man.* Maryknoll, N.Y.: Orbis Books.

Pannenberg, Wolfhart

1990. "Religious Pluralism and Conflicting Truth Claims: The Problem of a Theology of World Religions." In *Christian Uniqueness Reconsidered: The Myth of Pluralistic Theology of Religions,* ed. Gavin D'Costa, 96-106. Maryknoll, N.Y.: Orbis Books.

Parappally, J.

1995. *Emerging Trends in Indian Christology.* Bangalore: IIS Publications.

Parratt, John

1995. *Reinventing Christianity: African Theology Today.* Grand Rapids: Eerdmans.

Paul VI (Pope)

1964. *Ecclesiam Suam,* encyclical letter on dialogue.

1967. *Populorum Progressio,* encyclical letter on human progress.

1976. *Evangelii Nuntiandi,* apostolic exhortation, on evangelization in the modern world.

Pfürtner, S.

1984. "Die Paradigmen von Thomas und Luther: Bedeutet Luthers Rechtfertigungsbotschaft einen Paradigmenwechsel?" In *Theologie-wohin? Auf dem Weg zu einen neuen Paradigma,* ed. Hans Küng and David Tracy, 168-92. Zurich/ Cologne: Benziger Verlag. English translation, *Paradigm Change in Theology.* New York: Crossroad, 1989.

Pius XI (Pope)

1926. *Rerum Ecclesiae,* encyclical letter..

1931. *Quadragesimo Anno,* encyclical letter.

Pius XII (Pope)

1939. *Summi Pontificatus,* encyclical letter.

1951. *Evangelii Praecones,* encyclical letter.

1957. *Fidei Donum,* encyclical letter, on the present state of the Catholic missions, especially in Africa.

Power, John

1970. *Mission Theology Today.* Dublin: Gill & Macmillan.

Rahner, Karl

1966. "Christianity and Non-Christian Religions." *Theological Investigations,* 5:115-34. London: Darton, Longman and Todd.

1968. *Spirit in the World.* New York: Herder and Herder.

1974. *Theological Investigations.* Vol. 6. London: Darton, Longman and Todd.

1981. *Theological Investigations.* Vol. 20. London: Darton, Longman and Todd.

Raiser, Konrad

1997. *To Be the Church: Challenges and Hopes for a New Millennium.* Geneva: WCC.

Ratzinger, Josef

1982. *Theologiche Prinzipienlehre.* Munich.

Roest Crollius, Arij A.

1978. "What Is New about Inculturation." *Gregorianum* 59:721-38.

1980. "Inculturation and Meaning of Culture." *Gregorianum* 61:253-74.

Rosenkranz, G.
   1977. *Die Christliche Mission: Geschichte und Theologie.* Munich: Chr. Kaiser Verlag.
Rosin, H. H.
   1972. *Missio Dei: An Examination of the Origin, Contents and Function of the Term in Protestant Missiological Discussion.* Leiden: Inter-University Institute for Missiological and Ecumenical Research.
Rossano, Piero
   1968a. *Meeting African Religions.* Vatican City: Editrice Libreria.
   1968b. *L'uomo e la religione.* Città del Vaticano: Editrice Vaticana.
   1975. "Dialogue avec les Religions Non-Chrétiennes: contenu, facilité, conditions, limites." *Bulletin du Secretariatus pro non-Christianis* 10:26-28.
   1976. "Acculturazione del Vangelo." In *Evangelizzazione e Culture: Atti del Congresso Internazionale Scientifico di Missiologia* (5-12 October 1975, Rome), 104-16. Rome: Pontificia Università Urbaniana.
   1981. "Christ's Lordship and Religious Pluralism." In *Mission Trends*, ed. Gerald H. Anderson and Thomas F. Stransky, 5:20-35. New York: Paulist Press/Grand Rapids: Eerdmans.
Rütti, Ludwig
   1972. *Zur Theologie der Mission: Kritische Analysen und neue Orientierungen.* Munich: Chr. Kaiser Verlag.
   1974. "Mission—Gegenstand der Praktischen Theologie oder Frage an die Gesamttheologie?" In *Praktische Theologie Heute*, ed. F. Klostermann and R. Zerfass, 288-307. Munich: Chr. Kaiser Verlag.
Rzepkowski, Horst
   1985. "First Evangelization from the Perspective of Differing Missionary Approaches." *Verbum SVD* 26:95-120.
Sanon, Anselme T.
   1991. "Jesus, Master of Initiation." In *Faces of Jesus in Africa*, ed. Robert J. Schreiter, 85-102. Maryknoll, N.Y.: Orbis Books.
Saraiva Martins, J.
   1994. *La missione oggi: Aspetti teologico-pastorali.* Rome: Urbaniana University Press.
Scherer, James A.
   1971. "Missions in Theological Education." In *The Future of the Christian World Mission*, ed. William J. Danker and Wi Jo Kang, 143-55. Grand Rapids: Eerdmans.
   1985. "The Future of Missiology as an Academic Discipline in Seminary Education." *Missiology* 13:454.
Scherer, James A., et al.
   1997. "Evangelical Mission Theology." In *Dictionary of Mission: Theology, History, Perspective,* ed. Karl Müller et al., 146-51. Maryknoll, N.Y.: Orbis Books.
Schineller, Peter
   1976. "Christ and Church: A Spectrum of Views." *Theological Studies* 37:545-66.
   1990. *A Handbook on Inculturation.* New York: Paulist Press.
Schlette, Heinz Robert
   1966. *Toward a Theology of Religions.* New York: Herder.

Schmemann, Alexander
    1961. "The Missionary Imperative in the Orthodox Tradition." In *The Theology of the Christian Mission*, ed. Gerald H. Anderson, 250-57. London: SCM Press.
Schmidlin, Josef
    1917. *Einführung in der Missionswissenschaft.* Münster.
    1931. *Catholic Mission Theory.* Techny, Ill.: Mission Press. German orig., 1919.
    1933. *Catholic Mission History.* Techny, Ill.: Mission Press. German orig., 1924.
Schnackenburg, Rudolf
    1973-87. *Il Vangelo secondo Giovanni.* 4 vols. Brescia: Paideia.
Schoonhoven Jansen, E.
    1974a. *Variaties op het thema "zending."* Kampen: Kok.
    1974b. *De ontwikkeling van het Christendom in de nieuwste tijd.* Leiden: Inter-University Institute for Missiological and Ecumenical Research.
Schottroff, Luise, and Wolfgang Stegemann
    1986. *Jesus and the Hope of the Poor.* Maryknoll, N.Y.: Orbis Books.
Schreiter, Robert J.
    1989. "Teaching Theology from an Intercultural Perspective." *Theological Education* 26:13-34.
    1996. "Reconciliation as a Model of Mission," *Neue Zeitschrift für Missionswissenschaft* 52:6-15.
    1997. *The New Catholicity: Theology Between the Global and the Local.* Maryknoll, N.Y.: Orbis Books.
Schreiter, Robert J., ed.
    1991. *Faces of Jesus in Africa.* Maryknoll, N.Y.: Orbis Books.
SECAM (Symposium of Episcopal Conferences of Africa and Madagascar)
    1984. "The Church and Human Promotion in Africa Today: Communiqué, Resolutions and Recommendations." (Acts of the 7th Assembly, Kinshasa, 15-22 July 1984), *AFER* 26:376-82.
Senior, Donald, and Carroll Stuhlmueller
    1983. *The Biblical Foundations for Mission.* Maryknoll, N.Y.: Orbis Books.
Seumois, André
    1973/81. *Théologie Missionaire.* 5 vols. Rome: Bureau de Presse, O.M.I.
    1993. *Teologia missionaria.* Bologna: EDB.
Shenk, Wilbert R.
    1987. "Mission in Transition: 1972-1987." *Missiology* 15:415-30.
Shenk, Wilbert R., ed.
    2002. *Enlarging the Story: Perspectives on Writing World Christian History.* Maryknoll, N.Y.: Orbis Books.
Shorter, Aylward
    1972. *Theology of Mission.* Cork: Mercier Press.
    1988. *Toward a Theology of Inculturation.* Maryknoll, N.Y.: Orbis Books.
Spijker, G. T.
    1994. "Liberating the Church from Its Northern Captivity: Dialogue with Traditional Religion in Africa." *Studies in Interreligious Dialogue* 4:170-88.
Spindler, Marc
    1967. *La mission, combat pour le salut du monde.* Neuchâtel: Delachaux et Niestlé.

Stamoolis, James J.
  1986. *Eastern Orthodox Mission Theology Today.* Maryknoll, N.Y.: Orbis Books;
    Eugene, Ore.: Wipf & Stock, 2001.
Stark, Rodney
  1997. *The Rise of Christianity: How the Obscure, Marginal Jesus Movement
    Became the Dominant Religious Force in the Western World in a Few Cen-
    turies.* San Francisco: HarperSanFrancisco.
Sundermeier, Theo
  1986. "Konvivenz als Grundstruktur ökumenischer Existenz heute." *Oecumeni-
    scher Existenz Heute* 1:49-100.
  1997. "Theology of Mission." In *Dictionary of Mission: Theology, History, Per-
    spective,* ed. Karl Müller et al., 429-51. Maryknoll, N.Y.: Orbis Books.
Sundkler, Bengt
  1968. "Bedeutung, Ort und Aufgabe der Missiologie in der Gegenwart." *Evange-
    lische Missions-Zeitschrift* 25:113-24.
Swidler, Leonard, ed.
  1987. *Toward a Universal Theology of Religion.* Maryknoll, N.Y.: Orbis Books.
Testa, E.
  1985. "I principi biblici della missione." In *Missiologia oggi,* 11-47. Rome: Urba-
    niana University Press.
Thauren, J.
  1927. *Die Akkommodation im Katholischen Heidenapostolat.* Münster: Aschen-
    dorffsche Verlagsbuchhandlung.
Tillich, Paul
  1963. *Christianity and the Encounter of World Religions.* New York: Columbia
    University Press.
Tomko, Josef
  1998. *La missione verso terzo millennio.* Bologna: EDB.
Torres, Sergio, and Virginia Fabella
  1976. *The Emergent Gospel: Theology from the Underside of History.* Maryknoll,
    N.Y.: Orbis Books.
Tracy, David
  1975. *Blessed Rage for Order: The New Pluralism in Theology.* New York: Cross-
    road.
  1981. *The Analogical Imagination: Christian Theology and the Culture of Plural-
    ism.* New York: Crossroad.
Ukpong, Justin
  1984. *African Theologies Now: A Profile.* Eldoret, Kenya: Gaba Publications.
  1987. "What Is Contextualization?" *Neue Zeitschrift für Missionschaft* 43:161-
    68.
Uzukwu, Elochukwu E.
  1983. "Igbo World and Ultimate Reality and Meaning." *Lucerna* (Bigard Theo-
    logical Studies) 4:9-24.
  1996. *A Listening Church: Autonomy and Communion in African Churches.*
    Maryknoll, N.Y.: Orbis Books.
Vanhoye, A.
  1990. "Le origini della missione apostolica nel Nuovo Testamento." *La Civiltà
    Cattolica* 141:544-59.

Vatican II documents
  1964. *Lumen Gentium*, dogmatic constitution on the church.
  1964. *Unitatis Redintegratio*, decree on ecumenism.
  1965. *Nostra Aetate*, declaration on the relation to non-Christian religions.
  1965. *Dei Verbum*, dogmatic constitution on divine revelation.
  1965. *Ad Gentes*, decree on the church's missionary activity.
  1965. *Gaudium et Spes*, pastoral constitution on the church in the modern world.
Verkuyl, Johannes
  1987. *Contemporary Missiology: An Introduction*. Grand Rapids: Eerdmans.
Vicedom, Georg Friedrich
  1958. *Missio Dei: Einführug in eine Theologie der Mission*. Munich: Chr. Kaiser
    Verlag.
  1965. *The Mission of God: An Introduction to the Theology of Mission*. St. Louis,
    Mo.: Concordia.
Visser 't Hooft, Willem Adolph
  1963. *No Other Name*. London: SCM.
  1967. *Hauptschriften*. Vol. 2, *Ökumenischer Aufbruch*. Stuttgart: Kreuz Verlag.
Voulgarakis, Elias
  1965. "Mission and Unity from the Theological Point of View." *International
    Review of Missions* 54:298-307.
  1997. "Orthodox Mission." In *Dictionary of Mission: Theology, History, Per-
    spective*, ed. Karl Müller et al., 334-38. Maryknoll, N.Y.: Orbis Books.
Wagner, Peter C.
  1979. *Our Kind of People: The Ethical Dimensions of Church Growth in Amer-
    ica*. Atlanta: John Knox.
Waldenfels, Hans, ed.
  1978. ". . . denn Ich bin bei Euch" *(Mt 28, 20): Perspektiven im christlichen Mis-
    sionsbewusstsein heute*. Einsiedeln: Benziger.
Warneck, Gustav
  1892/1905. *Evangelische Missionslehre*. 5 vols. Halle: University of Halle/Martin
    Luther University.
  1906. *Outline of a History of Protestant Missions*. Edinburgh: Oliphant, Ander-
    son and Ferrier.
Warren, M., ed.
  1983. *Source Book for Modern Catechetics*. Winona, Minn.: St Mary's Press/
    Christian Brothers Publications.
Westermann, Claus
  1982. *Dieu dans l'Ancien Testament*. Paris: Cerf.
Wolanin, Adam
  1989. *Teologia della missione: temi scelti*. Casale Monferrato: Piemme.
Wong, Joseph
  1994. "Anonymous Christians: Karl Rahner's Pneuma Christocentrism and an
    East-West Dialogue." *Theological Studies* 55:609-37.
World Christian Database
  Published and available on the Internet at http://www.worldchristiandatabase.org
World Council of Churches (WCC)
  1967. *The Church for Others and the Church for the World*. Geneva: WCC.

1979. *Guidelines on Dialogue with People of Living Faiths and Ideologies.* Geneva: WCC.

1982. "Baptism, Eucharist, Ministry." Faith and Order Paper No. 111. Geneva: WCC.

Yannoulatos, Anastosios

1965. "The Purpose and Motive of Mission." *International Review of Missions* 54:281-97.

1989. "Orthodox Mission—Past, Present, Future." In *Your Will Be Done: Orthodoxy in Mission*, ed. George Lemopoulous, 63-92. Geneva: World Council of Churches.

Yates, Timothy

1994. *Christian Mission in the Twentieth Century.* Cambridge: Cambridge University Press.

INDEX

accommodation, 67, 68, 69
Ad Gentes, 4, 9
  on church unity, 159
  and fraternal dialogue, 172
  and missionary nature of the church,
    42
  and proclamation, 207
adaptation, 84, 85, 86
  in Catholic missiology, 99-110
  and creation, 85, 86
  criticism of, 98, 99, 105
  external and internal forms of, 101-2
  and incarnation, 85, 101
  and inculturation, 102
  and local culture, 104-5
  pre–Vatican II papal teaching on,
    106-10
  and relation of mission subject and
    mission object, 103-4
  subjective and objective, 100
  theology of, 18, 19, 104
Africa
  and interreligious dialogue, 127-28
  theology of liberation in, 194
  See also theologians, African; theol-
    ogy, African
African Traditional Religion(s), 127,
    195, 200
  and supernatural revelation, 127-28
Ahn, Byung-Mu, 192
Akademie der Wissenschaften, 44
Allen, Roland: on dependency struc-
    tures, 92
Amaladoss, Michael, 192
Amalorpavadass, D. S., 192
American Society of Missiology, 166,
    175
ancestor(s)
  in African theology, 194, 196, 197
  Christ as, 197, 198, 199
anonymous Christianity, 124, 125,
    126
apartheid, 74

Appiah-Kubi, Kofi, 184
Arrupe, Pedro: on inculturation, 20
arts and sciences: as area of collabora-
    tion, 174
assimilation, 67, 68
Augustine: on universality of the
    church, 155

Baago, Kaj, 37
Balz, H., 115
Bangkok study week, 36
Bantu: and adaptation, 101
baptism: in Christian churches, 176-
    77
Barth, Karl, 130, 131
  on mission as the activity of God
    (*actio Dei*), 29, 134-35, 146
  and Protestant theology of mission,
    130, 131
Basil the Great, 155
Bediako, Kwame, 204
Benedict XV, Pope: on mission, 106-7
Bettscheider, Heribert: on liberation,
    188-89
Bevans, Stephen: on contextual theol-
    ogy, 184-85
Bible: and mission, 66, 67
bishop of Rome: as ecumenical
    patriarch, 156
bishops
  African: and church as family, 201
  and inculturation, 111
  indigenous, 108
  local, 89
  role of, in evangelization, 6
Bonhoeffer, Dietrich, 32, 145
Bosch, David, 18, 43, 53, 70, 135, 146,
    159
Breckenridge, Charles, 44, 47
British-Irish Association for Mission
    Studies, 175
Bsteh, Andreas, 68
Bujo, Bénézet, 197, 198

232

Calvin, John, 72
Carey, William, 130
Catechesi Tradendae: on ecumenical
collaboration, 175
catechetical renewal, 36
Catholic Church
and charismatic renewal, 167
dialogue with Independent churches,
167-71
dialogue with other Christian religions, 159-60
and ecumenical formation, 178
and World Council of Churches, 159
CELAM (*Consejo Episcopal Latinoamericano*), 12, 187, 188
Cerularius, Michael, 156
Charles, Pierre, 91
and church planting, 82-86
Christ
as ancestor, 197, 198, 199
as fulfillment of human history, 125
and historical Jesus, 32
and non-Christian religions, 124-26
role of: in salvation, 21, 24, 25, 30,
35, 53, 123-26, 128, 129, 208
Unknown, 32
Christianity
advantages of adaptation for, 102
as general religion of humanity, 76-77
and non-Christian religions in
Protestant thought, 131, 132
relation to other world religions, 118
and replacement model of mission,
130-31
translation of, into culture, 112
as world religion, 77
Christology (Christologies)
African, 196-97
ancestor, 197-200
cosmic, 32, 191-92
illustrative, 197
Japanese, 193
Korean, 192
Logos, 32
and mission, 30-34
Omega, 32
of Rahner, 124-26
Spirit, 32
and Third World theologies, 181
trends in, 30-34
church(es)
as catholic, 155
and cultural diversity, 6

Ecumenical, 165
as family, 201-3
Independent, 165; and dialogue with
Catholic Church, 167-71
indigenous, 86-87
as instrument of mission, 135
as instrument of salvation, 142
local, 6, 8; and communion with
pope, 90, 91; and evangelization,
109; and universal church, 26, 91
mission-sending, 91
nature of, 5-6, 42
North Atlantic: decline in, 27; mission to, 7-8, 12
in Orthodox theology, 79
as political principle of liberty, 147
responsibility of: for all humanity, 9-
10
role of: in mission, 66
and salvation, 34-39, 78, 122
as sign of Christ's presence, 6
teachings on mission, 40
Third World: mission to North
Atlantic churches, 7-8
universal, 5, 100, 102, 108, 156, 157,
170; and church planting, 89, 90;
communion with, 111; and local
church, 26
whole, 170
young and mature, 91-92
See also ecclesiology
church growth
and Donald McGavran, 93-96
numerical approach to, 94
See also church planting
church planting, 18, 73
and the Louvain school, 82, 86
as purpose of missionary activity, 5
structures of, 89-90
and universal church, 89, 90
clergy
indigenous: and adaptation, 102;
training of, 87
local, 89, 106-9
collaboration
ecumenical, 171-78
at religious and pastoral level, 174-
75
social, 173
Collegium Orientale Theologicum, 44
*Collegium Urbanum de Propaganda
Fide,* 44

human promotion (*continued*)
  as source of missiology, 3, 4
  and Third World theologies, 181
  See also liberation theology
humanity
  christianization of, 76-77
  common origin of: in African theology, 195
humanization: as goal of mission, 144

implantatio ecclesiae. See church planting
incarnation
  and adaptation, 85, 101
  and inculturation, 19-20, 111
inculturation, 4, 16, 84
  and adaptation, 102
  in conciliar and postconciliar Catholic mission theology, 110-11
  and cultural anthropology, 110
  and evangelization, 20-21
  and incarnation, 19-20, 111
  from Judaeo-Christianity to Gentile Christianity, 17
  and mission, 17-20
  prophetic role of, 111
  as source of missiology, 3
indigenization, 86-87
  and mission thinking, 28-29
individual, emphasis on the, 75, 77
Instructio de Propaganda Fide (1659), 85
Instruction on Christian Freedom and Liberation, 190
International Association for Catholic Missiology, 175
International Missionary Conference (Whitby, Ontario, 1948), 136
International Missionary Council, 92
International Monetary Fund, 22

Jesus
  historical, 66
  love of, 74-75
  and the reign of God, 141
John Chrysostom, 155
John Paul II, Pope, 102, 129, 153, 166, 207
  on African theology, 201
  on church unity, 160
  on ecumenical collaboration, 175
  on human promotion, 23
  on missions, 8, 9, 10

  on new evangelization, 12, 13
  and religious pluralism, 30, 33
  and work of Cyril and Methodius, 78
John the Faster, 156
John XXIII, Pope
  on ecumenical dialogue, 172
  and liberation theology, 188
  on mission, 109-10
justification: by faith, 162, 163
Justin Martyr, 118, 121

Kappen, S., 192
Katigondo study week (1964), 36
Kitamori, K., 193
Knitter, Paul, 30, 119, 130-31
Koyama, Kosuke, 193
Kraemer, Hendrik, 113-14, 130
Kraft, Charles H.: and influence of anthropological studies in missiology, 115-16

laity, role of: in evangelization, 108, 109, 145
Lamb, Christopher: on missiology as theological discipline, 48, 49
Lange, René, 91
Lausanne Committee for World Evangelization, 168, 169, 170
Lausanne Covenant (1974), 166, 169
Legrand, Lucien: on culture, 116
liberation theology, 4, 146-47, 186-91
  See also human promotion
Libertatis Nuntius, 190
Lima statement (WCC), 176, 177
Linz, Manfred, 143
Loffeld, E., 90
logoi spermatikoi, 118, 119
López-Gay, J.: on mission and conversion, 37-39
Louvain school: and church planting, 62, 82, 83, 86, 90, 91
Lull, Raimon, 43
Lumen Gentium: and the role of the church in salvation, 34
Luther, Martin, 72, 163
Luzbetak, Louis J.: on adaptation and inculturation, 103-5

magisterium: as source of missiology, 3
Manila Manifesto, 169
Manila study week (1967), 36-37
Margull, H. J., 143
Marsden, George, 166

mission (*continued*)
  and Vatican II, 4-7
missionaries
  and cultural superiority, 112
  trained, 6, 92
missionary
  activity, purpose of, 4
  role of: in conversion, 39
  training of, 179-80
modernist movement, 19
Moltmann, Jürgen, 143, 146
moratorium, 27-28, 95
Moravianism, 168
Müller, Karl, 52, 53, 63, 65, 69-71, 90
Münster school, 90, 91
  and conversion, 60, 64, 65, 69, 82
Mwoleka, Christopher, 200

Neuner, Josef, 154
New Delhi Congress (1961), 29
New Testament, authority of: in Evangelical and Pentecostal churches,
  167
Nida, Eugene A.: and communication of
  the faith, 114-16
non-Christians
  and plan of God, 123-25
  salvation of, 122
  terminology of, 118
Nostra Aetate, 127, 129
Nyamiti, Charles, 197, 198, 200

Ohm, Thomas, 64-69
oikoumenē, 153-58
Okolo, Barnabas: on liberation theology, 22
oppression: and Latin American theology, 187

pagans: as saints, 121
Pan-African Conference of Third World
  Theologians, 195
Panikkar, Raimon, 191-92
partnership in obedience, 92, 136
Paul VI, Pope, 34, 96, 166, 187, 207,
  209
  on church unity, 160
  on ecumenical dialogue, 172
  and human development, 71
  on human promotion, 23
  on universal mission, 9, 10
peace, collaboration on, 173-74
Pentecostalism, 166-67
  Independent, 165-67

people of God, missionary role of, 89
Pickett, J. Wascom, 93-94
Pietism, 74, 75, 130, 139, 156, 168
Pius XII, Pope, 27
  and African churches, 109
  on mission, 107-9
plantatio ecclesiae. *See* church planting
Plath, C. H., 44
pluralism, religious, 30-33
politics: as arena for mission studies,
  147
pope: and communion with churches,
  16, 90, 91
Populorum Progressio, 23, 71
praeparatio evangelica, 21, 99, 119-20
predestination, 74
priesthood: of all believers, 163, 164
primacy: and church unity, 160, 161
Princeps pastorum, 109
proclamation: and mission, 36-37, 72,
  206-9
Protestantism
  and concept of "ecumenical," 156-57
  and missionary cooperation, 15

Rahner, Karl, 47, 51
  and Christology, 124-26
  on non-Christian religions, 124-26
  and the supernatural existential, 68
Ratzinger, Joseph (Benedict XVI): and
  church unity, 160
Rayan, Samuel, 183-84, 192
reconciliation: as area of collaboration,
  173-74
Redemptoris Missio, 6, 8, 10, 11, 12,
  30, 33, 102, 129, 166, 207
reevangelization. *See* evangelization,
  new
reign of God
  and Jesus Christ, 141
  and mission, 139, 140
religion(s)
  differences among, 128
  fulfillment theory of, 119-32
  non-Christian: and church fathers,
  118, 119; and Protestant theology,
  130-32
  pagan, 118
  as *praeparatio evangelica*, 21
Rerum Ecclesiae, 107, 108
revivals: and Evangelical churches, 168
Rossano, Piero: and interreligious
  dialogue, 126-29